Understanding Modern Money

'This book is a "must read" for those calling for the abandonment of the floating exchange rate policy and a return to fixed exchange rates, a gold standard, or capital controls. The achievement of zero unemployment, price stability, and a market economy for the long term as advanced by Wray is viable only with floating exchange rates. As economic policy that clearly does not understand the operation of floating rate currencies drives the world into economic decline, the understanding of the principles advanced in *Understanding Modern Money* can both halt the decline and lead the world into an era of unprecedented, long term, economic achievement.'

– Warren Mosler, Director of Economic Analysis, III Finance

'This is a most important work, one that should be read by all serious economists regardless of their particular theoretical persuasions. Wray not only presents a most innovative study of the relationship among money, public policy, employment, and the price level, but develops a position on how a modern monetary economy works that is clear, insightful, and useful. This book, in my opinion, is the most important theoretical study in decades.'

– John F. Henry, California State University, Sacramento

'Extremely well written and persuasively argued. . . It turns economics from a dismal science into a positive science, capable of clear policy recommendations that cut the gordian knot of the unemployment–inflation tradeoff.'

– Jan Kregel, Universita degli Studi di Bologna, Italy

'*Understanding Modern Money* breathes a whiff of fresh air over the desert of unimaginative, and only too often irrelevant though lofty sophisticated technicalities, in which macroeconomic writing has landed us in the last decades.'

– Y. S. Brenner, Utrecht University, The Netherlands

'An innovative and carefully argued proposal for solving the most pressing economic issue of our times – how to eliminate unemployment without reigniting inflation.'

– Paul Dalziel, Lincoln University, New Zealand

'This book is to be recommended to any reader interested in both economic theory and macroeconomic policy, whether the person be an academic economist or policy maker. The book is, for the first time, exposing an original theory of money without any unnecessary controversies, in the tradition of Keynes's *Treatise on Money*. The major proposition of the book, encompassing the chartalist approach, is that the *sine qua non* for the existence of a monetary economy is the state power to create money and to ensure its general acceptance by imposing taxes. By far the most important feature of the book is that it is deducing from this chartalist theory of money a comprehensive program of economic policy that reconciles full employment with the absence of inflationary pressures. It is a major advancement in the elaboration of an heterodox macroeconomic theory along Post-Keynesian lines.'

– Alain Parguez, Professor of Economics, University of Franche-Comté, France
and Adjunct Professor of Economics, University of Ottawa, Canada

Understanding Modern Money

The Key to Full Employment and Price Stability

L. Randall Wray

Bard College
Annandale on Hudson, NY 12504

Edward Elgar
Cheltenham, UK • Northampton, MA, USA

Published by
Edward Elgar Publishing Limited
Glensanda House
Montpellier Parade
Cheltenham
Glos GL50 1UA
UK

Edward Elgar Publishing, Inc.
6 Market Street
Northampton
Massachusetts 01060
USA

HG
221
.W894
1998

A catalogue record for this book
is available from the British Library

Library of Congress Cataloguing in Publication Data

Wray, L. Randall, 1953–
    Understanding modern money : the key to full employment and price stability / L. Randall Wray.
    1. Money. 2. Monetary policy. 3. Prices. 4. Full employment policies. I. Title.
HG221.W894   1998
332.4'6—DC21   98–37874
                                                          CIP

ISBN 1 84064 007 3 (cased)

Printed and bound in Great Britain by Bookcraft (Bath) Ltd.

Contents

Preface

> The Conservative belief that there is some law of nature which prevents men from being employed, that it is 'rash' to employ men, and that it is financially 'sound' to maintain a tenth of the population in idleness for an indefinite period, is crazily improbable – the sort of thing which no man could believe who had not had his head fuddled with nonsense for years and years . . . Our main task, therefore, will be to confirm the reader's instinct that what <u>seems</u> sensible <u>is</u> sensible, and what <u>seems</u> nonsense <u>is</u> nonsense. We shall try to show him that the conclusion, that if new forms of employment are offered more men will be employed, is as obvious as it sounds and contains no hidden snags; that to set unemployed men to work on useful tasks does what it appears to do, namely, increases the national wealth; and that the notion, that we shall, for intricate reasons, ruin ourselves financially if we use this means to increase our well-being, is what it looks like – a bogy. (Keynes 1972, pp. 90–92)

In a letter to George Bernard Shaw on 1 January 1935, Keynes wrote 'I believe myself to be writing a book on economic theory which will largely revolutionise – not, I suppose, at once but in the course of the next ten years – the way the world thinks about economic problems.' Keynes's claim turned out to be true; his book did indeed revolutionize economic theory and in far less than a decade. However, by the late 1970s, the Keynesian paradigm had splintered into 'Keynesian', 'monetarist' and 'supply-side' factions, and by the end of the 1990s very little of the Keynesian revolution remained. In some respects, the theory presented here returns to the analysis of Keynes, but I have purposely avoided doctrinal debates in the hope that there would be nothing in this book that Keynesians, monetarists or supply-siders should have difficulty in accepting.

As I note at the end of this section, there are a number of other economists who are developing similar arguments, primarily for publication in academic journals. My purpose here is to introduce these ideas in a manner that will make them clear to a reader with a strong, but not necessarily academic, background in economics. Perhaps more importantly, this book synthesizes theoretical and policy-oriented research that investigates modern money, government spending and deficits, inflation and employment into what is intended to provide a coherent and unified exposition. It is hoped that this present analysis is only the opening 'salvo' of what may become a revolution in the way that we think about the economy and, especially, economic policy.

The primary policy conclusion that comes out of this analysis is, perhaps, shocking, but it can be stated simply: It is possible to have truly full employment without causing inflation. This will appear to be a desirable goal, but a preposterous claim; no self-respecting Keynesian, monetarist or supply-sider would allow herself to entertain such hopes. But if the analysis here is correct – and it goes without saying that I am sure it is – then the logical conclusion is that we can move immediately to full employment with enhanced price stability. Indeed, as I will argue, the two goals are inextricably linked: the policy that is recommended to achieve full employment will also increase price stability.

That policy is to have government operate as 'employer of last resort'; it has also been called 'government job assurance' and 'government buffer stock employment' by others. Quite simply, the government would announce that it will hire anyone ready, willing and able to work at a stated fixed money wage. This is not a new idea; it can be traced back at least as far as the Great Depression. The novelty here lies in the economic analysis that shows that this employment policy must at the same time enhance price stability. 'Employer of last resort' workers act as a 'buffer stock' of employable labour, available for hire by the private sector at a mark-up over a known, fixed wage (the government's stated wage). This serves to anchor wages and, thus, prices. The reader will not be convinced at this stage; certainly careful analysis is required to convince readers of the validity of such claims. That is what I attempt to do.

Even if one accepts the argument that truly full employment (as discussed in Chapter 1, this is to be distinguished from 'NAIRU' – the non-accelerating inflation rate of unemployment) can be achieved without setting off inflation, there are still many objections that can be raised. What is the cost? Won't the budget deficit explode? If it does, how will the government finance its deficits? Won't government spending and borrowing for this programme 'crowd out' private spending and borrowing? How will the programme affect competition with foreign firms in the new global economy? I attempt to deal with these objections in the chapters that follow. As it happens, most concerns – particularly those having to do with programme costs, government finance and 'crowding out' – disappear once one understands the nature of 'modern money'.

In all modern economies the government defines money by choosing what it will accept in payment of taxes. Once it has required that the citizens must pay taxes in the form of money (say, dollars), the citizens must obtain money in order to pay taxes. In order to obtain 'that which is necessary to pay taxes', or money, they offer labour services or produced goods to the government (as well as to markets). This means the government can buy anything that is for sale for dollars merely by issuing dollars. The government does not 'need' the 'public's money' in order to spend; rather, the public needs the 'government's money' in order to pay taxes. Once this is understood, it becomes clear that neither taxes nor government bonds 'finance' government spending. Instead, taxes are required to give value to money, while bond sales are a part of monetary or interest rate policy (providing an interest-earning alternative to non-interest-earning currency to be held as a store of value).

When readers first encounter this argument, they typically believe I am calling for full-tilt operation of the 'printing presses', to finance all the government's spending by 'printing money', which is believed to be a sure-fire path to hyperinflation. And indeed it would be. My point is that, in reality, all government spending is 'financed' by 'money creation', but this money is accepted because there is an enforced tax liability that is, by design, burdensome. Without that onerous tax liability, the government could run the printing presses until the cows come home, but would find nothing for sale for dollars! Thus government spending can be too large (but also too small); government deficits can be excessive (but also deficient); there is a real danger that government activity could crowd out private activity; and there is a danger that government spending can cause inflation when too large, or deflation when too small.

The key, then, is to ensure that government spending is at just the right level so that neither inflationary nor deflationary forces are induced. As I will show, the design of the employer of last resort programme ensures that government spending will be at the correct level. Further, the price-stabilizing feature of the programme allows the government to 'dictate' to markets the wage at which it will hire all those ready, willing and able to work. In sharp contrast, current policy requires that the government pay 'market prices' for most things it buys, which means that the government has no choice but to force slack, or unemployment, on markets in order to fight inflation. In other words, under the current system full employment and price stability are inconsistent, exactly as many economists argue. However, with the policy changes advocated here, we can move immediately to full employment and greater price stability.

The book provides examination of the historical record, institutional analysis and some history of economic thought. These may be 'bells and whistles' for those who are willing to be persuaded by the logic alone. But academic economists, in particular, expect, even demand, history, authority and empirical results before revolutions are undertaken. Thus the arguments of Adam Smith and others and the examples of colonial Africa, the

Southern Confederacy and other remote experiences are provided to supplement the theoretical and policy analyses.

The book is organized as follows. Chapter 1 provides an overview of the theoretical arguments and policy recommendations. It also shows how different the view presented in this book is from conventional policy analysis. Chapters 2 and 3 present an alternative view of money – which could be called the 'state theory of money'. Chapters 4 through 6 then examine the important policy implications that derive from this view of money. Chapter 7 provides a summary through the use of an abstract, yet not mathematical, model. When this book is used in the undergraduate classroom, Chapter 7 can probably be omitted; however, the understanding developed in the previous six chapters should make the exposition of Chapter 7 accessible even to the non-academic audience. The book closes with Chapter 8, which offers a brief summary and conclusion.

One final note. In this preface I have used the first person singular, but have used the plural form in the remainder of the book. This is because I have received so much help from a group of individuals who have worked with me to develop the major arguments that I must share the credit for what follows with Warren Mosler, John Henry, Jan Kregel, the late Hyman Minsky, Mat Forstater, Stephanie Bell and Pavlina Tcherneva. I have also benefited from discussions with Jay Levy, Dimitri Papadimitriou, Wynne Godley, Bill Mitchell, John Adams, Anne Mayhew, Karl Widerquist, Alain Parguez, participants of the PKT and AFEEMAIL discussion groups,[1] Robert Guttmann, Helen Ginsburg, Sumner Rosen, members of the National Jobs for All Coalition, Tom Ferguson, Robert Heilbroner, Steve Fazzari and Paul Davidson. Barbara Slater, Desk Editor at Edward Elgar Publishing, and Judy Kahn, Editor at the Levy Institute, offered editorial assistance, while Irene Culver, Marc-Andre Pigeon and Sandy Nelson helped with the word processing. I received helpful suggestions on the manuscript from several anonymous readers, as well as from Philip Arestis, Malcolm Sawyer, Geoff Harcourt, Peter Groenewegen, Philip Harvey, E.J. Nell, Y.S. Brenner and Paul Dalziel. Needless to say, none of the above should be held responsible for my errors. Finally, I would like to acknowledge the financial support of the Center for Full Employment and Price Stability.

NOTES

1. AFEEMAIL is an institutionalist Internet discussion group operated by the Association for Evolutionary Economics (afeemail@crcvms.unl.edu), while PKT is a Post Keynesian Internet discussion group organized by Ric Holt (pkt@csf.colorado.edu).

1 Introduction

In this book, we will explore the implications that follow from an understanding of the role played by modern money in any developed capitalist economy. Many of the most important topics of current economic debate take on a completely new light when exposed to critical analysis informed by this understanding. For example, we shall see that our analysis helps to clarify issues in the following areas:

Government deficits   Most economists and policymakers (in the US and elsewhere) have become convinced that government deficits must be reduced. Indeed, in the US many support a balanced budget amendment that would require that temporary deficits be offset by surpluses in following years; and the Maastricht Treaty specified maximum permissible deficit-to-GDP and dept-to-GDP ratios. Most have cheered as the US budget moved toward balance and they debate about 'what to do with the surplus'.

Our analysis, however, shows that a balanced budget is the theoretical minimum possibility that is sustainable; the practical lower limit is a continuous deficit and any surplus will be short-lived because it will unleash strong deflationary forces. Further, there is no 'optimal' or even 'maximum' internal deficit or dept-to-GDP ratio consistent with fiscal prudence. The balanced budget amendment would impose unnecessary and impossible fiscal restraint on the US.

Value of the currency   Most economists and policymakers believe that monetary policy is responsible for maintenance of the domestic value of the currency (the international value of the currency is now determined by 'dirty float'). Indeed, two pieces of legislation (the Employment Act of 1946 and the 'Humphrey-Hawkins' Act of 1978) are interpreted as instructing the Fed to maintain the domestic value of the currency. The predominant consensus is now that the Fed can do this by targeting the inflation rate of an index, such as the Consumer Price Index (CPI).

Our analysis will show, however, that the responsibility for the value of the currency lies with the Treasury. 'Prudent' fiscal policy, then, lies not in 'balancing the budget', but rather in maintaining the value of the currency while withdrawing resources from the private sector to be used in the public sector. This is done by ensuring the currency is sufficiently difficult to obtain that the public will provide to the government those goods and services it desires, at more or less stable prices, to undertake public policy. We will propose that the government should stabilize the domestic value of the currency in terms of the nominal wage it pays in a buffer stock, employer of last resort programme.

Monetary policy   As discussed above, most economists and policymakers erroneously assume or believe the Fed determines the rate of inflation through control over the money supply. However, adoption by the Fed of explicit money targets for most of the past decade and a half did not permit it to control the money supply in the desired manner. Many other countries also experimented with money targets, with results similar to that in the US. Still, the majority of economists believe the Fed can at least control the quantity of reserves.

We will see that the conventional view misunderstands the reserve-supply process. No central bank is able to control the quantity of reserves, which must be supplied on demand. The modern central bank policy instrument is always and everywhere an overnight lending rate at which reserves are supplied. Most central bank activity is defensive, necessitated by activities of the Treasury.

Government bond sales   Sales of government bonds by the Treasury are generally seen as 'financing' operations required whenever the government runs a deficit. According to this view, the government must borrow at a rate dictated by markets, and there is great fear that a continuous deficit could expose the government to the possibility that it might offer debt to finance a deficit only to find that there are no buyers – causing a fiscal crisis. The problem is thought to be compounded when a government is 'forced' to rely on foreign 'lenders' to finance the government deficit.

We will show that this is an unwarranted fear. Rather, bond sales can be seen as nothing more than a reserve clearing drain required to allow the central bank to hit its interest rate target. This means that (1) bond sales are undertaken as part of monetary policy, not to finance deficits, (2) the interest rate on government bonds can be any rate above zero desired by the central bank, and (3) this interest rate cannot be market determined, as it is determined by central bank policy.

Employment policy   While the Employment and Humphrey-Hawkins Acts commit the US government to high, if not full, employment, the government has never adopted policy that would guarantee this result. Rather, it has adopted a variety of 'supply-side' policies (tax incentives, training programmes) and some 'demand-side' policies (primarily, those designed to raise the level of aggregate demand) in the hope that markets would operate at a sufficiently high level to ensure high employment. Because markets have almost never operated at the desired level, the government has been forced to supplement these policies with various 'welfare' programmes to provide a safety net (unemployment compensation, AFDC, food stamps, general assistance).

We will show that there is an alternative that recognizes the important role of work in creating positive feelings of self-worth and also ensures that those who can contribute to society will contribute. In short, we propose a true full employment policy: The government will act as 'employer of last resort' by offering a job to anyone who wants to work at a nominal wage fixed by government.[1]

Exogenous pricing Currently, the US government (like all other 'free market' governments around the world) decides how many resources (including labour) it wishes to purchase and then pays market prices for virtually everything it buys. In other words, it generally fixes quantity exogenously (determines outside markets the quantity of aircraft carriers, miles of interstate highway, hours of janitorial services), but lets prices 'float' endogenously (pays prices dictated by suppliers – either by going directly to markets or through a 'competitive' bidding process). If inflation results (and it is not hard to see why it might), the government must then force slack on the private sector in an attempt to reduce 'market pressure' on prices. This slack shows up as unemployed labour, idle plant and equipment, and rising inventories of raw materials and consumer goods. In other words, as is well recognized, unemployment is the enforced cost of maintaining some degree of price stability.

There is an alternative. The government can instead let quantity 'float' and fix prices exogenously. While the government can, in principle, set the price of anything and everything that it wants to buy, it is probably preferable and certainly sufficient (for reasons discussed below) for the government to fix only one important price. The market would then establish all other prices relative to that price. In the past governments fixed the price of gold or some other precious metal. In the modern economy it is far preferable to stabilize the price of labour. This is done by creating and maintaining a 'buffer stock' of labour in the 'employer of last resort' (ELR) programme, with the price of that labour fixed by government. This will provide for full employment without inducing the kinds of inflationary pressures that can result when the government pays market prices for everything. Just as a gold buffer stock is believed to impart some price stability (while ensuring that gold is always 'fully employed'), the ELR labour buffer stock would also improve price stability (while ensuring that labour is always fully employed). In a real sense, full employment becomes a 'by' product of price stability, the reverse of the current situation, in which unemployment is required to maintain price stability.

These examples are offered to indicate how far this analysis departs from the conventional wisdom. Although at least some of the above will no doubt appear far-fetched to many readers, careful analysis leads inexorably to these results. Let us very briefly present the main arguments that lead to these conclusions.

We can begin with the recognition that the modern state imposes and enforces a tax liability on its citizens, and, importantly, chooses 'that which is necessary to pay taxes' (twintopt).[2] If a state decided that it would accept only beaver pelts in payment of taxes, the population would have to organize itself to ensure that it obtained the requisite number of beaver pelts; if the tax liability were sufficiently difficult to meet, beaver pelts would carry high relative value. Of course, all modern states impose a monetary tax liability and generally accept only money in payment of taxes. Not coincidentally, all modern states require that these monetary tax payments be made in the form of the state's own currency.[3] That currency, in turn, is nothing more than the government's liability.

Because the public needs the government's money (government liabilities, which are currency), it is willing to provide things to the government in order to obtain twintopt. Just as people would struggle to obtain beaver pelts if they were the required twintopt, citizens of the modern economy devote efforts to obtaining currency in order to pay taxes.[4] This means that the government can, if it chooses to do so, dictate the terms on which currency can be obtained (that is, the 'effort' required to obtain it). Note that it would be senseless for the government to impose a tax, and then to refuse to supply the currency required, for this could only mean imprisonment of the citizenry for tax evasion![5] At a minimum, the government will have to ensure that it supplies an amount of currency equal to the tax liability over the longer run. Indeed, it could probably provide more currency than absolutely necessary for taxes without danger. Many citizens would gladly accumulate small holdings of extra currency in any given year, just in case currency is harder to come by in following years and just in case some currency is lost in the wash. The 'normal' case, then, is for the government to 'run a deficit', that is, to provide more currency than it collects in taxes.[6] To repeat, in the modern economy, currency (or, more specifically, government liabilities – often called high-powered money – Treasury coin, Federal Reserve notes and bank reserves, in the case of the US) is always money.

The government creates a demand for the currency by imposing a tax liability; as is the case in all modern economies, the US government itself is the monopoly supplier of the currency, which is supplied when it purchases goods, services and assets from the public.[7] The government decides how much 'effort' is required when it sets the terms on which it provides currency, for example, the price it is willing to pay times the quantity it purchases (or, total government spending).[8] Note also that the government can choose to devalue its currency by reducing the effort required to obtain currency. If the government holds the tax liability constant, but announces it will pay twice as many units of currency to obtain the same amount of goods, services and assets, it should not be surprised to find that its money has become 'less valuable'. Looked at from a different angle, the government would find that 'prices' of everything it bought had risen; an index of the prices of the items the government purchased would register 'inflation' in terms of the currency. Similarly, the government could hold constant the effort required to obtain each unit of currency (that is, hold prices constant), but cut the tax liability in half. It probably would then find, all else equal, that fewer goods and services would be offered for sale to the government.[9]

At this point, the reader may object that this appears to be far too simple: money is used for many things in addition to paying taxes; even individuals with no tax obligations demand money; government is not the only source of money; government does not, alone, determine what must be done to obtain money. Although these objections are valid, they change nothing of significance. If beaver pelts were twintopt, we would expect that they would also be used as a medium of exchange and means of payment in transactions between citizens. Even if the government were to announce a new policy that beaver pelts would be replaced by bison pelts as twintopt, we would expect that at least for some time beaver pelts might continue to be used in private transactions. However, after the announced change, all the advantages that beaver pelts had formerly enjoyed would now be transferred to bison pelts, and we would expect that over time private markets would abandon beaver for bison pelts.

All modern states can and do reserve the right to determine twintopt, and in all well-functioning states twintopt is the currency used. While many, indeed most, transactions do not require use of the currency by the parties to the transaction, final settlement of accounts among banks takes place in the form of the government's currency.[10] That is, when one buys something by writing a cheque, this results in a 'clearing drain' from one bank to another that occurs on the books of the nation's central bank and in the form of 'bank reserves' that are nothing but the government's liability. Within the borders of the US, then, almost all monetary transactions take place in the dollar unit of account, a unit chosen by the state as the unit in which it denominates its own liabilities, which, in turn, are required in payment of taxes. The use of other dollar-denominated liabilities (such as bank deposits) in private transactions derives from the US government's imposition of a dollar-denominated tax liability payable in the form of dollar-denominated government liabilities. Once dollar-denominated government liabilities (and dollar-denominated bank liabilities) are used in private transactions, then currency will have additional uses beyond the ability to serve as twintopt. This would probably increase the public's desire to accumulate net claims against the government, in the form of currency hoards.[11]

Note, also, that even in this 'expanded' economy, in which most money is used in private transactions and in which most money takes the form of private liabilities (such as bank deposits), government still has the power to devalue (or revalue) the currency. Suppose the government had been paying $10 000 per year per full-time worker (say, for 2000 hours of work) to obtain secretarial services, but now announces it will pay $20 000 per year, even while it maintains the tax liability at a constant $1000 per capita. Not only do citizens find it easier to meet the tax liability (it used to take one-tenth of a year, or 200 hours, to earn the currency required to meet the liability, but now it takes only one-twentieth, or 100 hours), but the private sector will find that, all else equal, it must compete with a public sector wage for secretarial services that has doubled. It would be quite surprising if one found that these forces did not lead to 'inflation', or reduction of the value of the currency.[12] Even if the government bought only secretarial services, other private sector prices would tend to rise as labour was reallocated. In other words, the government's doubling of prices it paid would affect relative prices (that is, relative rates of remuneration), tending to place upward pressure on other wages and thus prices through competition and arbitrage (all else equal, if one has a choice of producing toilet seats to specification for sale to the government at prices that have doubled or producing toilet seats for the private sector, one will produce for the private sector only if prices rise).[13] We conclude that even if currency is only a portion of the total money supply, and even if government spending is only a small portion of total spending, government spending decisions generally affect the value of the currency, or, prices.

As to the objection that taxes do not fall on all those who might use currency, in a strict theoretical sense, even if the government imposed taxes on only one individual, that would be sufficient to generate a demand for currency. Realistically, however, if the US government were to impose a trillion-dollar tax on you, alone, the likely result would be that it would find no demand for its currency (other than your demand), that it would collect no taxes, and that you would spend the rest of your life in prison. If, however, the government imposed a tax on half of its citizens, even those with no tax liability would be willing to accept the government's money because the half with a tax liability would be willing to do things for the half without a tax liability to obtain currency. Thus, it is by no means necessary to impose a tax on all citizens in order to create a widespread demand for currency.

To sum up, with a sufficiently high tax liability (and a sufficiently severe penalty for failure to pay taxes), the government can transfer to itself the desired portion of a nation's output (although we make no claim that total GDP would be as high under a government-takes-all scheme as it is under the current system). However, this is not because the government needs the tax payments in order to purchase the nation's output, but rather because the tax liability is required to force the citizens to provide things to the government to obtain currency.[14] As the monopoly supplier of the currency, the government can set the price of those things it is willing to buy since this is the only source of the currency needed by the public to pay taxes.[15]

There are, however, disadvantages to government attempts to set prices exogenously for all things it wishes to buy. Even if we take a simple case in which government announces it will pay, say, $32 per ounce of gold and $10 per ounce of silver, it is easy to see that government might run into what is known as the 'two-price problem'. If the private sector finds that, at these prices, it is relatively easier to mine silver, then production would be shifted toward silver until the private sector has supplied all the silver that the government is willing to buy. So long as citizens have not yet met their tax liability, production would then be shifted to gold. As the deadline for tax payment nears, gold would become highly valued relative to silver as the population desperately tried to supply gold to the government. Even if the private sector were perfectly planned to avoid such problems, relative prices would be disrupted unless the government happened to set the gold-to-silver nominal price ratio at the private market's relative price ratio; further disruptions would occur as technology changed or as new resources were discovered. If the government buys thousands of different types of goods and services, each at an announced fixed price, it is exceedingly unlikely that the government's nominal price ratios would reflect market-relative price ratios; thus the government's fixed nominal prices would disrupt the market's relative price system.

But this does not mean that a wise government should merely accept market-determined prices for all that it buys, for then it could do little to reduce market price inflation except to impose slack. It might find that the prices of the things it buys would be rising, requiring ever-expanding budgets and ever-rising tax liabilities to avoid contributing to inflation pressures (although it is unlikely that tax revenues would have to rise exactly in step with spending as desired saving in the form of net claims on government would probably rise as well).[16] Such a system would have no price anchor, although the government could try to deflate the economy by reducing its orders of goods and services relative to the tax liability (that is, moving the budget toward surplus) – causing unemployment of resources such as labour. Thus resorting to 'market-determined' prices eliminates direct government influence over prices and forces it to use slack to fight inflation.

The government could, instead, try to create a price anchor through use of a buffer stock. For example, many governments in the past operated a 'gold standard', without recognizing this could be used as a buffer stock price anchor.[17] The government could announce buy and sell prices for gold, agreeing to buy gold at, say, $32.02 and to sell gold at, say, $32.04. When the public needed currency, it would sell gold to the government, thereby increasing the supply of currency. When the public had more currency than it desired, it could buy gold from the government. The gold standard would impart some stability to prices so long as the government kept its buy price constant. When there was inflation of prices generally, the price of gold (which would be held constant) would fall relative to other prices and gold would be substituted for other commodities in consumption (for example, gold would replace other precious metals in jewellery) and in production processes. The stabilized price of gold would serve as an anchor for prices, although to the extent that gold's substitutability is low, the effect would be limited.[18]

The problem, then, with a gold standard is that gold is a relatively minor commodity in the modern economy so far as its use in production and consumption goes. Stabilizing the price of gold does not generate strong forces to stabilize the prices of other commodities. It would be far preferable to choose a more important commodity to serve as the basis of a buffer stock policy. For example, petroleum products enter into the production of most other commodities, making oil a strong candidate for a buffer stock policy.[19] Stabilizing the price of oil would be a much greater stabilizing force in the modern economy than would be obtained by returning to a gold standard, or gold buffer stock regime. The government would announce that it would stand ready to buy oil at $20.00 per barrel and to sell it at $20.05 per barrel. During inflationary periods the government would sell oil, which would be substituted for relatively more expensive inputs; this would also reduce the supply of currency and would cause resources to move out of oil production and refining. During deflationary periods the government would buy oil, whose relative price would be rising, supplying more currency and inducing greater use of resources in the oil producing and refining industries.

There is, however, an even better commodity to serve as a buffer stock, and that commodity is labour. One of the advantages of a buffer stock policy is that the commodity that serves as a buffer stock is always fully 'employed'. Under a gold standard, one would never find 'idle' gold just lying around; if the private economy could not find a use for the gold, it would be sold to the government at the fixed price. Likewise, with an oil buffer stock programme, oil not needed in the private market would be sold to the government at the fixed price; no one would be forced to hold 'unwanted' oil, as the government would guarantee a market.[20] There are thus two reasons why labour is the preferred 'commodity' to be used in a price-stabilizing buffer stock programme.[21] First, labour is a basic input into virtually all conceivable production processes. Second, idleness of labour (that is, unemployment) generates a great number of problems for individuals and for society in general.

We recognize, of course, that labour is not a 'homogeneous' input to production, as is gold; oil is less homogeneous than gold, but perhaps more homogeneous than labour. Those individuals who are currently unemployed (whether officially or unofficially) in the US could not immediately perform all those tasks associated with production in a modern economy; some individuals might never be suited for more than a few of the required tasks; some tasks might require the specific skills, education, dexterity or temperament that only a handful of Americans could possess. To the extent that the unemployed are not, and cannot be made to be, substitutes for labour already employed, the buffer stock will be less successful at stabilizing prices. However, even if there were no existing job that could be performed by the currently unemployed (and this is quite unlikely), employers could devise new processes to utilize the unemployed under the right incentives. For example, it might be possible to replace some processes that require highly skilled workers with processes that require little skill (as the handicrafts were replaced with factory production). To some degree, unemployed labour is, or could be, a substitute for existing labour in at least some occupations. This is why it is believed that unemployment helps to stabilize prices, and why policy currently relies on rising unemployment in order to reduce inflation, for otherwise unemployment would do little to fight inflation. As we will argue, if those who are currently unemployed do help to fight inflation, then a buffer stock policy involving employed labour will do a better inflation fighting job.

The employer of last resort (ELR) policy is really a 'buffer stock' scheme that helps to anchor prices. It also provides for full employment. The government would announce a fixed price for labour, agreeing to 'buy' all labour at the announced wage or to 'sell' it at a slight mark-up over the announced wage. Anyone who could not find a job in the private and public sector could show up for ELR work and would receive the ELR wage. The private sector could always hire workers out of the ELR pool by paying a wage sufficiently high to make private sector employment preferable to ELR employment. As discussed in Chapter 6, ELR workers would receive training to make them more desirable (relative to the unemployed) to private sector employers; at the same time, they would receive income from work. The specifics of such a programme are treated below in Chapter 6; here we summarize only the macroeconomic implications.

Under this scheme, the government 'defines the currency' by setting the ELR wage.[22] If the government changes the ELR wage, it will redefine the currency, just as an announced change of the price of gold under a gold standard would devalue or revalue the currency. So long as the ELR wage is held constant, it will serve as a 'price anchor' for the economy with other prices determined 'relative' to this price. For example, a firefighter might receive a wage equal to five times the ELR wage; as market conditions change, as institutions change, as bargaining power changes, this ratio might change; the firefighter might come to receive six times the ELR wage. We do not claim that other prices (whether for labour or for produced goods and services) would be perfectly stable under such a system, just as they were not held stable under a gold standard. However, we believe that with an ELR buffer stock, price stability would be much greater than under the current system and even greater than under the old gold standard. At the same time, the ELR buffer stock scheme would automatically achieve continuous full employment.[23]

ELR workers are a better buffer stock than are unemployed workers because, at the very least, they must show up ready, willing and able to work (unlike unemployed workers, who may not be ready, willing and able). As will be discussed in Chapter 6, the ELR programme can be designed to make ELR workers even more desirable to the private sector by providing on-the-job training and teaching remedial reading, writing and maths skills as necessary. This is why full employment under an ELR scheme will be less inflationary than is the current system which relies on unemployment to stabilize prices. One could even think of the ELR labour force as a 'price-stabilizing pool' of available workers, that is in contrast to the current 'reserve army of the unemployed' that is supposed to fulfil the same function, but with much suffering and social ills caused by the unemployment. The ELR programme will more successfully stabilize prices, and at the same time will guarantee full employment.

Not only would the ELR policy generate greater price stability and full employment, but it would also create a powerful 'automatic stabilizer' to reduce business cycle fluctuations. As we will show, the ELR pool of workers will grow and shrink countercyclically. When private markets are depressed, displaced workers will flow into the ELR pool, increasing government spending and the supply of currency while helping to maintain consumption.[24] When the private economy booms, workers will be hired out of the ELR pool, shrinking government spending.[25] Thus government spending (on the ELR programme) would fluctuate in a strongly countercyclical manner.[26]

In some respects, this book presents a modest proposal that would generate incremental improvement over the current situation. At the very least, we can immediately move to full employment without generating more inflation than the current system generates. Even if there were no other benefits, this would seem to be sufficient cause to give the proposal a try. We expect that we would also achieve much greater price stability, much higher economic growth, reduction of crime and other social problems, and improvement of many indicators of social well-being. But even if that were not the case, we think that it would be much easier to discuss solutions to various social and economic problems in the US if we could first solve the unemployment problem once and for all.

DEFINITIONS

In the remainder of this chapter, let us define a few key words that will be used in later chapters.

State money will be defined as that which is accepted by the state in discharge of liabilities to the state (primarily, taxes). State money may, or may not, be legal tender. State money today consists of state liabilities and some private liabilities, although 'full-bodied' coin (commodity money) may have been used as state money in the past.

Commodity money will be defined as a given quantity of a precious metal which when stamped circulates as a means of payment and medium of exchange. Often its supply is monopolized in some manner by government. Commodity money consists of coins whose value is determined by the quantity of precious metal they contain; however, even in the case of full-bodied coin, the state determines the value of the precious metal in terms of the state money of account. For example, under a gold standard, the state announces that gold will be 'worth' $32 per ounce and then operates as a 'marketmaker' to ensure that gold remains at that nominal value. A full-bodied one-dollar coin then must contain one-thirty-second of an ounce of gold. Thus even full-bodied coin can be a state money, with a nominal value determined by the state. As discussed in Chapter 3, most precious metal coins throughout history have not been full-bodied. Coins that contain some precious metal, but whose face value is above that dictated by precious metal content, are really a fiat money (unless the state promises to convert them on demand at par to precious metal).

Fiat money will be defined as state liabilities issued to purchase goods, services or assets, or to discharge government liabilities, with no promise to convert. It is itself nothing more than a debt. Most importantly, fiat money can be used to retire liabilities to the government – such as tax liabilities. In the US, fiat money consists of currency or cash (Federal Reserve notes, Treasury coin, and a few remaining Treasury notes) and bank reserves (which consist of currency held by banks in vaults, but also – and more importantly – of bank deposits at the Federal Reserve banks). Note, as above, that a coin which contains gold may still be nothing more than a fiat money even under a gold standard where the coin is not full bodied and cannot be redeemed for gold.[27]

It is often said that the value of fiat money is determined by 'trust' in the state. In some sense, this is true: as we will discuss below, what is necessary is that one 'trust' that the state will impose and enforce a tax liability, payable in the form of the state money which is accepted at par at state pay offices. For example, a coin with a face value of one dollar must be accepted by the state in payment of taxes at a value of one dollar. However, this is just as true of commodity money as it is of fiat money; there is no significant difference between a fiat money coin and a full-bodied coin.[28] On the one hand, it is probably preferable to use the term 'currency' rather than 'fiat money', dispensing with any distinction between 'fiat money' and 'commodity money' ('commodity money' is not used any more, in any case). On the other, 'currency' has the disadvantage that most people do not think of bank reserves as currency, while we can stretch the definition of fiat money to include bank reserves. Perhaps our definition of fiat money comes closest to what economists call 'high-powered money' or 'base money'.

Bank money will be defined as bank liabilities that are accepted as means of payment or media of exchange; today, this is primarily deposits on which cheques can be drawn, although in the past it consisted primarily of banknotes. Some bank money – especially in modern times – is convertible without much delay and with little loss of value to fiat money and/or to commodity money; today, conversion is always done at par with fiat money, although in the past bank money often circulated without convertibility. Just as the state agrees to accept fiat money at its pay offices, banks accept bank money in payment to retire liabilities to the banking system. This explains why convertibility is not necessary to allow bank money to circulate. However, so long as bank money was not convertible at par, individual banks were selective in accepting money issued by other banks. This problem was solved through the development of clearing houses which would allow banks to clear accounts among each other at par; this allowed each bank to accept money issued by any bank, thus increasing acceptability by the public. The acceptability of bank money increases further when it becomes a state money, accepted in payment of taxes. Indeed, this is the key to development of par clearing, for if the state accepts bank deposits in payment of taxes without distinguishing among banks, then bank deposits clear at par. Note that bank money can circulate (and indeed did circulate) even when it is not a state money; while acceptability in payment of taxes is a sufficient condition to give demand to a money, it is not a necessary condition.

The *unit of account* is the unit in which the monies, prices and monetary contracts are denominated. It was originally a weight unit – shekel, lira, pound – based on the weight of a given quantity of grains of wheat or barley. In the modern economy, it is purely notional – the dollar, the mark, the franc. The modern state issues its fiat money denominated in the unit of account, accepting the fiat money in payment of tax liabilities that are always stated in terms of the same unit of account. In the US, the unit of account is, of course, the dollar; tax liabilities, all important domestic prices (including the prices of liabilities and assets), and most domestic monetary contracts are denominated in the dollar. As we discuss, fiscal policy plays a large role in determining the domestic value of the dollar, or, how much the dollar can buy domestically.

Full employment According to many economists, 'full employment' means a rate of unemployment that is associated with a constant inflation rate, that is, NAIRU or the non-accelerating inflation rate of unemployment. Other economists associate full employment with a 'natural rate' of unemployment that is supposed to be determined by the equilibrium real wage (at the intersection of aggregate labour demand and supply curves) such that all unemployment is voluntary in the sense that it is unwilling to work at the equilibrium wage. During the 1960s, many economists assumed that the natural rate of unemployment was about 4 per cent, but that was raised to more than 5 per cent by the early 1980s. Estimates of NAIRU vary considerably, but most economists believed that in the US during the 1980s, NAIRU was well above 6 per cent. Other economists associate full employment with a situation in which only frictional unemployment (for example, those who are temporarily between jobs) and perhaps structural unemployment (for example, due to a mismatch between the skills required to fill job vacancies and the skills of the unemployed) remain. On this definition, full employment would be consistent with an unemployment rate of perhaps 1or 2 per cent. Some economists adopt a definition according to which full employment is consistent with a situation in which the number of unemployed equals the number of job vacancies; although comprehensive job vacancy data for the US is not generally available, surveys show that even in recent years with unemployment rates below 5 per cent, the number of unemployed is several times greater than the number of job vacancies.

There are different ways to go about defining the unemployed. Obviously, many and perhaps most of those who are not working should not be classified as unemployed. Official US statistics count only those who are currently looking for work (with specified search requirements), thereby excluding many who might wish to work but who, for whatever reason, are not actively seeking work (these are classified as out-of-the-labour-force). Economists would generally wish to distinguish between voluntary and involuntary unemployment: those who are unemployed simply because they refuse to work at the 'market wage' they can obtain are classified as voluntarily unemployed. There are also employed workers who are working fewer hours than desired, or who are working in a job that does not require their skills, education or training; these could be said to be partially unemployed, or, underemployed.

In February 1998, the official US unemployment rate was 4.6 per cent (or 6.4 million persons), with 137.6 million in the civilian labour force (a labour force participation rate of 67 per cent) and 131.2 million employed (the employment–population ratio was 64.2 per cent). Another 1.5 million persons were marginally attached to the labour force, meaning they wanted to work, were available for work, and had looked for a job sometime in the prior 12 months but had not searched for a job in the four weeks preceding the survey (thus were not counted as unemployed). These represent a subset of the approximately 67 million adults (over age 16) who were classified as out-of-the-labour-force. Obviously, the official statistics do not necessarily count as unemployed those that economists would want to count. Some of the officially unemployed may be enjoying a vacation while collecting unemployment benefits, while some of those who are out-of-the-labour-force would happily accept employment if a job were offered. Others could be drawn into the labour force if, for example, adequate child care or health benefits were made available (in the US, such benefits are not usually available at the low end of the wage scale, while health benefits may be available to those who are unemployed or out-of-the-labour-force).

Much has been written about these issues and much more analysis could be done. For the purposes of this book, however, we adopt a rather simple approach. Full employment and zero unemployment are defined as a situation in which all who wish to work at a nominal wage fixed by the government will be provided with a full-time job. Certainly, some individuals will choose to remain officially unemployed, perhaps while searching for a higher-paying job; some individuals will accept the government's job offer, but will work below skill level; others will remain outside (or will drop out of) the labour force. We will discuss the employer of last resort programme in detail in Chapter 6, but the idea is very simple: the government offers to hire anyone who shows up for work, at a wage of $6.25 per hour. We expect that many of the officially unemployed at the time of the programme's start-up will accept the offer; in addition, many of those who were previously counted as out-of-the-labour-force will also accept the offer. If the government's wage is above the minimum wage, or if the government jobs are perceived to be better jobs than private sector jobs, some of the employed will quit their jobs to accept buffer stock work.

As we will discuss, it is impossible to predict beforehand how many of the officially unemployed, employed and out-of-the-labour force will accept the offer of a job at $6.25, nor can we predict how many will choose to remain officially unemployed or out-of-the-labour force, but we will call this a state of full employment because there will be a job made available to anyone who wishes to take an employer of last resort job. Nor do we wish to minimize the problems faced by a worker who loses a high-paying job and must choose between a government job at $6.25 per hour or unemployment. We realize this does not address, much less solve, all unemployment problems. However, it does address what we believe to be the primary unemployment problem of modern economies: the inability to provide sufficient jobs at the bottom of the wage and skill level. Other programmes may be required to address other employment and unemployment problems, but for the most part, they are beyond the scope of this study.[29]

NOTES

1. See the discussion in Chapter 6, as well as the definition of full employment provided at the end of this chapter.

2. This follows from the state theory of money, presented in Chapter 2 below. We apologize for the neologism 'twintopt', but thank an anonymous referee for improving our original, which was 'twintpt'.

3. See Chapter 3 below for a discussion of the 'history' of money. While it appears to most Americans that taxes are paid in the form of a cheque drawn on a private bank, every such payment leads to a drain of bank reserves; reserves are comprised solely of US Treasury and Fed liabilities. Here, as discussed below, we consolidate the Treasury and central bank accounts; there is no significant difference between Treasury liabilities and central bank liabilities in the modern economy.

4. Here we can distinguish between necessary and sufficient conditions. We are claiming that taxes are a sufficient condition to induce the public to provide things to government in order to obtain money (or any other twintopt). Taxes may not be a necessary condition, however; see Chapters 2 and 3 below.

5. Note that in the beaver pelt example one can always hunt to obtain twintopt. However, when government liabilities are the only twintopt, they can be obtained only from the government. If the government refuses to supply its liabilities, taxes cannot be paid. Note also that in the case of beaver pelt twintopt, those who are unemployed can always become self-employed by hunting beaver pelt 'money'; however, when money is supplied by the government in the form of its own liabilities, the government defines what can be done to obtain twintopt. If the government refuses to supply it, the unemployed have no recourse. In the case of modern money, unemployment results when the government spends too little.

6. See Chapter 4 for a detailed analysis of deficit spending.

7. As we discuss in Chapter 7, a head tax is the easiest way to generate a demand for government supplied currency. Income taxes or other transaction taxes complicate the analysis because one can avoid the tax by avoiding the taxed activity. See also Chapter 3 for a discussion of the methods used to monetize real world economies.

8. See Chapters 6 and 7 for analysis of the determinants of the value of the currency.

9. Note that one cannot jump to the conclusion that cutting the tax liability in half would devalue the currency by half. If the government holds prices constant, the value of the currency may remain constant, but the public might obtain all the currency it desires at a lower quantity of sales to the government. The government can also 'revalue' (increase value of) the currency by lowering the price it pays; however, the adjustment process through which the economy deflates can be quite disruptive. The process is also complicated by the central bank intervention that would probably be required due to impacts of deflation on the banking system. See Chapters 5, 6 and 7. Note also that tax liabilities must be enforced to generate a demand for twintopt; however, some degree of laxity is possible. For example, it is estimated that less than half of the taxes levied in Russia are collected, but this has not (yet) eliminated demand for the rouble. In most modern states, enforcement plus some degree of civic responsibility results in much higher rates of collection of tax levies. One suspects, however, that if the Internal Revenue Service in the US were abolished (as some of its critics advocate), civic pride alone would not be sufficient to generate high rates of compliance, so that eventually the domestic value of the dollar would decline.

10. Chapter 5 provides a detailed treatment of these issues.

11. Once we allow for bank deposits, the public can accumulate deposits while banks will accumulate the net claims on government as 'bank reserves'.

12. Admittedly, one could construct scenarios in which the increased price paid by government did not spill over into higher private sector prices. If, for example, the secretaries were homogeneous (or if the government did not attempt to distinguish among heterogeneous secretaries) then a doubling of government salaries might not affect private wages directly.

13. As noted above, there is a symmetry: the government can lower the prices it offers to increase the value of the currency. This will impose deflationary pressures on the economy. While it might appear that if the government were to offer prices below market prices, then it would find no offers, since the public needs the government's money, the private sector would have to 'deflate' until goods and services were provided to the government.

14. Nor can the government always increase its share by offering to pay higher prices (while holding the tax liability and preferences of the public regarding currency holdings constant), for this could merely generate inflation and even fewer goods and services offered.

15. As discussed in Chapter 5, the central bank can supply currency when it purchases financial assets, thus government purchase of goods and services is not the only source of currency. This complicates the analysis, especially in the case where the government tries to impose deflation on the economy.

16. Of course, if government requires too much effort on the part of taxpayers to obtain money, prices could be falling.

17. See Chapters 3 and 7 for discussion of the gold standard.

18. Indeed, the relatively stable prices under the gold standard had more to do with tight fiscal policy than with the operation of the gold buffer stock. See Chapter 3 below.

19. Indeed, the US has operated a buffer stock policy for oil and for many other important raw materials to help stabilize their prices, although this has not been used much since the early 1970s.

20. Of course, this presumes that the government''s buffer stock price is above the minimum supply price.

21. Chapter 6 presents the labour buffer stock proposal.

22. For example, an hour of unskilled labour time is paid $6.25 per hour; a dollar is then defined as being equal to or valued at 9.6 minutes of unskilled labour time.

23. Again, see our definition of full employment at the end of this chapter.

24. Consumption will fall because the lost private sector jobs probably will have paid more than the ELR jobs, but the fall will not be as great as under the current system wherein unemployment rises.

25. The fall of government spending would almost certainly be greater than under the current system because spending on ELR workers would be greater than current government spending on the unemployed, at least in the case of the US where unemployment benefits are low and do not cover the majority of the unemployed.

26. An ELR buffer stock programme would also allow the government to react in a sensible manner to displacement of workers caused by downsizing, technological changes or trade deficits. With an ELR policy in place, displaced US workers will be able to find ELR jobs; admittedly, the ELR wage could be far below the wage of the jobs lost, but the worst problem (unemployment) would be removed, and ELR training could prepare displaced workers for alternative private sector work. Tax cuts or spending increases could be used to stimulate the private economy, reduce the size of the ELR pool, and create jobs to replace those lost. See Chapter 6.

27. In the unlikely case that the market value of gold is above the nominal value of the coin, the coin would disappear from circulation to be melted.

28. However, a 'gold standard' system operates much differently from the modern money system, as we will discuss in later chapters (see Chapters 5, 6 and 7).

29. As we will discuss in Chapters 4 and 6, one way to encourage generation of higher wage and skill level jobs is to stimulate the private economy.

2 Money and Taxes: The Chartalist Approach

INTRODUCTION

In conventional analysis, money is used to facilitate exchange; its value is supposed to have been long determined by the value of the precious metal it represented, although under a fiat money system its value is said to be determined by the quantity of commodities it can purchase. This, in turn, is a function of the rate of inflation, which is presumed to be under the control of the central bank. In this view, monetary policy has to do, primarily, with control of the money supply, while fiscal policy has to do with government spending, taxing and borrowing.

This is quite different from the Chartalist approach, which can be traced from Adam Smith through to John Maynard Keynes. Rather than restricting our focus to the better-known Chartalists, in this chapter we choose instead to bring out the related ideas of Smith, Knapp and Keynes, and the later ideas of the theorists who follow the 'endogenous money approach', as well as related work by Hyman Minsky, Abba Lerner and Kenneth Boulding. This is the view that informs the analysis of money presented in this book, which we will call the 'taxes-drive-money' view, but which we might as well call the Chartalist approach.

In the Chartalist approach, money is a creature of the state; at least in the case of modern money, examples of stateless money are hard to come by.[1] The state defines money as that which it accepts at public pay offices (mainly in payment of taxes). This has important policy implications. Once the state imposes a tax on its citizens, payable in a money over which it has a monopoly of issue, it can influence the value of that money by setting the conditions under which the population can obtain it. The government does not 'need' the public's money in order to spend; rather, the public needs the government's money in order to pay taxes. This means that the government can 'buy' whatever is for sale in terms of its money merely by providing that money. As we discuss in Chapter 4, because the public will normally wish to hold some extra money, the government will normally have to spend more than it taxes; in other words, the normal requirement is for a government deficit. Government deficits do not require 'borrowing' by the government (bond sales); rather (as we show in Chapter 5), the government provides bonds to allow the public to hold interest-bearing alternatives to non-interest-bearing government money. Thus the Chartalist view of money, if fully understood, would lead to a very different view of appropriate monetary and fiscal policy goals. Most notably, it would be recognized that rather than striving for a balanced budget, deficits would be accepted as the 'norm'. And rather than trying to use monetary policy to achieve stable prices, monetary policy would recognize that its role is to establish the short-term interest rate, while fiscal policy would be used to increase stability of the value of the currency.

SMITH ON MONEY

Let us first examine Adam Smith's views of money. Smith's views – particularly on bank creation of money and on the determination of the value of an inconvertible currency – are quite similar to views presented below (especially in Chapter 5). It is thus worth the effort to explore the arguments of the 'father' of economics in detail; our exposition later might then be easier to follow.

According to Smith, convertible banknotes can substitute for commodity money:

> When the people of any particular country have such confidence in the fortune, probity, and prudence of a particular banker, as to believe that he is always ready to pay upon demand such of his promissory notes as are likely to be at any time presented to him; those notes come to have the same currency as gold and silver money . . . (Smith [1776] 1937; p. 277)

At this point, the bank can 'create (bank) money' by lending its own notes. In most countries, banknotes enter the economy as banks discount bills of exchange; however, in Scotland, banks had gone one step further:

> They invented, therefore, another method of issuing their promissory notes; by granting, what they called, cash accounts, that is by giving credit to the extent of a certain sum . . . to any individual who could procure two persons of undoubted credit and good landed estate to become surety for him . . . (Ibid., pp. 282–3)

In other words, banks issued notes and held IOUs of borrowers, with the 'surety' of two creditworthy persons. These banks would then accept their own notes in payment of bank loans. This ensured demand for banknotes by merchant sellers in order to make payments on loans ('cash accounts').

> The banks, when their customers apply to them for money, generally advance it to them in their own promissory notes. These the merchants pay away to the manufacturers for goods, the manufacturers to the farmers for materials and provisions, the farmers to their landlords for rent, the landlords repay them to the merchants for the conveniences and luxuries with which they supply them, and the merchants again return them to the banks in order to balance their cash accounts, or to replace what they may have borrowed of them; and thus almost the whole money business of the country is transacted by means of them. (Ibid., p. 283)

Because notes circulate as if they were money, the banker need hold only a fractional reserve against them.

> Though he has generally in circulation, therefore, notes to the extent of a hundred thousand pounds, twenty thousand pounds in gold and silver may, frequently, be a sufficient provision for answering occasional demands . . . [T]he whole circulation may thus be conducted with a fifth part only of the gold and silver which would otherwise have been requisite. (Ibid., p. 277)

Thus in Scotland, 'The business of the country is almost entirely carried on by means of the paper of those different banking companies, with which purchases and payments of all kinds are commonly made' (ibid., p. 281).

Banknotes 'free up' specie, which is not needed domestically, to go abroad

> in order to seek that profitable employment which it cannot find at home. But the paper cannot go abroad; because at a distance from the banks which issue it, and from the country in which payment of it can be exacted by law, it will not be received in common payments. Gold and silver, therefore. . . will be sent abroad, and the channel of home circulation will remain filled with . . . paper . . . (Ibid., p. 278)

Not only does the paper money substitute for gold and silver, it actually increases the volume of trade. 'By means of those cash accounts every merchant can, without imprudence, carry on a greater trade than he otherwise could do' (ibid., p. 283). This is because the merchant with a 'cash account' (or credit line) can safely keep nearly zero precautionary balances. 'The merchant in Edinburgh . . . keeps no money unemployed for answering such occasional demands. When they actually come upon him, he satisfies them from his cash account with the bank, and gradually replaces the sum borrowed with money or paper which comes in from the occasional sales of his goods' (ibid., p. 284). This does not mean that the volume of paper money will exceed the volume of gold and silver that would be necessary to circulate the same output. 'Should the circulating paper at any time exceed that sum, as the excess could neither be sent abroad nor be employed in the circulation of the country, it must immediately return upon the banks to be exchanged for gold and silver' (ibid., p. 284).

Occasionally, however, banks do issue too much paper money. This could occur because a bank did not actually require its loans to be repaid; for example, a bank might allow a customer to deliver a bill of exchange rather than either commodity money or banknotes. Further, these were often 'fictitious' bills with no commodities circulating behind them.

> [T]he value which had been really advanced upon the first bill, was never really returned to the banks which advanced it; because, before each bill became due, another bill was always drawn to somewhat a greater amount . . . than the bill which was soon to be paid; and the discounting of this other bill was essentially necessary towards the payment of that which was soon to be due. This payment, therefore, was altogether fictitious. (Ibid., pp. 295–6)

This process would increase interest owed (due to compounded discounts on the bills submitted for payment) beyond the ability to pay. Further, excessive note issue would increase reflux, draining reserves and forcing the bank to increase its reserve holdings – which earn less interest – lowering its profitability. Thus, for the most part, market pressures would ensure that there would be a tendency to issue the 'correct' amount of paper – which would be equivalent to the quantity of gold and silver required for circulation – but more than the amount that would have been circulated if specie were actually used in circulation (because the volume of trade would be larger).

So long as paper money is redeemed on demand for gold (or silver), it circulates at par with the gold coin. 'Whatever is either bought or sold for such paper, must necessarily be bought or sold as cheap as it could have been for gold and silver' (ibid., p. 308). If it is not redeemable on demand, then it may circulate at a discount. He discussed the case where redeemability might be uncertain, or might require a wait: 'Such a paper money would, no doubt, fall more or less below the value of gold and silver, according as the difficulty or uncertainty of obtaining immediate payment was supposed to be greater or less; or according to the greater or less distance of time at which payment was exigible'[2] (ibid., p. 309).

As an example, Smith offered the case of the American colonies, which typically offered conversion only after a wait of several years and did not pay interest on the paper for the waiting period. Still, these colonies passed legal tender laws 'to render their paper of equal value with gold and silver, by enacting penalties against all those who made any difference in the price

of their goods when they sold them for a colony paper, and when they sold
them for gold and silver . . .' (ibid., p. 311). Smith decried such regulations
as 'tyrannical' and ineffectual, for the colony currency would fall relative to
the English pound. However, he also noted that Pennsylvania 'was always
more moderate in its emissions of paper money than any other of our
colonies. Its paper currency accordingly is said to never to have sunk below
the value of the gold and silver which was current in the colony before the
first emission of paper money' (ibid., p. 311). Here there is some ambiguity,
for he had not previously argued that the depreciation of a non-convertible
currency was a function of the quantity of the currency issued, but now he
seemed to argue that the more moderate emission of Pennsylvania
forestalled depreciation.

In the following paragraph he seems to have solved the puzzle. If a
paper money whose redeemability is uncertain (or is subject to conditions –
such as a waiting period) is accepted in payment of taxes, and if it is not
excessively issued relative to the tax liability, then it need not depreciate
relative to specie.

> The paper of each colony being received in the payment of the provincial taxes,
> for the full value for which it had been issued, it necessarily derived from this
> use some additional value, over and above what it would have had, from the real
> or supposed distance of the term of its final discharge and redemption. This
> additional value was greater or less, according as the quantity of paper issued
> was more or less above what could be employed in the payment of the taxes of
> the particular colony which issued it. It was in all the colonies very much above
> what could be employed in this manner. (Ibid., p. 312, emphasis added)

Thus the depreciation noticed in the colonies occurred precisely because the
note issue was well above what was required in payment of taxes.

A wiser government could not only prevent depreciation, it might even
cause paper money to carry a premium over specie!

> A prince, who should enact that a certain proportion of his taxes should be paid
> in a paper money of a certain kind, might thereby give a certain value to this
> paper money; even though the term of its final discharge and redemption should
> depend altogether upon the will of the prince. If the bank which issued this
> paper was careful to keep the quantity of it always somewhat below what could
> easily be employed in this manner, the demand for it might be such as to make it
> even bear a premium, or sell for somewhat more in the market than the quantity
> of gold or silver currency for which it was issued. (Ibid., p. 312)

In summary, an essentially non-redeemable paper money could actually
circulate above par even under a gold standard if it was legally required by

the state in payment of taxes, and if the quantity issued were kept 'somewhat below what could easily be employed in this manner'.[3] The key, then, is not really redeemability, nor is it 'legal tender laws' that attempt to 'render their paper of equal value with gold and silver'; rather, it is the acceptance of the paper money in payment of taxes and the restriction of the issue in relation to the total tax liability that gives value to the paper money. Importantly, Smith recognized that this paper money need not be government fiat currency, for his argument was predicated upon the recognition that the paper money is the liability of the banking system. All that mattered was that the state accepted these banknotes in payment of taxes, in which case they could circulate at par, or even at a premium, relative to specie. Note also that this is the real reason that 'paper' remains at home while 'specie' can go abroad. If there are gold or silver standards abroad, then specie will always be accepted outside the country since it can be 'monetized' and accepted in payment of taxes in the foreign country. On the other hand, paper money is denominated only in the domestic unit of account and cannot be 'monetized' or accepted for tax payments abroad.

Finally, while Smith did not explicitly recognize it, payment of taxes is a form of reflux that removes paper money (and specie) from circulation just as bank money (notes or deposits) is refluxed when notes and cheques are presented for payment or clearing. It is not really convertibility, but rather reflux that removes 'unwanted' paper money.

In the next section, we will examine Knapp's more general theory of money, which is consistent with, but expands significantly upon, the observations of Smith.

KNAPP AND THE STATE THEORY OF MONEY

Georg Friedrich Knapp put forward a state theory of money similar to, but more general than, what is now known as the Chartalist approach. This approach is opposed to the metallist view, according to which the value of money derives from the value of the metal standard (for example, gold or silver) adopted. More generally, according to Knapp, metallists try to 'deduce' the monetary system 'without the idea of a State'. This, he believes, is 'absurd' for 'the money of a state' is that which is 'accepted at the public pay offices' (Knapp [1924] 1973, pp. vii–viii; see also Goodhart, 1989). It is thus impossible to separate the theory of money from the theory of the state. Knapp's exposition is quite complex and required the creation of a classificatory scheme with hundreds of terms. We will try to keep our summary simple; to some extent we will have to paraphrase rather than use

extensive quotes, for otherwise we would have to define the numerous
terms he coined.

According to Knapp, debts are expressed in a unit of value, 'the unit in
which the amount of the payment is expressed' (ibid., p. 8) and discharged
with means of payment 'a movable thing which has the legal property of
being the bearer of units of value' (ibid., p. 7). What, then, determines
which things will act as means of payment to discharge debts? Knapp
noticed that means of payment are occasionally changed; sometimes one
type of material (say, weighed or coined gold) has been accepted but
'suddenly' another (say, weighed or coined silver) takes its place.
Therefore, while the means of payment may be a definite material, it is not
bound to any particular material, for it may be changed (ibid., pp. 8–25). 'A
proclamation is made that a piece of such and such a description shall be
valid as so many units of value' (ibid. p. 30). 'Validity by proclamation is
not bound to any material. It can occur with the most precious or the basest
metals . . .' (ibid. p. 30). The fundamental insight was his recognition that
these transitions always require that the state announce a conversion rate
(say, so many ounces of gold for so many ounces of silver). The debts were
always nominal and were never actually 'metallic': all debts are converted
to the new metal, which proves that all units of account must be nominal.
Hence, the Chartalist, and more specifically, state theory of money, since
the proclamation is made by the state.

Knapp examined the transition from use of weights of gold, to stamped
coins that are weighed to determine value, to stamped coins that are
accepted at face value, and finally to paper money; he found that the state
played the major role in much of this transformation – but we shall skip this
historical evolution. We will begin with the modern system, where Chartal
money has developed.

> When we give up our coats in the cloak-room of a theatre, we receive a tin disc
> of a given size bearing a sign, perhaps a number. There is nothing more on it,
> but this ticket or mark has legal significance; it is a proof that I am entitled to
> demand the return of my coat. When we send letters, we affix a stamp or a ticket
> which proves that we have by payment of postage obtained the right to get the
> letter carried. The 'ticket' is then a good expression . . . for a movable, shaped
> object bearing signs, to which legal ordinance gives a use independent of its
> material. Our means of payment, then, whether coins or warrants, possess the
> above-named qualities: they are pay-tokens, or tickets used as means of payment
> . . . Perhaps the Latin word 'Charta' can bear the sense of ticket or token, and we
> can form a new but intelligible adjective – 'Chartal'. Our means of payment
> have this token, or Chartal, form. Among civilized peoples in our day, payments
> can only be made with pay-tickets or Chartal pieces. (Knapp [1924] 1973, pp.
> 31–2)

Note that like the tin disc issued by the cloakroom, the material used to manufacture the Chartal pieces is wholly irrelevant – it can be gold, silver or common metal; it can be paper.

> It is, therefore, impossible to tell from the pieces themselves whether they are Chartal or not. This is at once evident in the case of warrants. As to coins, we must always refer to the Acts and Statutes, which alone can give information . . . if the pieces gain their validity through proclamation, they are Chartal. (Ibid., pp. 34–5)

Finally, 'Money always signifies a Chartal means of payment. Every means of payment we call money. The definition of money is therefore a Chartal means of payment' (ibid., pp. 34–8).

Chartalism is often identified with the proposition that legal tender laws determine that which must be accepted as means of payment. However, Knapp's analysis went further.

> If we have already declared in the beginning that money is a creation of law, this is not to be interpreted in the narrower sense that it is a creation of jurisprudence, but in the larger sense that it is a creation of the legislative activity of the State, a creation of legislative policy. (Ibid., p. 40)

And what is the nature of this 'legislative activity' that determines what will be the Chartalist money accepted within the jurisdiction of the state?

> What forms part of the monetary system of the State and what does not? We must not make our definition too narrow. The criterion cannot be that the money is issued by the State, for that would exclude kinds of money which are of the highest importance; I refer to bank-notes: they are not issued by the State, but they form a part of its monetary system. Nor can legal tender be taken as the test, for in monetary systems there are very frequently kinds of money which are not legal tender . . . We keep most closely to the facts if we take as our test, that the money is accepted in payments made to the State's offices. Then all means by which a payment can be made to the State form part of the monetary system. On this basis it is not the issue, but the acceptation, as we call it, which is decisive. State acceptation delimits the monetary system. By the expression 'State-acceptation' is to be understood only the acceptance at State pay offices where the State is the recipient. (Ibid., p. 95)

Thus it is the decision of the state to accept at state pay offices, and not legal tender laws, that creates a Chartal money.

According to Knapp, 'centric' payments, or those involving the state, are decisive; these take the form of either (1) 'payments to the State as receiver; these we call epicentric' or (2) 'payments made by the State, these we will call apocentric' (ibid pp. 96–7). On the other hand payments between private persons ('paracentric') 'are not so important as is generally supposed, for they mostly, so to speak, regulate themselves' (ibid., p. 96). Indeed, the actions of the state play a large role in determining that which will serve as ('paracentric') means of payment in private transactions.

> In the monetary system of a State there must be one kind of money which is definitive, as opposed to provisional (convertible) money . . . Money is definitive if, when payment is made in it, the business is completely concluded . . . The payer is no longer under an obligation, the recipient has no further rights either against the payer or against the State, if the State has issued the money [ibid., p. 102] . . . That kind of definitive money which is always kept ready and can be insisted on for apocentric payments [payments made by the State] . . . we call *valuta*; all other kinds of money . . . we call *accessory* (p. 105).

The definitive money is that which the state insists it will accept at pay offices, while valuta money is a component of definitive money, namely that which it will provide in payment.[4]

> In Germany our gold pieces were valuta, not because they were made of gold . . . but only because the State, when it made a payment, was ready in the last resort to pay in gold pieces, and, if it found it at all inconvenient, totally to refuse any other means of payment which the recipient might happen to want. (Ibid., p. 107)

However, once the state has decided to declare one type of money as valuta, then that type will become the 'decisive' money used in private transactions.

> So, if from political necessity the State announces that henceforth it will pay in State notes, as fountain of law it must equally allow the State notes to suffice for other payments . . . The consequence is, in a legal dispute the means of payment which the creditor is compelled to accept is always that which the State has put in the position of valuta . . . Apart from friendly agreement, all payments eventually have to be made in valuta money. (Ibid., p. 110)

Thus it is not simply a 'legal tender' law that makes state notes acceptable in private transactions, but it is the fact that the state first decides what it will use or accept as money in its own transactions, and that this must then be acceptable as means of settlement of private debts. 'The laws do not decide what shall be valuta money, they merely express a pious hope, for they are powerless against their creator, the State . . .' (Ibid., p. 111).

Knapp extended his analysis to include bank money. 'The bank makes notes and offers them in payment to its customers. Issuing notes is not a special business . . . but a special way in which the bank endeavours to make its payments . . . . It tries to pay in its own notes instead of in money issued by the State, because then with a comparatively small capital it can make greater profits than it otherwise could' (ibid., p. 131). Acceptability of banknotes in private transactions is not (as was commonly believed) due to the bank promise to convert these to specie. In other words, bank money did not derive its value from the gold reserves or specie coin, or even valuta money, into which it promised redemption. 'A bank-note is a chartal document, which specifies a sum of valuta money; and the bank issuing it is pledged by law to accept it for a payment of that amount' (ibid. p. 134). Whether banknotes are convertible is irrelevant. 'An inconvertible bank-note, then, is not a nullity, but has this in common with the convertible bank-note, that it is a till-warrant of the bank' (ibid.). What is important is that the note 'is a private till-warrant available for payments to the bank . . . but clearly the customers of the bank can use it for payments between themselves, as they are sure it will be taken at the bank. These customers and the bank form, so to speak, a private pay community; the public pay community is the State' (ibid.).

Knapp goes further than Smith in his recognition that banknotes do not derive their value from the reserves (whether gold or government fiat money) held for conversion, but rather from their use in the 'private pay community' and 'public pay community'; this, in turn, is a function of 'acceptation' at the bank and public pay offices. Within the 'private pay community' (or 'giro'), bank money is the primary money used in payments; however, payments in the 'public pay community' require state money. This can include bank money, but note that generally delivery of bank money to the state is not final, or definitive, because the state will present it to banks for 'redemption' (for valuta reserves). Bank money, when used in the public pay community is not 'definitive' unless the state also uses it in its own purchases.

What makes banknotes state money? 'Bank-notes are not automatically money of the state, but they become so as soon as the State announces that it will receive them in epicentric payments [payments to the state]' (Knapp [1924] 1973, p. 135). If the state accepts notes in payment to the state, then the banknotes become 'accessory' and the business of the bank is enhanced, 'for now everybody is glad to take its bank-notes since all inhabitants of the State have occasion to make epicentric payments (e.g. for taxes)' (ibid. p. 137). The banknotes then become 'valuta' money if the state takes the next step and makes 'apocentric payments [payments by the State] in bank-notes' (ibid., p. 138). However, states often required that banks make their notes convertible to state-issued money: 'one of the measures by means of which the State assures a superior position to the money which it issues itself' (ibid., p. 140), and thus maintained banknotes in the role of accessory money (rather than allowing them to become valuta money). If the state accepts banknotes in payment, but does not make payments in these banknotes, then the notes will be redeemed – leading to a drain of 'reserves' of valuta money (indeed, governments and central banks used redemption or threat of redemption to 'discipline' banks).

In times of distress (frequently during wars that required finance provided by banks), however, governments would pass laws ending convertibility, announce that the state would henceforth make payments in terms of the banknotes, and thereby declare that the banknotes were valuta money (Knapp [1924] 1973, p. 143). Usually, this was for one bank only – the bank which became the central bank. Through action of the state, then, paper money can become valuta money. 'At first bank-notes and Treasury notes are employed only as accessory money . . . The mournful hour arrives when the State has to announce that it can no longer pay in the money that was till then valuta [say, coined gold] and that those warrants themselves are now valuta'[5] (ibid., p. 196).

At this point we have a Chartalist, non-convertible, paper money, as do all modern developed countries. Of course, this extreme development came nearly three-quarters of a century after Knapp's book was first published (1905). However, he had recognized that the money of a state did not derive its value from metal, and indeed, that no metal was needed domestically. He did argue, on the other hand, that in the international sphere 'To dispense with specie money altogether would only be possible for very large federations of States [and, therefore, is] probably impracticable. On account of foreign trade specie money is still necessary', (ibid., p. xv) a point similar to that made by Smith. Within a state, however, specie is not necessary, for 'state money may be recognised by the fact that it is accepted in payment by the State'; as Keynes said (see below), the state not only enforces the dictionary (legal tender laws) but writes it (decides what is to be accepted as money).[6]

It can be seen that Knapp's analysis is consistent with Smith's. Most paper money (today, mostly deposits) is privately issued and derives its demand not from a promise of redeemability but rather from state acceptance at pay offices. Knapp goes further, for he argues that the state eventually realizes (usually during a crisis) that it can also make payments in that which it promises to accept. Once freed from domestic convertibility on a metallic standard, the state's spending domestically would not be constrained by the quantity of the metal available. Abandonment of the metallic standard internationally would eliminate metallic constraints on countries. The state thus moved to a paper money system domestically, making its apocentric payments in central bank notes and accepting epicentric payments in private bank notes (today, deposits) that would have to be redeemed (today, cleared) for the valuta central bank notes (today, reserves). Precious metals were then used only for international purposes until the US finally abandoned the gold standard altogether in the early 1970s.

KEYNES'S *TREATISE ON MONEY*

While Keynes's *General Theory* presented the theory of aggregate effective demand that is now identified as 'Keynesian theory', his earlier *Treatise on Money* provided a more detailed treatment of his monetary theory. The first volume of that work presents definitions of money that would be used in his analysis; a brief examination of these provides insights into the view of money adopted by Keynes.

According to Keynes, the 'money of account' is the 'primary concept' of a theory of money; the money of account 'comes into existence along with Debts, which are contracts for deferred payment, and Price-Lists, which are offers of contracts for sale or purchase' (Keynes, 1930, p. 3). In turn, 'Money itself, namely that by delivery of which debt-contracts and price-contracts are discharged, and in the shape of which a store of General Purchasing Power is held, derives its character from its relationship to the Money-of-Account, since the debts and prices must first have been expressed in terms of the latter' (ibid.). He further clarifies the distinction between money and the money of account: 'the money-of-account is the description or title and the money is the thing which answers to the description' (ibid., pp. 3–4).

Following Knapp, Keynes argued that the state determines what serves as the money of account as well as dictates what 'thing' will be accepted as money.

The State, therefore, comes in first of all as the authority of law which enforces the payment of the thing which corresponds to the name or description in the contracts. But it comes in doubly when, in addition, it claims the right to determine and declare what thing corresponds to the name, and to vary its declaration from time to time – when, that is to say, it claims the right to re-edit the dictionary. This right is claimed by all modern states and has been so claimed for some four thousand years at least. (Ibid., p. 4)

The 'Age of Chartalist or State Money' had been reached, when the state 'claimed the right not only to enforce the dictionary but also to write the dictionary' (ibid., p. 5). Let us emphasize that Keynes believed the 'Age of State Money' to have begun 'at least' four thousand years ago, as such, the state theory of money would certainly apply to all the 'modern' economies including those living under the gold standard in the last century – even a gold-based commodity money is state money.

Privately issued debt – such as that issued by banks – might be accepted in settlement of transactions even if it is not declared by the government to be money; it can circulate 'side by side' with 'state money' (ibid., p. 6). However, the state might 'use its chartalist prerogative to declare that the [bank] debt itself is an acceptable discharge of a liability' (ibid.). Bank money then becomes a 'Representative Money' (ibid.). 'At the cost of not conforming entirely with current usage, I propose to include as State-Money not only money which is itself compulsory legal-tender but also money which the State or the central bank undertakes to accept in payments to itself or to exchange for compulsory legal-tender money' (ibid.). In a footnote to this passage, he goes on: 'Knapp accepts as "Money" – rightly I think – anything which the State undertakes to accept at its pay-offices, whether or not it is declared legal-tender between citizens' (ibid. pp. 6–7). Therefore, like Knapp, Keynes's analysis goes beyond legal tender laws to identify state 'acceptation' as the key to determining what will serve as money.

Finally, state money may take any of three forms: '*Commodity Money*, *Fiat Money* and *Managed Money*, the last two being sub-species of *Representative Money*' (ibid., p. 7). Commodity money is defined as 'actual units of a particular freely-obtainable, non-monopolised commodity which happens to have been chosen for the familiar purposes of money', or 'warehouse warrants for actually existing units of the commodity' (ibid.). Fiat money is representative money 'which is created and issued by the State, but is not convertible by law into anything other than itself, and has no fixed value in terms of an objective standard' (ibid.). This is distinguished from managed money, which 'is similar to Fiat Money, except that the State undertakes to manage the conditions of its issue in such a way that, by convertiblity or otherwise, it shall have a determinant value in terms of an objective standard'[7] (ibid., p. 8).

Managed money is, according to Keynes, the most generalized form of money, which can 'degenerate into Commodity Money on the one side when the managing authority holds against it a hundred per cent of the objective standard, so that it is in effect a warehouse warrant, and into Fiat Money on the other side when it loses its objective standard' (ibid.). In other words, a full-bodied – say, one ounce – gold coin valued at one currency unit would qualify as commodity money, while a paper note which is convertible to gold against which a fractional gold reserve is held would qualify as managed money – even if the conversion rate is one currency unit per ounce of gold. Thus a gold standard system can be operated as either a commodity money or as a managed money. On the other hand, a representative money can take the form of either a managed money (a paper note convertible on demand to gold, or even to a foreign currency – for example a currency board system) or a fiat money (no promise to convert at a fixed exchange rate to precious metals or foreign exchange). Note that Keynes argued that even a gold standard, whether a commodity money system or a managed money system, operates as a state money system. In either case, the state can always 'rewrite the dictionary', for example, by adopting a silver standard and a conversion rate (say, one ounce of gold for four ounces of silver).

State money can be held by banks, by the central bank, and by the public.

> The State-Money held by the central bank constitutes its 'reserve' against its deposits. These deposits we may term Central Bank-Money. It is convenient to assume that all the Central Bank-Money is held by the Member Banks – in so far as it may be held by the public, it may be on the same footing as State-Money or as Member Bank-Money, according to circumstances. This Central Bank-Money plus the state money held by the Member Banks makes up the Reserves of the Member Banks, which they, in turn, hold against their Deposits. These Deposits constitute the Member Bank-Money in the hands of the Public, and make up, together with the State-Money (and Central Bank-Money, if any) held by the Public, the aggregate of Current Money. (Keynes, 1930 pp. 9–10)

Any payments to the state using 'Member Bank-Money' will cause member banks to lose 'Central Bank-Money' or 'State Money held by the Member Banks' – that is, reserves.

As we will explore in more detail in Chapter 5, and as Knapp recognized, 'Member Bank-Money' is the primary 'thing' answering to the 'description' – money – used in private transactions (or, within the 'private pay community'). When accepted in payment of taxes, it is also used in the 'public pay community' – but it is not 'definitive' or valuta money from the perspective of member banks because they must deliver reserves (mainly 'Central Bank-Money') whenever taxes are paid using 'Member Bank-Money'.

In summary, with the rise of the modern state, the money of account ('the description') is chosen by the state, which is free to choose that which will qualify as money ('the thing' that answers to the description). This goes beyond legal tender laws – which establish what can legally discharge contracts – to include that which the state accepts in payment at its 'pay offices'. The state is free to choose a system based on commodity money, fiat money or managed money. Even if it chooses a strict commodity system, the value of the money does not derive from the commodity accepted as money, '[f]or Chartalism begins when the State designates the objective standard which shall correspond to the money-of-account'. (ibid., p. 11). '[M]oney is the measure of value, but to regard it as having value itself is a relic of the view that the value of money is regulated by the value of the substance of which it is made, and is like confusing a theatre ticket with the performance' (Keynes, 1983, p. 402). Once it is recognized that the state may 'write the dictionary', it becomes obvious that the nominal value of a commodity (or managed) money cannot be derived from the value of the 'objective standard'; it is then a small step to a 'fiat money' with no 'objective standard', for in all three cases, the state determines the nominal value of money. This is done when the state establishes what it will accept at public pay offices, as well as the nominal value of the thing accepted.

RECENT CONTRIBUTIONS IN THE CHARTALIST TRADITION

In recent years, many theorists have contributed to the development of an 'endogenous money' approach that is in many respects related to the Chartalist position and to the view presented in this book.[8] There are two fundamental precepts of the endogenous money view: (1) the 'supply' of money generally expands to meet the 'demand' for money; and (2) the central bank has no direct, discretionary, control over the quantity of money. To some extent, all the economists examined here, as well as most economists until the present century, at least implicitly adopt an endogenous money approach. It is only in this century that the majority of economists have come to accept the 'exogenous' money view that the central bank can directly control the quantity of money and that the money stock can be taken to be 'fixed' such that it does not respond to 'money demand'. In this section we examine only briefly contributions directly related to arguments made above. In Chapter 5, we will show that both the 'exogenous' and the 'endogenous' views can contribute to our understanding of the money-supply process, but that to some extent the debate between the two camps has been at cross purposes, for they have each examined different parts of that process.

The view that the 'supply' of money expands to meet the 'demand' for money can be traced back at least to the Banking School in the early nineteenth century (if not to Adam Smith as discussed above), although this terminology was not used (Wray 1990). The Banking School believed that banknotes are issued to meet the needs of trade (essentially a 'real bills' argument), that banknotes could never be excessive so long as they were redeemable on demand and, thus that no other restrictions on note issue would be required. Their contemporary opponents, the Currency School, wanted to regulate strictly the quantity of notes issued so that it would equal the quantity of coin specie – essentially, a 100 per cent reserve backing – to make the system operate as if all circulation were conducted on the basis of full-bodied coin (Keynes's 'commodity money', with money no more than a warehouse receipt for specie). This, they thought, would tame or eliminate the business cycle, which they believed to be caused by excessive note issue. In contrast, the Banking School concluded that private banknote issue could never be excessive, so long as notes were convertible, because they would reflux to banks (a position quite similar to that of Smith, examined above); however, a non-convertible (government) fiat money could be excessive because it would not reflux.[9]

Others after this controversy similarly held the Banking School view that the supply of credit expands more or less in step with the needs of trade. Marx, for example, argued that during an expansionary phase, credit substitutes for money, functioning as the primary medium of exchange and allowing the volume of transactions to rise. In a crisis, however, only 'narrow money' (Knapp's 'definitive' money) is desired, where it functions primarily as a means of payment to retire debts (and pay taxes) rather than as a medium of exchange. In crisis, 'the circulation of [bank] notes as a means of purchase is decreasing' even though 'their circulation as means of payment may increase' (Marx, 1909, p. 542). 'It is by no means the strong demand for loans . . . which distinguishes the period of depression from that of prosperity, but the ease with which this demand is satisfied in periods of prosperity, and the difficulties which it meets after a depression has become a fact' (ibid p. 532). In other words, banks readily advance loans (creating 'member bank money') in expansion but refuse to grant credit in the downturn.

As discussed above, Keynes also recognized that banks can normally increase loans to finance an increase of spending.[10] Many of his followers later held similar positions. This was developed by Kaldor (1985) into what has come to be known as the 'horizontalist' endogenous money approach (Moore, 1988). A similar, but mainly independent, path led to the modern Circuitiste approach. Before Keynes, Schumpeter had developed a view of dynamic and innovative banks, in which credit expansion was the key to allow entrepreneurs to finance innovation. Indeed, credit was seen as 'essentially the creation of purchasing power [by banks] for the purpose of transferring it to the entrepreneur' (Schumpeter, 1934, p. 107). Building on Schumpeter's views, the Circuitiste approach to money reached independently many of the same conclusions as did the 'horizontalist' endogenous money approach.[11]

What is important to note is that if money supply responds to money demand, this means that the 'quantity of money' is not 'exogenous' in the sense of being determined either through monetary policy (such as control by the central bank over bank reserves) or by the quantity of a precious metal reserve (as under a 'commodity money' or 'managed money' system).[12] While the state defines money, it does not control the quantity. The state is able to control its initial emission of currency, but this is through fiscal policy rather than through monetary policy. That is, the quantity of currency created is determined by purchases of the state (including goods, services and assets purchased by the Treasury and the central bank); much of this currency will then be removed from circulation as taxes are paid. The rest ends up in desired hoards, or flows to banks to be accumulated as bank reserves. Monetary policy then drains excess reserves, removing them from member bank accounts, and replacing them with bonds voluntarily purchased. As Boulding (1950) had argued, fiscal policy has more to do with the quantity of money issued by the government, while monetary policy has to do with regulation of financial markets (most importantly, with determination of short term interest rates).

Hyman Minsky presented a view of money that was based on the Chartalist approach.[13] His approach emphasized the 'endogeneity' of money, that is, the view that money is created during the normal, and important, processes of a capitalist economy – and is not created and dropped by helicopters (as in Milton Friedman's famous exogenous, helicopter, money story). For the most part, bank money is created as banks 'make loans'.

> Money is unique in that it is created in the act of financing by a bank and is destroyed as the commitments on debt instruments owned by banks are fulfilled. Because money is created and destroyed in the normal course of business, the amount outstanding is responsive to the demand for financing. (Minsky, 1986, p. 249)

A 'loan' is nothing more than an agreement by a bank to make payments 'now' on the basis of a promise of the borrower to 'pay later'. 'Loans represent payments the bank made for business, households and governments in exchange for their promises to make payments to the bank at some future date'[14] (ibid p. 230).

All of this occurs on the balance sheets of banks; the 'money' that is created by a bank is nothing more than a credit to another bank's balance sheet.[15] According to Minsky, there is a pyramid of liabilities, with those of the central bank at the top. Bank liabilities are convertible on demand into central bank liabilities, which are used for interbank clearing (as well as for conversion of bank liabilities to 'cash' held by the public, resulting in a net reserve drain).

> The payments banks make are to other banks, although they simultaneously charge the account of the customer. In the receiving bank, the payments are credited to a depositor's account.
>
> For member banks of the Federal Reserve System, the interbank payments lead to deposits shifting from the account of one bank to the account of another at Federal Reserve banks. For nonmember banks, another bank – called a correspondent – intervenes, so that the transfer at the Federal Reserve banks are for the accounts of correspondents. (Minsky, 1986, pp. 230–1)

Thus 'payments' among banks occur on the balance sheet of the Fed as banks use 'Fed money' (reserves) to settle net debits from their accounts. 'Whereas the public uses bank deposits as money, banks use Federal Reserve deposits as money. This is the fundamental hierarchical property of our money and banking system' (ibid., p. 231). This is, of course, the same hierarchical arrangement noted by Knapp (in his public and private pay communities) and by Keynes (a point to which we will return in Chapter 5).

In an argument very similar to Knapp's Chartalist view, Minsky explained that people accept bank money in part because they can use it to meet their own commitments to banks. 'Demand deposits have exchange value because a multitude of debtors to banks have outstanding debts that call for the payment of demand deposits to banks. These debtors will work and sell goods or financial instruments to get demand deposits' (ibid.). In other words, according to Minsky, bank money has (nominal) value precisely because it can be used to retire debts to banks – it is, so to speak, accepted at 'bank pay offices'. The 'borrower' retires his/her promise to the bank by delivering bank liabilities at the future date, and the need for bank liabilities to retire one's own liabilities to banks leads one to accept bank liabilities in payment for goods and services delivered. Rather than focusing on money as a medium of exchange, this focus is on money as means of payment – to retire liabilities.

This led Minsky back to the Smith/Knapp recognition that taxes give value to the money issued by the government.[16]

> In an economy where government debt is a major asset on the books of the deposit-issuing banks, the fact that taxes need to be paid gives value to the money of the economy . . . [T]he need to pay taxes means that people work and produce in order to get that in which taxes can be paid. (Ibid.)

And even though most taxes are actually paid using bank money, because of the hierarchical arrangement, Keynes and Minsky emphasize that banks can make these payments to government only by using central bank money, that is, by losing reserves.

Returning to the primary Chartalist theme, Abba Lerner insisted that

> [W]hatever may have been the history of gold, at the present time, in a normally well-working economy, money is a creature of the state. Its general acceptability, which is its all-important attribute, stands or falls by its acceptability by the state. (Lerner, 1947, p. 313)

Just how does the state demonstrate acceptability?

> The modern state can make anything it chooses generally acceptable as money . . . It is true that a simple declaration that such and such is money will not do, even if backed by the most convincing constitutional evidence of the state's absolute sovereignty. But if the state is willing to accept the proposed money in payment of taxes and other obligations to itself the trick is done. Everyone who has obligations to the state will be willing to accept the pieces of paper with which he can settle the obligations, and all other people will be willing to accept these pieces of paper because they know that the taxpayers, etc., will accept them in turn. (Ibid.)

This seems to be about as clear a statement as one can find: even if it has not always been the case, it surely is now true and obvious that the state writes the 'description' of money when it denominates the tax liability in a money of account, and defines the 'thing' that 'answers to the description' when it decides what will be accepted at public pay offices. The 'thing' which answers to the 'description' is widely accepted not because of sovereignty alone, not because of legal tender laws and not because it might have (or have had) gold backing, but because the state has the power to impose and enforce tax liabilities and because it has the right to choose 'that which is necessary to pay taxes' ('twintopt'). This right, as emphasized by Keynes, 'has been so claimed for some four thousand years at least' (Keynes, 1930, p. 3). While Keynes is no historian and while one might quibble over the exact number of years since states first claimed these rights, there can be no doubt but that all modern states do have these rights. As Lerner said 'Cigarette money and foreign money can come into wide use only when the normal money and the economy in general is in a state of chaos' (Lerner, 1947, p. 313). One might only add that when the state is in crisis and loses legitimacy, and in particular loses its power to impose and enforce tax liabilities, 'normal money' will be in a 'state of chaos', leading, for example, to use of foreign currencies in private domestic transactions. In all other cases, it is state money which is used, and state money is that which the state accepts in payment of taxes.

CONCLUSION

In the Chartalist approach, the public demands the government's money because that is the form in which taxes are paid. It is not a coincidence that the modern state uses the same valuta money in its apocentric payments that it accepts in epicentric payments – it uses taxes as a means of inducing the population to supply goods and services to the state, supplying in return the money that will be used to retire the tax liability. In the modern economy, it appears that taxes are paid using bank money, but analysis of reserve accounting shows that tax payments always lead to a reserve drain (that is, reduce central bank liabilities), so that in reality only the government's money is definitive (finally discharging the tax liability).

We turn next to a history of money before moving on to examine the policy implications of the Chartalist or taxes-drive-money view.

NOTES

1. Some might wonder whether the Eurodollar is an example of a stateless money, as these appear to be stateless dollars. Actually, however, Eurodollars are created when the holder of a US commercial bank demand deposit opens a Eurodollar account, transferring funds (for example, to a London-based commercial bank). This creates a dollar-denominated deposit in a foreign bank offset by an asset which is a dollar-denominated demand deposit held against a US bank. Sometimes these Eurodollars are then lent to the US banking system, causing a shift of reserves among US banks; the Eurodollar market can never be a net source of reserves to the US banking system, because Eurodollars are really just liabilities that 'leverage' US bank reserves and currency (see Chapter 5 for discussion of such leveraging activity). Clearly, however, the Eurodollar derives its value from the US dollar, which itself derives its demand from US tax liabilities. This is not to say that foreigners who demand Eurodollars do so in order to pay US taxes (clearly that is almost never the case), rather, Eurodollars are demanded because the dollar has become an international reserve currency.

2. He went on to give the example of banks in Scotland which adopted an 'optional clause' which allowed them the option of withholding redemption for six months after presentation (in which case they paid interest for the period). These notes typically suffered a discount of 4 per cent relative to specie in trade.

3. In the sidebar to Smith's discussion of the relation between the value of the currency and taxes, Cannan wrote 'A requirement that certain taxes should be paid in particular paper money might give that paper a certain value even if it was irredeemable' (Edwin Cannan, in Smith, 1937, p. 312). Earlier, Cannan had applied 'the theoretical apparatus of supply and demand to units of a currency,' arguing 'Given a certain demand, increase of supply, in case of any article, reduces value, and currency is no exception' (Cannan 1983 [1921], pp. 3, 9). In that article, he recognized that currency is supplied by government 'in exchange for commodities and services', but also 'in doles and pensions without getting any return' (ibid, p. 9); the demand for currency was functionally related to many factors, including population, wealth distribution, introduction of currency economizing practices, uncertainty

about the future, and exchange rate speculation, however, he did not relate demand to the tax liability.

4. A money can be both definitive and valuta if the state makes payments in it and accepts it at pay offices. Note that there is some inconsistency in Knapp's argument, for what is important is 'acceptation' at public pay offices. He should thus define valuta to indicate both acceptation by the state and use by the state in its own payments.

5. This often comes after the bank has purchased government debt and issued notes that promised conversion; in times of war or other distress, the government would 'encourage' banks to issue far more notes (to 'finance' government spending) than they could conceivably convert. Thus suspension of convertibility served the interests of government as well as the bank.

6. Of course, the type of monetary system envisioned by Knapp is similar to the one adopted shortly thereafter by the US: a 'gold standard' without domestic convertibility, but with a specie reserve to satisfy international purposes. Knapp did not foresee the time when metals could be dropped altogether in favour of foreign currency reserves and flexible exchange rates.

7. The employer of last resort programme examined in Chapter 6 below is a managed money system on Keynes's definition.

8. See Davidson (1978), Kaldor (1985), Minsky (1986), Moore (1988), Rousseas (1986), and Wray (1990).

9. Note that neither school appeared to recognize that state fiat money does indeed reflux as taxes are paid – which, as Smith recognized, is the mechanism that can ensure state note issue is not excessive. The Currency School also did not appear to recognize Smith's argument that the volume of real trade would be higher if the quantity of notes issued were to exceed the quantity of gold reserves as its proponents saw the extra money in circulation as excessive given the needs of trade.

10. This is even clearer in his 1937 articles, after publication of *The General Theory*. See Keynes (1973).

11. See Deleplace and Nell (1996). In Chapter 5 we will return to an examination of the theory behind the approach.

12. Note that most 'money' is credit money; here we are using the term 'money' in its broad sense.

13. In private conversation, Minsky acknowledged his intellectual debt to the Chartalists and especially to Knapp.

14. In 1913, Mitchell Innes presented a view quite similar to Minsky's. 'Debts and credits are perpetually trying to get into touch with one another, so that they may be written off against each other, and it is the business of the banker to bring them together . . . There is thus a constant circulation of debts and credits through the medium of the banker who brings them together and clears them as the debts fall due. This is the whole business of banking as it was three thousand years before Christ, and as it is today' (Innes, 1913, pp. 402–3).

15. As the borrower spends the created money, a cheque drawn on the first bank is deposited with another.

16. This has been recognized by Goodhart, who argues that 'The use of such state-issued fiat currency was supported by several factors. First the state levies taxes and can insist that these be paid in state-issued money. This ensures that such fiat currency will have some value' (Goodhart, 1989, p. 36). Similarly, James Tobin argues that 'By its willingness to accept a designated asset in settlement of taxes and other obligations, the government makes that asset acceptable to any who have such obligations, and in turn to others who have obligations to them, and so on' (Tobin, 1998, p. 27).

3 An Introduction to a History of Money

TALLIES AND COINS

Most money and banking texts begin with a story about the origins of money, according to which early exchange was based on barter until humans discovered that certain commodities could be used as a medium of exchange to eliminate the 'double coincidence of wants' required for barter to take place. An early caricature of this belief is presented by A. Mitchell Innes (1913); while it is somewhat long, it cannot be improved upon:[1]

> The fundamental theories on which the modern science of political economy is based are these:
>
> That under primitive conditions men lived and live by barter;
>
> That as life becomes more complex barter no longer suffices as a method of exchanging commodities, and by common consent one particular commodity is fixed on which is generally acceptable, and which therefore, everyone will take in exchange . . . ;
>
> That this commodity thus becomes a 'medium of exchange and measure of value'.
>
> That many different commodities have at various times and places served as this medium of exchange, – cattle, iron, salt, shells, dried cod, tobacco, sugar, nails, etc.;
>
> That gradually the metals, gold, silver, copper, and more especially the first two, came to be regarded as being by their inherent qualities more suitable for this purpose than any other commodities and these metals early became by common consent the only medium of exchange;
>
> That a certain fixed weight of one of these metals of a known fineness became a standard of value, and to guarantee this weight and quality it became incumbent on governments to issue pieces of metal stamped with their peculiar sign . . . ;
>
> That Emperors, Kings, Princes and their advisors, vied with each other in the middle ages in swindling the people by debasing their coins . . . and that this

situation produced serious evils among which were a depreciation of the value of money and a consequent rise of prices . . . ;

That to economize the use of the metals and to prevent their constant transport a machinery called 'credit' has grown up in modern days, by means of which, instead of handing over a certain weight of metal at each transaction, a promise to do so is given, which under favourable circumstances has the same value as the metal itself. Credit is called a substitute for gold. (Innes, 1913, p. 377)

However, 'modern research in the domain of commercial history and numismatics' demonstrates that 'none of these theories rest on a solid basis of historical proof – that in fact they are false' (ibid., p. 378). Briefly, there is no evidence that markets operated on the basis of barter (except in extraordinary circumstances such as prisoner-of-war camps), there is no evidence that 'many different commodities' have exchanged hands as media of exchange (that is, to purchase commodities on the market), there is no evidence that the value of early coins was determined by certain fixed weights of precious metals, and there is no evidence that credit 'has grown up' as an 'economizing' substitute for precious metal coins for use as a medium of exchange.

In this chapter we will outline an alternative to the conventional view. It is of course impossible to present an adequate 'history of money' in one chapter. We will instead provide a few anecdotes and alternative interpretations of well-known folklore regarding the origins and evolution of money. In some respects it might have been sufficient to simply ignore the history of money and to focus only on money as it stands at the end of the twentieth century. However, as Keynes argued, 'Chartal' or modern money is at least 4000 years old, and it is our proposition that the analysis contained in this book is not merely of a 'special case' to be applied only to the US at the end of this century, but rather that it can be applied much more generally to the entire era of Chartal, or state, money. Instead of trying to locate the origins of money in a supposed primitive market originally based on barter, we find the origins in the rise of the early palace community, which was able to enforce a tax obligation on its subjects. We thus believe that a brief examination of the history and evolution of money does shed light on the nature of modern money.

Historical evidence suggests that virtually all 'commerce' from the very earliest times was conducted on the basis of credits and debits. Innes writes of the early European experience: 'For many centuries, how many we do not know, the principal instrument of commerce was neither the coin nor the private token, but the tally[2]' (ibid. p. 394). This was a 'stick of squared hazel-wood, notched in a certain manner to indicate the amount of the purchase or debt', created when the 'buyer' became a 'debtor' by accepting a good or service from the 'seller' who automatically became the 'creditor' (ibid.). 'The name of the debtor and the date of the transaction were written on two opposite sides of the stick, which was then split down the middle in such a way that the notches were cut in half, and the name and date appeared on both pieces of the tally' (ibid.). The split was stopped about an inch from the base of the stick so that one piece, the 'stock' was longer than the other, called the 'stub' (also called the 'foil'). The creditor would retain the stock (from which our terms capital and corporate stock derive) while the debtor would take the stub (a term still used as in 'ticket stub') to ensure that the stock was not tampered with. When the debtor retired his debt, the two pieces of the tally would be matched to verify the amount of the debt.

Of course, wooden tallies were not the only records as there was nothing unique about hazelwood (indeed, it appears to have been used because it was common in England and Northern Europe). Pieces of copper dating from 1000 to 2000 BC have been found in Italy which appear to be tallies, purposely broken at the time of manufacture so that creditor and debtor would have their stock and stub (Innes, 1913, p. 394). Some of the earliest records of tallies come from Babylonia, on clay *shubati* ('received') tablets; these indicated a quantity of grain, the word *shubati*, the name of the person from whom received, the name of the person by whom received, the date, and the seal of the receiver or of the king's scribe (when the king was the receiver). Unlike the wooden tally, these tablets would not be split to give the debtor a stub. This problem was solved in two ways: the tablets were either stored in temples where they would be safe from tampering, or they were sealed in cases which would have to be broken to reach them. All the inscriptions listed above would be repeated on the case, but the enclosed tablet would not contain the name and seal of the receiver. Thus if the case were broken, the tablet would not be complete. Only when the debt was repaid would the case be broken (allowing the debtor to observe that the inscription on the case matched that of the enclosed tablet). Unlike the tablets stored in temples, the 'case tablets' could circulate.

And, indeed, the tallies did circulate as 'transferable, negotiable instruments'. One could deliver the stock of a tally to purchase goods and services, or to retire one's own debt. 'By their means all purchases of goods, all loans of money were made, and all debts cleared' (Innes, 1913, p. 396). A merchant holding a number of tally stocks of customers could meet with a merchant holding tally stocks against the first merchant, 'clearing' his tally stub debts by delivery of the customers' stocks. In this way, great 'fairs' were developed to act as 'clearing houses' allowing merchants 'to settle their mutual debts and credits'; the 'greatest of these fairs in England was that of St. Giles in Winchester, while the most famous probably in all

Europe were those of Champagne and Brie in France, to which came merchants and bankers from all countries' (ibid.). Debts were cleared 'without the use of a single coin'; it became common practice to 'make debts payable at one or other of the fairs', and '[a]t some fairs no other business was done except the settlement of debts and credits', although retail trade was often conducted at the fairs. While conventional analysis views the primary purpose of the fairs as retail trade, Innes postulates that the retail trade originated as a sideline to the clearing house trade.[3] He also notes that clearing house fairs were held in ancient Greece and Rome, and in Mexico at the time of the conquest.

Even if one accepts that much or even most trade took place on the basis of credits and debts, this does not necessarily disprove the story of the textbooks. Perhaps coins existed before these tallies (records of debts), and surely the coins were made of precious metals. Perhaps the debts were made convertible to coin, indeed, perhaps such debt contracts were enforceable only in legal tender coin. If this were the case, then the credits and debts merely substituted for coin, and net debts would be settled with coin, which would not be inconsistent with the conventional story. There are several problems with such an interpretation.

First, the tally debts (in the form of clay tablets) are at least 2000 years older than the oldest known coins.[4] It seems very unlikely that clay tablets would outlast coined precious metal. Second, it has long befuddled economic historians that the denominations of all the early precious metal coins (even the least valuable) were far too high to have been used in everyday commerce. For example, the earliest coins were electrum (an alloy of silver and gold) and the most common denomination would have had a purchasing power of about ten sheep, so that 'it cannot have been a useful coin for small transactions' (Cook, 1958, p. 260). They might have sufficed for the wholesale trade of large merchants, but they could not have been used in day-to-day retail trade.[5] Furthermore, the reported nominal value of coins does not appear to be closely regulated by precious metal content (see below). It is also quite unlikely that coins would have been invented to facilitate trade, for 'Phoenicians and other peoples of the East who had commercial interests managed satisfactorily without coined money' for many centuries (ibid. p. 260). Indeed, the introduction of coins would have been a less efficient alternative in most cases.

Finally, while we are accustomed to a small number of types of coins (always issued by government, with perhaps one coin for each denomination), the typical case until recently was a plethora of coins, sometimes including many with the same face value but different exchange value, issued by a wide variety of merchants, kings, feudal lords, barons, ecclesiastics and others. Indeed, 'in [feudal] France there were beside the royal monies, eighty different coinages . . . each entirely independent of the other and differing as to weights, denominations, alloys and types [and] twenty different monetary systems' (Innes, 1913, p. 385). According to MacDonald, in Merovingian Gaul there were '1200 different moneyers', the great majority of whom were private individuals; this 'epoch of private coinage' seems to have been 'brought to an end by Pepin and Charlemagne' (MacDonald, 1916, pp. 29–35).

Note that the textbook story relies on choice of a particular precious metal by 'common consent' to be used as money precisely to reduce the transactions costs of barter. However, in reality, the poor consumer (if such existed) was faced with a tremendous number of coins of varying weight, denomination, alloy and fineness with which he would not be able to cope.[6] Indeed, it is difficult to believe that the typical member of these societies would be more able to assess the value of a coin than he would be able to assess the value of, say, a cow.[7] Rather than reducing transactions costs by using precious metals, it would probably have reduced transactions costs to use cows! And it does no good to argue that cows are less divisible, for as noted above, the precious metal coins were far too valuable to have been used in daily transactions anyway. That at least some were not used in frequent transactions is evidenced by 'the excellent state of preservation in which they are usually found' (Grierson, 1965, p. 536). We know that 'wear and tear' on coins in circulation is quite high – perhaps 1 per cent per year (Munro, 1979, pp. 181–2) – but 'Carolingian coins seem to have circulated surprisingly little' (Grierson, 1965, p. 536). Finally, Grierson notes that it was frequently necessary to impose 'legislation forcing people to use coin; if they refused it they laid themselves open to severe penalties, a heavy fine if they were free men or a flogging if they were unfree' (ibid.). This hardly seems consistent with the textbook story of 'common consent'.[8]

It is also difficult to understand why precious metal coins were virtually always 'worth more' than would be dictated by their precious metal content if it is true that the value of the precious metal determines the value of the coin. Indeed, it would be strange if the value of coined metal were no more than the value of the metal coined. If the nominal value of the coin were below the relative value of precious metal contained therein, the coin would be removed from circulation to be used as metal. Further, given the costs of coinage, if the mint were to issue coins whose value were little more than that of the embodied metal, this would provide very little purchasing power to the mint. While the textbook story argues that paper 'credit' developed to economize on precious metals, we know that metal coins were a late development. In other words, lower-cost alternatives to full-bodied coin were already in use. Surely hazelwood tallies or clay tablets had lower non-monetary value than did precious metals. Thus it is unlikely that metal coins would be issued to circulate competitively (for example, with hazelwood tallies) unless their nominal value were well above the value of the embodied precious metal.[9]

What then are coins, what are their origins, and why are they accepted? Coins appear to have originated as 'pay tokens' (in Knapp's colourful phrase), as nothing more than evidence of debt. It is possible that these originated in the 'private sector', perhaps derived from medals that were common in some traditional societies. The earliest 'coins' then, may have been nothing more than gifts with an imprint to signify the giver; it is conceivable that these were given to recognize a personal debt to the receiver.[10] We will return below to this view, although it seems to be an unlikely source for the earliest coins.

Many believe that the first coins were struck by government, probably by Pheidon of Argos about 630 BC (Cook, 1958, p. 257). Given the large denomination of the early coins and uniform weight (although not uniform purity – which probably could not have been tested at the time), Cook argues that 'coinage was invented to make a large number of uniform payments of considerable value in a portable and durable form, and that the person or authority making the payment was the king of Lydia' (ibid. p. 261). Further, he suggests 'the purpose of coinage was the payment of mercenaries' (ibid.).[11] This thesis was modified 'by Kraay (1964) who suggested that governments minted coins to pay mercenaries only in order to create a medium for the payment of taxes'[12] (Redish, 1987, pp. 376–7). Crawford has argued that the evidence indicates that use of these early coins as a medium of exchange was an 'accidental consequence of the coinage', and not the reason for it (Crawford, 1970, p. 46). Instead, Crawford argued that 'the fiscal needs of the state determined the quantity of mint output and coin in circulation', in other words, coins were intentionally minted from the beginning to provide 'state finance' (ibid.). So, early governments did, indeed, understand that '[m]inting and taxing were two sides of the same coin of royal prerogative' (Davies, 1997, p. 146).

Similarly, Innes argued that '[t]he coins which [kings] issued were tokens of indebtedness with which they made small payments, such as the daily wages of their soldiers and sailors' (Innes, 1913, p. 399). This explains the relatively large value of the coins – which were not meant to provide a medium of exchange, but rather were evidence of the state's debt to 'soldiers and sailors'. The coins were then nothing more than 'tallies' as described above – evidence of government debt – and not deserving of the inordinate concern shown by modern economists. And, relative to the quantity of hazelwood tallies, and other forms of money, the quantity of coins was quite small:

[i]ndeed so small was the quantity of coins, that they did not even suffice for the needs of the Royal household and estates which regularly used tokens of various kinds for the purpose of making small payments. So unimportant indeed was the coinage that sometimes Kings did not hesitate to call it all in for re-minting and re-issue and still commerce went on the same[13] (Innes, 1913, p. 389).

Let us step back for a moment and ponder the implications. In our view, coins are mere tokens of the Crown's debt, a small proportion of the total 'tally'.

Just like any private individual, the government pays by giving acknowledgments of indebtedness – drafts on the Royal Treasury, or some other branch of government. This is well seen in medieval England, where the regular method used by the government for paying a creditor was by 'raising a tally' on the Customs or some other revenue-getting department, that is to say by giving to the creditor as an acknowledgment of indebtedness a wooden tally. (Ibid., p. 397–8)

The 'tallia divenda' developed to allow the king to issue an exchequer tally for payment for goods and services delivered to the court.[14] But why on earth would the Crown's subjects accept hazelwood tallies or, later, paper notes or token coins?

The government by law obliges certain selected persons to become its debtors. It declares that so-and-so, who imports goods from abroad, shall owe the government so much on all that he imports, or that so-and-so, who owns land, shall owe to the government so much per acre. This procedure is called levying a tax, and the persons thus forced into the position of debtors to the government must in theory seek out the holders of the tallies or other instrument acknowledging a debt due by the government, and acquire from them the tallies by selling to them some commodity or in doing them some service, in exchange for which they may be induced to part with their tallies. When these are returned to the government Treasury, the taxes are paid. (Ibid., p. 398)

Innes went on to note that the vast majority of revenues collected by inland tax collectors in England were in the form of the exchequer tallies:

[p]ractically the entire business of the English Exchequer consisted in the issuing and receiving of tallies, in comparing the tallies and the counter-tallies, the stock and the stub, as the two parts of the tally were popularly called, in keeping the accounts of the government debtors and creditors, and in cancelling the tallies when returned to the Exchequer. It was, in fact, the great clearing house for government credits and debts.[15] (Ibid.)

Each taxpayer did not have to seek out individually a Crown tally, for matching the Crown's creditors and debtors was accomplished 'through the bankers, who from the earliest days of history were always the financial agents of government' (Innes, 1913, p. 399). That is, the bank would intermediate between the person holding Crown debt and the taxpayer who required Crown debt in order to pay taxes. The exchequer began to assign debts owed to the king whereby 'the tally stock held in the Exchequer could be used by the king to pay someone else, by transferring to this third person the tally stock. Thus the king's creditor could then collect payment from the king's original debtor' (Davies, 1997, p. 150). Further, a brisk business developed to 'discount' such tallies so that the king's creditor did not need to wait for payment by the debtor. Note, also, that use of the hazelwood tallies continued in England until 1826. Ironically, the tallies went out in a blaze of glory, or of ignominy, depending on one's point of view. After 1826, when tallies were returned to the exchequer, they were stored in the Star Chamber and other parts of the House of Commons. 'In 1834, in order to save space and economize on fuel it was decided that they should be thrown into the heating stoves of the House of Commons. So excessive was the zeal of the stokers that the historic parliament buildings were set on fire and razed to the ground' (Davies, 1997, p. 663).

The inordinate focus of economists on coins (and especially on government-issued coins), market exchange and precious metals, then, appears to be misplaced. The key is debt, and specifically, the ability of the state to impose a tax debt on its subjects; once it has done this, it can choose the form in which subjects can 'pay' the tax. While government could in theory require payment in the form of all the goods and services it requires, this would be quite cumbersome. Thus it becomes instead a debtor to obtain what it requires (and note that this is no different from the way in which most buyers became debtors), and issues a token (hazelwood tally or coin) to indicate the amount of its indebtedness; it then accepts its own token in payment to retire tax liabilities.[16] Certainly its tokens can also be used as a medium of exchange (and means of debt settlement among private individuals), but this derives from its ability to impose taxes and its willingness to accept its tokens, and indeed is necessitated by imposition of the tax (if one has a tax liability but is not a creditor of the Crown, one must offer things for sale to obtain the Crown's tokens).

If money did not originate as a cost-minimizing alternative to barter, what were its origins? In the next section we will summarize research into the origins and early development of money. This is, of course, a difficult task. As Grierson notes,

Study of the origins of money must rely heavily on inferences from early language, literature, and law, but will also take account of evidence regarding the use of 'primitive' money in modern non-western societies. Such evidence, of course, has to be used with care. (Grierson, 1977, p. 12)

Grierson also recognizes that the history of money is much more complex than the history of coins, for there is the danger that one might try to find money in societies which did not even use it. 'Some systems, while employing shells or other commodities frequently used as 'money', may not necessarily be monetary at all'[17] (ibid. p. 13). It is difficult for modern economists to agree even on a definition for money, and most economists recognize several different functions of money. It is possible that one might find a different 'history of money' depending on the function that one identifies as the most important characteristic of money. While many economists (and historians and anthropologists) would prefer to trace the evolution of the money used as a medium of exchange, our primary interest is in the unit of account function of money.[18] In the next section, we will speculate on the origins of money, and specifically, on the money of account.

ANCIENT MONIES

In the previous chapter, we noted Keynes's claim that state money is 'at least' four thousand years old. In his analysis of ancient currencies, Keynes argued that even as early as the third millennium BC, one finds 'very advanced indeed' the Babylonian use of money. He examined in detail the monetary 'reforms' of Solon (*circa* 590 BC) and Pheidon (seventh century BC) which set the values of coins. However, these values were based on weight units that could be traced back to approximately 3000 BC, if not earlier. Keynes noted that the

mna, or mina, which Dungi prescribed for Ur in the middle of the third millennium BC is, within the limits of our positive knowledge, the earliest standard of weight. Recent discoveries have, however, thrown back the genesis of organised economic life to a date so much earlier than was previously supposed, that weights must have existed centuries, and, perhaps, even millennia before Dungi, in whose reign money, interest, contracts, receipts, and even bills of exchange are fully established . . . (Keynes, 1982, p. 232)

Indeed, Keynes argued that 'the fundamental weight standards of Western civilisation have *never* been altered from the earliest beginnings up to the introduction of the metric system' (ibid., p. 239); without exception,

'All weight standards of the ancient and also of the medieval world in Babylonia, the Mediterranean Basin and Europe have been based on either the wheat grain or the barley grain as their monad' (ibid.).[19] The basic 'monad' was then '60 x 60 x 3' grains of wheat for the mina of the 'Egyptian system', or 60 x 60 x 2 barley grains for the 'Lydian or Euboic system' (ibid., p. 236). 'Similarly, the avoirdupois grain is by contemporary definition the medieval wheat grain and the troy grain is the medieval barley grain' (ibid., p. 237). Whether we speak of the mina, shekel or pound, all the early money units were weight units based on either wheat or barley grains, with the nominal value of gold usually measured in wheat units, and the nominal value of silver usually measured in barley units.[20]

That Solon and Pheidon could proclaim the number of grams of metal that would henceforth be equal to the mina, talent or drachma is proof that the age of 'state money' had already arrived. It could not have been the case that the 'value of the precious metal' contained in the coins could have determined the value of the money, for the reforms changed the value of the metal relative to the money units of account.[21] Further, just as Knapp and Keynes had argued, the state is free to change the money of account; Solon's 'reform' was to switch from the 'Egyptian' iron standard to the earlier 'Lydian – Euboic' silver/copper standard (that is, the reform consisted of a 'rewrite' of the 'dictionary'). (Keynes, 1982, p.267) However, once a king had established a new money of account, setting a nominal value for a precious metal, he was usually powerless to maintain the value of the metal. Rather, the price of the precious metal tended to rise relative to the money of account (although it could fall); when faced with the choice of allowing the money unit to depreciate relative to the gold price or of trying to fix the money price of gold, the Crown until quite recently almost always chose to let the money depreciate – for reasons we will discuss below.

In other words, the king might establish the 'mina' monetary unit by initially setting it equal to so many grains of gold, but as the price of gold rose, the market price of that quantity of gold would rise without causing official proclamation to set a new monetary standard.[22] The 'mina' would remain defined as the same number of grains of gold regardless of the actual price of gold in terms of any particular mina money. Note also that, as Innes argued, 'The monetary units, the *livre*, *sol*, and *denier*, are perfectly distinct from the coins and the variations in the value of the latter did not affect the former' (Innes, 1913, p. 386). That is, coins could also depreciate (or appreciate) relative to the monetary unit (by 'crying down' the coins, as will be discussed below). In some cases, the monetary unit might never be coined.[23] It is thus quite difficult to maintain that metal determines the value of things used as money.

To recap: the state announces the money unit and may define its value as so many grains of gold. The actual coins, even though they may contain precious metal, do not necessarily carry a nominal value that is fixed relative to either the nominal value of the embodied gold nor even to the money of account. Indeed, the nominal value of the coin would almost always exceed the value of the embodied gold – except in the case when it was no longer a 'token' of the debt of the issuer (in which case, the coin might be taken from circulation and melted for the bullion). And, for reasons discussed below, the coin could depreciate relative to the unit of account by proclamation of the issuer. Finally, if the price of the precious metal changed, this would not necessarily change the nominal value of either the coin or the unit of account.

Monetary units, then, appear to be derived from weight units but do not derive their value from precious metal. Why weight units? It is possible that the weight units were just taken over because they offered well-known and objective standards. However, we know, for example, that 'there is plenty of evidence for corn-wages and corn-rents from the Babylonian age onwards' (Keynes, 1982, p. 258), and for barley taxes in Mesopotamia (Hudson, 1998). Is it possible that the choice of the wheat and barley grains as the bases of monetary units had a more concrete origin? And did they arise out of barter exchange or out of early debt relations?

The measurement units may have first developed in the elaborate rules governing *wergeld*, the practice of paying a compensation for injuries inflicted on others.[24] 'The general object of these laws was simple, that of the provision of a tariff of compensations which in any circumstances their compilers liked to envisage would prevent resort to the bloodfeud' (Grierson, 1977, p. 19). 'Compensation in the Welsh laws is reckoned primarily in cattle and in the Irish ones in cattle or bondmaids (*cumhal*) . . . In the Germanic codes it is mainly in precious metal . . . In the Russian codes it is silver and furs' (ibid., p. 20). The compensations required were quite specific, with different compensations for different offences.[25] These compensations 'were established in public assemblies, and the common standards were based on objects of some value which a householder might be expected to possess or which he could obtain from his kinsfolk' (ibid.).

However, even though payment of compensation required social consensus on the form of payment, there was no need to settle on a 'universal equivalent', for each specific injury inflicted put a specific debt on the individual transgressor. Thus while *wergeld* may have been the original source of the notion of debt and measurement of indebtedness, it probably could not have directly generated monetary payments because there was little private incentive for standardization of the terms.[26] If our monetary standards came from the practice of measuring wealth, paying compensations for injuries, or paying bride wealth, then it is not surprising that the units would be large (for example, representing the value of six sheep).

As these compensatory payments do not appear to have been originally measured in a unit of account, it seems more likely that money as a unit of account first appeared as a means of standardizing tribute or taxes levied by rulers.[27] The first evidence of writing, on clay tablets, appears to be records of taxes levied and collected. 'This combination of a) writing (e.g. farmer's name), b) numerical quantities and c) an accounting record offers the x that writing, numbers, and money . . . all have a common origin in these tablets' (John Adams, private correspondence, 27 January 1998). If so, the 'origins' of money may have been in the tax levies of the palaces of the great granary empires, eventually standardized in the wheat, or barley, weight units of account. The practice of paying in order to 'pacify' or eliminate one's debt for injuries inflicted on another seems to have accustomed the population to the notion of measuring value and the palace would have had a great incentive to standardize the measure of value (even though neither individuals nor even 'social consensus' would have had such an incentive). While the palace could have obtained whatever it needed by imposing 'in-kind' taxes with a list of every item it wished and imposing specific taxes on specific producers (for example a sheep tax on the sheep producer, and so on), imposing a 'five mina' head tax on each, then using mina-denominated state money to purchase needed items while accepting the same mina-denominated state money in payment of taxes would be a far simpler process.

The wheat or barley money of account, then, long pre-dates the use of precious metals. Indeed, evidence suggests that Pheidon's coins replaced earlier iron spits (*oboloi*) that had been used as currency.[28] These had been issued in the barley or wheat weight units of account with a stamp to indicate the issuing temple. Moving to precious metals seems to have been done to reduce counterfeiting – since scarce metals would be harder to obtain (Heinsohn and Steiger, 1983). The precious metal 'veil' that has clouded monetary thought ever since apparently resulted from this purely technical consideration. Coinage was a later development still, often with a stamp to indicate the issuer but only very rarely (at least until recently) with a stamp to indicate nominal value. As Innes notes,

> What has really happened is that the government has put upon the pieces of gold a stamp which conveys the promise that they will be received by the government in payment of taxes or other debts due to it . . . . In virtue of the stamp it bears, the gold has changed its character from that of a mere commodity to that of a token of indebtedness. (Innes, 1913, p. 402).

Similarly, Mommsen argued that in the case of Roman coinage,

> It may be regarded as a law which gives the . . . piece of metal its conventional
> value by legal decree, quite irrespective of whether the effective value
> corresponds with this or not. In this, so to speak, statutory validation, the coin of
> the realm . . . is already enshrined in republican law: only this coinage is money
> – all others are commodities of trade. (Mommsen, 1860, quoted in Heinsohn and
> Steiger, 1983, p. 22)

Heinsohn and Steiger argue that 'In the ancient world, at all events, there
was a full awareness of this gold fog obscuring the true nature of money.
Aristotle, for instance . . . writes: "In some respects, however, money is a
pure sham, a creature of convention established in law" ' (ibid. p. 23).

Much of this is, admittedly, speculative. However, we do have a lot of
evidence of the financial transactions from Mesopotamia from 2500–1200
BC. From this evidence, Michael Hudson concludes that 'debts preceded
money, not the other way around. The first obligations calling for
settlement were fines for inflicting personal injury' (Hudson, 1998, p. 7).
With the development of large palace communities, heavy taxes in the form
of barley were imposed on producers (initially on villages rather than on
individuals).[29] At this time, Mesopotamia had a dual standard, barley and
silver, although the silver was not coined; the 'ruler' announced the
conversion rate of silver to barley and accepted either in payment of taxes.
However, normally producers did not have access to silver, so typically
only merchants paid taxes in the form of silver.

It is suspected that the temples played a further role by acting as neutral
witnesses, recorders and enforcers of private wheat or barley transactions
(including compensation for damages and payment of bride wealth), and by
acting as depositories for grain.[30] At first these actions would have been
recorded on the clay tablets in the wheat or barley or cow that they directly
represented, with a wheat or barley fee imposed for the functions provided
by the temple. Over time, however, the units would have become
standardized (in either the wheat or barley unit), so that transactions in cows
would have been recorded in wheat or barley equivalent, and with fees
recorded in wheat or barley units (but payable in their equivalents).

To sum up, early money units appear to have been derived from weight
units which probably developed from the practice of *wergeld*. Palaces
created the money units to standardize payment of taxes. Use of money in
private transactions derived from tax debts, encouraged by the palaces
which could record and enforce private transactions. Once a money tax was
levied on a village, and later on individuals, the palace would be able to
obtain goods and services by issuing its own money-denominated debt in

the form of tallies (initially, clay tablets and later wooden tallies). Coins came much later, but were, like the tallies, evidence of the Crown's debt. Use of precious metals in the coins was adopted simply to reduce counterfeiting.

DEBASEMENT OF THE CURRENCY

Throughout history, devaluation of coins, rising prices of precious metals and attempts to restore 'strong money' have been commonplace. This is often linked to efforts of the Crown to obtain 'seigniorage' by purposely 'debasing' the coin (reducing the precious metal content in order to produce more coins per ounce of metal). The problem is said to have been resolved through rigorous enforcement of a gold standard, whereby 'full-bodied' coin (or notes with full precious metal backing) was minted. However, this interpretation may be incorrect, perhaps suffering from the 'veil of gold' to which we alluded above.

Innes argued that, until recently, there was little relation between the nominal value of a coin and its precious metal content. Even

> [i]n Amsterdam and in Hamburg in the eighteenth century, an exchange list was published at short intervals, and affixed in the Bourse, giving the current value of the coins in circulation in the city, both foreign and domestic, in terms of the monetary unit . . . The value of these coins fluctuated almost daily . . . Coins of similar weight and fineness circulated at different prices, according to the country to which they belonged'. (Innes, 1913, p. 388)

He offers both earlier examples (France during the reign of Saint Louis, ancient Gaul and Britain, ancient Greece) and later examples (the US in 1782 before adopting the dollar) to demonstrate that 'there never was a monetary unit which depended on the value of a coin or on a weight of metal; that there never was until quite modern days, any fixed relationship between the monetary unit and any metal' (ibid., p. 379).

Further, 'the general idea that the kings wilfully debased their coinage, in the sense of reducing their weight and fineness is without foundation' (ibid. p. 386).[31] Instead, kings were quite protective of the 'quality' of their coinage – not because this determined the value of the coin, but because 'towards the end of the thirteenth century, the feeling grew up that financial stability depended somehow on the uniformity of the coinage' (ibid.). According to Innes, coins were devalued not by reducing precious metal content, but by royal proclamation that consisted of 'crying down' the nominal value of the coin.[32] When a king wanted to increase his purchasing power, 'he decreed a reduction of the nominal value of the coins. This was a perfectly well recognized method of taxation acquiesced in by the people, who only complained when the process was repeated too often'[33] (ibid. p. 385). It is a method of taxation because by reducing the nominal value of the coins, the king would increase the number of coins that had to be delivered in payment of taxes, which would increase the quantity of goods and services offered by subjects in order to obtain the king's coins to pay the tax. Note that the king would not change the monetary unit, but would only change the monetary value of his 'tokens', thereby avoiding disruption of private markets (which for the most part were carried-on using tallies, bills of exchange or other debts denominated in the money of account). Further, although the nominal value of the coins would now be lower, whether or not this would result in a general inflation would depend on the prices paid by the king. If nominal spending and taxes were held constant, the so-called debasement of the currency could occur without affecting prices significantly.

However, as a result of crying down the coins, as well as the general upward trend of prices (sometimes called the 'price revolution') and the rising price of precious metals (only relieved with discoveries in the new world), a belief developed in late – medieval times that there was a connection among 'the fall in the value of money', 'the rise of the value of the metals', and the 'deplorable condition of the coinage' (Innes, 1913, p. 400). It came to be believed that if only the price of the precious metals could be controlled and the 'quality' of the coins improved, might the steady rise of prices be averted. Until the nineteenth century, however, governments were not able to stabilize gold prices. This could not be done by proclamation, but only by an active 'buffer stock' policy (and an enormous increase in production of gold). Nor were they able to stabilize the value of coins – even through imposition of legal tender laws (or floggings). As Chief Justice Chase recognized in a Supreme Court case of 1872, '[r]eceivability for debts due the government', and not legal tender laws, determines the nominal value of coins (Innes, 1913, p. 406).

During the nineteenth and early twentieth centuries, governments finally adopted gold standards and intervened to fix gold prices.[34] Because they established a gold standard that fixed the value of coins and all other state 'tokens' and debts relative to the unit of account, which in turn was fixed relative to a quantity of precious metal, they could no longer 'cry down' the value of a coin. Thus, we finally achieved an approximation to the monetary system that the textbook hypothesized for the origins of money – by the purposeful intervention of government rather than by the 'common consent' of our bartering forebears.

This is a quite brief summation of the 'origins' of money, much of it relying on speculation because of its ancient origins. However, we can also examine a few more recent cases of attempts to develop a monetary system. We will look at cases of the colonial governor, colonial America, and America during the Civil War to further examine the relation between money and taxes.

A HYPOTHETICAL GOVERNOR

We will begin with a stylized, hypothetical example of the way in which an economy can be monetized. In this section, we are not attempting to present 'history', but rather we are showing how money might be introduced to an economy while at the same time demonstrating some propositions that will be discussed again in following chapters. In the real world, as we will discuss in sections below, monetization of an economy is much more difficult and complex.

Let us suppose that a woman were appointed governor of a colony that had not been previously introduced to money, prices and markets. This colony has a fully functioning, although traditional (that is, tribal), economy that is able to provide more than sufficient food, clothing and shelter for its inhabitants. The new governor arrives with her chequebook and several bags of paper money and coin. Her charge is to organize the indigenous peoples to build the governor's mansion, to provide the necessary food and services for the governor and her family, and to accomplish a few tasks enumerated by the home office (a new road, for example). The governor announces various job openings and pay scales. To her surprise, no one shows up for work; higher wage offers still produce no takers. She calls the home office for troops and uses the threat of violence to induce the indigenous peoples to provide labour. However, she finds the indigenous population to be 'lazy, untrustworthy, unmotivated' (although they had been quite successful at providing for themselves before she arrived!).

It did not have to be this way. As real-world colonial governors discovered, the way to introduce money into the economy (and, in particular, to generate a supply of labour offered for money wages) is to impose a monetary tax. In many cases, the indigenous population would already have been familiar with the payment of taxes or tribute, albeit in non-monetary form. Once taxes have been imposed, the governor need only define what must be done to obtain 'that which is necessary to pay taxes'; she announces that so much 'twintopt' can be obtained for construction work on the mansion, so much 'twintopt' for delivery of food to her family, so much 'twintopt' for work on the new road, and so on. Note also that there is no need to carry bags of paper money and coin from home, for the indigenous peoples would readily accept anything the governor paid, provided she would accept the same in payment of taxes. For example, the governor could photocopy a picture of herself to use as paper money, which could be called 'govs'.

The govs would not require any precious metal 'backing', nor would the governor have to hold any home currency reserves against govs. The govs need not be legal tender 'acceptable in payment of all debts, public and private', for all that is necessary is that they are acceptable in payment of taxes. Note, finally, that it does not matter whether the indigenous population is accustomed to 'market mechanisms', to 'financial contracts', to use of 'money', nor does it matter whether there is 'trust' in the governor or the gov. That is to say, all the explanations normally given in economic textbooks for public use of government's money do not apply to our example. The only requirement is that the governor imposes and enforces a tax, payable in govs.

The governor could set the value of the govs at any level she liked: whether it is one gov per hour of construction work or one thousand govs per hour of construction work is entirely irrelevant to the indigenous peoples. What matters, of course, is to set the rate of remuneration relative to the tax liability in a manner that will call forth the amount of work 'effort' required by the governor. Note that if the governor did not get as much effort as she desired, it would do no good to raise the rate of pay – that would merely 'devalue' the gov and she would find fewer hours of work supplied by the indigenous peoples, at any given tax liability. Instead, she should increase the tax liability or lower the rate of remuneration to increase the amount of labour offered.

Finally, the governor would realize that she did not 'need' the govs provided by indigenous peoples in payment of taxes; rather, the indigenous peoples needed the govs to pay taxes. This also means that the governor would never worry about 'financing' her spending (through tax revenues); nor would she ever worry about her 'deficits' that would result if the indigenous peoples decided to earn more govs than required to meet tax payments. Indeed, she would expect that the indigenous peoples would normally want to hold some extra govs (for example, to pay taxes in the future, or just in case some govs are 'lost in the wash'), so that she would normally run deficits. And she could perhaps encourage them to accumulate govs as saving by offering to pay interest on gov hoards.

This could be done, for example, by offering to trade one interest-paying 'govbond' for every ten govs saved, paying one gov interest each year and promising to return the ten govs principal at the end of five years. Over time, her outstanding govbond 'debt' would grow to the extent the indigenous population desired to save govs and exchange them for govbonds. She would not lose any sleep about her 'growing indebtedness' to her subjects; indeed she would have no reason even to keep track of her deficits and outstanding govbond debt. Nor would she ever be deluded into believing that 'financial markets' dictated to her what interest rate she would have to pay on her govbonds, for it would be obvious that she, alone, set that rate. She would realize that no useful information could possibly come from the interest rate she paid on govbonds, from her annual deficits, from her debt, or even from the prices she paid for the goods and services obtained. All that would matter to her would be the quantity of real goods and services offered by the indigenous population. If insufficient (for example, if her own needs were not being met), she could raise the tax liability; if in excess of her requirement (for example, if the indigenous population was not producing enough for its own survival), she could lower taxes and reduce her purchases to reduce the 'work effort' of the indigenous peoples.

Of course, the govs could also be used in private exchanges, or what Knapp called the 'private pay community'. An individual with a tax liability might agree to perform services for his neighbour to obtain govs that neighbour might have accumulated. Private markets could develop to allow producers of goods and services to obtain govs needed for payment of taxes. A greater proportion of each individual's day might come to be devoted to market activities in search of govs, not only to pay taxes, but also to purchase on the market goods and services that raise the standard of living. (As we will discuss below, 'real-world' traditional economies might require much greater 'inducement' to produce for the market.)

Once the governor has introduced gov money over which she has the monopoly of issue, unemployment can develop when individuals offer labour to her but find no work.[35] It would be pretty silly to leave the unemployed begging the governor to allow them to provide goods and services to her so that they might obtain govs; after all, the cost to the governor of issuing govs would be nearly zero (consisting of the photocopying costs of govs). The clever governor should quickly realize that the solution is to accept the offers, that is, to hire the unemployed labour.

If she found that too much labour was offered (for example, the indigenous peoples were working sixteen-hour days and neglecting their families), she could always reduce taxes and her spending to reduce the supply of labour. She would find that 'government spending' can be too large and too small, as indicated by excessive effort devoted to obtaining govs at one extreme, or by excessive numbers of offers to work that are not met by job offers at the other extreme. The governor would not be able to judge whether government spending were too large (or too small) merely by adding up the govs she had spent, nor by tallying the size of her deficits, nor even by measuring total government spending as a percentage of the colony's 'gross national product' – these data provide no useful information to her. Again, the governor needs only to determine that she is able to obtain the goods and services required to fulfil the functions her office is supposed to perform, while ensuring that the population is neither working too much nor too little, as evidenced by neglect of other activities at one extreme, or by queues of unemployed seeking jobs at the other.

That may strike readers as a nice story, but did real-world colonial governors really create a labour supply willing to work for money wages by imposing taxes? As we will show below, they did indeed. Still, this does not prove that this is the way that money originated; it is one thing to argue that a governor who is accustomed to use of money might discover that taxes provide one means to help monetize an economy, but it is quite another matter to argue that this is the way economies were first monetized. Further, as we will note, there is no evidence to support an extreme position that taxes alone will be sufficient to create a monetary economy out of a traditional economy. Real-world governors also relied on force. Even though taxes would generate a supply of labour, development of 'private' markets required destruction of the traditional economy. Note, also, that it is not apparent that any real-world governor fully understood the implications of the taxes-drive-money view, even though many of them did explicitly acknowledge that taxes were imposed to induce indigenous populations to offer goods and labour services in exchange for 'twintopt'. In the next section we will briefly examine a few historical examples that appear to be consistent with our general argument.

REAL WORLD COLONIAL GOVERNORS

William Henry Furness reported the case of the island of Uap (part of the Caroline Islands), which came under the control of Germany in 1898. The islanders used *fei*, 'large, solid, thick stone wheels, ranging in diameter from a foot to twelve feet, having in the centre a hole sufficiently large and strong to bear the weight and facilitate transportation' in ceremonial exchange[36] (Furness, 1910, p. 93). In any case, the only background that is necessary is to understand that the islanders placed great ceremonial value on the *fei*, and that the German government used this as a means of obtaining labour services.

There are no wheeled vehicles in Uap, and consequently, no cart roads; but there have always been clearly defined paths communicating with the different settlements. When the German Government assumed ownership of the Caroline Islands . . . many of these paths or highways were in bad condition, and the chiefs of the several districts were told that they must have them repaired and put in good order. The roughly dressed blocks of coral were, however, quite good enough for the bare feet of the natives; and many were the repetitions of the command, which still remained unheeded. At last it was decided to impose a fine for disobedience on the chiefs of the districts. In what shape was the fine to be levied? It was of no avail to demand silver or gold from the chiefs – they had none – and to force them to pay in their own currency [*fei*] would have required, in the first place, half the population of the island to transport the fines; in the second place, their largest government building could not hold them; and finally, *fei* six feet in diameter, not having been 'made in Germany', were hardly available as a circulating medium in the Fatherland. At last, by a happy thought, the fine was exacted by sending a man to every *failu* and *pabai* throughout the disobedient districts, where he simply marked a certain number of the most valuable *fei* with a cross in black paint to show that the stones were claimed by the Government. This instantly worked like a charm; the people, thus dolefully impoverished, turned to and repaired the highways to such good effect from one end of the island to the other, that they are now like park drives. Then the Government dispatched its agents and erased the crosses. Presto! the fine was paid, the happy *failus* resumed possession of their capital stock, and rolled in wealth. (Furness, 1910, pp. 98–100)

Thus the simple act of 'fining' (or, taxing) generated the labour supply desired by the colonialists; the indigenous peoples worked to remove the 'tax liability' in order to restore their wealth.[37]

Mat Forstater recently argued that colonial Africa offers an excellent source of examples of monetization of economies through imposition of taxes because these are recent cases with accurate records. As he said,

One of the goals of the colonial policy of demanding taxes be paid in a government-issued currency was to compel Africans to offer their "labor" power for sale in exchange for wages denominated in that currency (as well as to force movement from subsistence to cash-crop production and to create new markets for European goods). (Mathew Forstater, PKT, 25 September 1996)

We will examine a few cases that are particularly clear demonstrations of this.

Throughout colonial Africa, colonists found it difficult to draw the indigenous peoples into the 'labour force'. 'The difficulties faced by early settlers and other employers in securing wage labour are well known . . . The chief mechanisms in the creation of a semi-proletariat may be simply listed. First, the conquest and active administration of African societies was usually accompanied by a) taxation' (Stichter, 1985, p. 25). Walter Neale examined the specific case of the British colonial government of Central Africa.

> The immediate needs of the Pioneers were for land and the labor to make that land productive. Conquest provided the Pioneers with the land . . . Labor was another matter. Slavery, seizing local people and forcing them to work on the land, had become reprehensible in European eyes . . . In any case, in the beginning the Pioneers assumed – it seemed obvious to them – that labor would be forthcoming to work the land if wages were offered. Wages were offered, but Bantu did not come forth to work the land. (Neale, 1976, p. 79)

This African society was not monetized, so the question was how to do this. 'The solution imposed by the Pioneers was a requirement that a head tax be paid in money, thus requiring that Bantu work to earn the money to pay the tax' (ibid.). This was a nearly universal experience throughout Africa. For example, Magubane examined the case of South Africa:

> H.J. and Ray Simons, in their book *Class and Colour in South Africa, 1850–1950* point out that after the Anglo–Boer War, . . . Every adult African male was required to pay a labour tax of two pounds, with another two pounds for the second and each additional wife of a polygamist . . . (Magubane, 1979, p. 48)

As another example, a huge labour force was needed to work in the gold mines in the Cape, but the Africans refused to work, so 'the 1893 Commission of Labour in the Cape Colony suggested that every male African should be taxed, with full remission if he could show he had been employed away from home during the year' (ibid., p. 78). Similarly, in West Africa, the French imposed a monetary tax to create wage labour (Stichter, 1985, p. 40). In the Belgian Congo, 'direct force tended to be used in the early stages of labour recruitment before the indirect but powerful effects of taxation' (ibid., p. 94). A colonial administrator in South Africa noticed

> they have nothing but their grain for subsistence and the payment of their taxes. Corn, when they are able to sell it, brings about 5 shillings a bag and in many cases a woman or man will have to travel 20 miles with a bag of corn on their heads for which they will receive 9 pence or 1 shilling and then have to travel back again for 20 miles and thus raise their tax. (Colonial Administrator of Ciskei, South Africa, 1865, quoted in Iliffe, 1987, p. 73)

As still another example,

In 1922, to increase the economic pressure on the African peasants, the Native Taxation and Development Act (number 41 of 1922) forced all African males between the ages of eighteen and sixty-five to pay a poll tax of £1 per annum and every male occupant of a hut in the reserves to pay a local tax of ten shillings. (Magubane, 979, p. 83)

According to figures supplied by Colin Leys for post-WWI Kenya, taxes averaged approximately three-quarters of annual money wages (Leys, 1975, pp. 31–32). As the colonial administrators seemed to recognize, the purpose of the taxes was not to provide revenue to the colonial government, but rather to 'increase economic pressure' on the indigenous population.

Returning to the case of Central Africa, as Neale notes, imposition of taxes to obtain labour 'was not a happy solution'; the indigenous peoples ran off 'as soon as they had earned the money required to pay the tax'; the pioneers 'quite rightly as they saw the world, thought the Bantu shiftless, lazy, dishonest, incompetent, and irresponsible', while the Bantu 'quite rightly as they saw the world, thought the Pioneers threatening, brutal, and at least somewhat crazy' (Neale, 1976, pp. 79–80). Over time, tribal life was destroyed. As Neale argues 'to "blame it all on money" would be wrong', but the indigenous people increasingly 'came to need and then to want money and the things money would buy . . . money was certainly an important element in changing the lives of the descendants of both white and black in Central Africa' (ibid., 1976, pp. 80–81).

Thus taxation in the form of money in the colonies not only destroyed the traditional economies, but helped in the development of monetary economies. This is not meant to imply that taxation alone would be sufficient to induce market production for money. Colonists sometimes found it necessary to eliminate alternatives to markets, for example, by destroying crops that allowed self-sufficiency. Or, colonists created a demand for luxury or status goods that could be obtained only from markets by destroying egalitarianism in order to create an upper class. That other means were used in addition to imposition of monetary taxes shows just how incorrect the textbook story is. Far from a 'social consensus' to use money as an efficient alternative to barter, in reality development of a monetary economy required imposition of taxes and use of force. As Rodney argued only a 'minority eagerly took up the opportunity' (Rodney, 1974, p. 157) to produce cash crops in order to obtain European goods – and this is after they have been exposed to them. It is far more difficult to believe that individuals in a traditional society would hit upon the idea of producing crops for market to obtain money in order to obtain goods which did not even exist!

In conclusion, the colonial authorities were faced with the problem of inducing indigenous populations to supply labour; they realized that simply offering money – even if in the form of gold or silver coins – would not call forth the required labour. Nor was enslavement, or other forms of compulsion, generally acceptable or successful at this time. Thus they relied on imposition of taxes, payable (usually) in the form of the European currencies that could only be obtained from the colonizers. This would not only generate the labour needed by the colonialists, but it would also help lead to the destruction of tribal society and the creation of a monetary economy.[38] Furthermore, while it is clear that colonial governors understood that taxes would monetize the economy, it is not clear that they understood all the implications of this. They did understand that higher taxes would induce more work effort, and that tax increases should be used to increase labour supply rather than to raise more revenue. Clearly, as the European money had to come initially from the colonists, taxes could, at best, only return money the governor had spent; however, later, with the development of production of cash crops for export, money could flow from the home country, modifying this result. In any case, the purpose of the tax was not to raise monetary revenue, but to provide real goods and services to the governor (and, eventually, to induce cash crop production).

Finally, the case of the colonial governors may be a more powerful test of the taxes-drive-money thesis than is readily apparent, for here is a case in which taxes are imposed by an external authority whose only legitimacy in the eyes of the population might be threat of use of force. The transition might have been smoother if the state's authority to levy taxes had been seen as derived from democratic principles. However, the power to tax and to define the form in which the tax would be paid set in motion the process of monetization of the economy. The important point is that 'monetization' did not spring forth from barter; nor did it require 'trust' – as most stories about the origins of money claim.[39]

AMERICA: COLONIALS, FISCAL PRUDENCE, AND THE CONFEDERATE MONEY

Finally, let us examine the case of the US, which is quite interesting because of its tumultuous monetary history. Except during periods of war, the American government adopted 'fiscal prudence' as its guiding principle during the late eighteenth and throughout the nineteenth centuries. Very large deficits would be run during war, generating substantial public debt; this would then lead to an attempt to run fiscal surpluses after the war in order to retire the debt, which, in turn, would generate severe contractionary forces, problems for the banking system, and deep recessions or depressions that restored government deficits – thwarting the effort to retire the debt. Only once (1835) did 'fiscal prudence' succeed in eliminating the interest-paying government debt, and this was followed by a particularly severe depression.

America to the Civil War

A wide variety of monies circulated in the American colonies, including 'official' British coin and 'unofficial' foreign coin (primarily Spanish and Portuguese coins). Only one colonial mint of any consequence operated, in Massachusetts from 1652 to 1684, when it was forced to close.[40] Even though frowned upon by Britain, and periodically prohibited, the colonial governments also issued large quantities of paper notes, denominated in the pounds, shillings, and pence of the imperial system. These were often declared legal tender (in 1775 alone, North Carolina declared 17 different types of money legal tender) and accepted in payment of taxes (Davies, 1997, pp. 458–60). However, colonial note issue was, in almost every case, greatly in excess of tax liabilities that could be imposed by the colonial governments. As Adam Smith recognized at the time, it was this mismatch that generated the 'inflation' or devaluation of colonial notes relative to British coin. A series of Acts by Parliament finally banned the issue of legal tender paper money by the colonies in 1764.

At the start of the Revolutionary War, the new American government believed it literally had no choice but to 'finance' it by 'printing money'. 'Taxation was hated by the Americans, for that had been a major cause of the revolt' (Davies, 1997, p. 464). In addition, the American governments did not have in place 'appropriate administrative machinery' for tax collection, and in any case the 'British army occupied much of the land while the Royal Navy blockaded the ports' (ibid.). Besides, the Continental Congress did not have the power to impose taxes; only the individual colonies could do so. Further, it was not possible to borrow enough: at most $100 million was raised by domestic borrowing, with almost $90 million of this raised in the form of paper notes, and perhaps less than $8 million was raised from foreign borrowing. The central government issued $241 million in 'Continentals', with state governments issuing another $210 in their own notes (ibid., p. 465). Without a sufficient tax liability, the notes depreciated quickly in spite of attempts to fix prices in terms of the notes. Continentals eventually fell to one one-thousandth of their face value, leading to the phrase 'not worth a Continental'.

Happily, the war effort was more successful than its finance would have suggested. After the war, although the Continentals were still considered legal tender, merchants refused to accept them at face value. When the Constitutional Convention was held in May 1787, one of the important items considered concerned the state of the new country's money and finances. The Constitution, ratified in 1789, is noteworthy in that Article 1 links by proximity, if not in theory, money and taxes in two clauses: 'Congress shall have power to coin money, regulate the value thereof and of foreign coin' and Congress will have 'the power to lay and collect taxes, duties and excises, and to pay the debts . . . of the United States' (Davies, 1997, p. 466). As we now understand, these powers are inextricably linked (Congress could not regulate the value of the money without the power to levy taxes), although it is not clear that the framers of the Constitution linked the two (as we argued in the previous chapter, Adam Smith did make the connection, at least in passing). For his part, Alexander Hamilton argued that 'A national debt, if it is not excessive, will be to us a national blessing' in part because 'the taxes needed to pay and service the debt would . . . force the masses to worker harder to pay those taxes', an 'argument made often at the time' (Stabile and Cantor, 1991, p. 16).

It was not until the Coinage Act of 1792, however, that the dollar, based on the decimal system, was officially adopted and successfully coined.[41] Reflecting the current belief that a strong currency had to be based upon precious metals, the dollar was defined as equivalent to 371.25 grains of silver or 24.75 grains of gold (the ratio was thus 15:1), valuing silver somewhat higher than abroad. The Act set up a national mint, made gold and silver coins legal tender (with some legal tender status also given to copper coins), and would remove legal tender status for foreign coins after three years (Davies, 1997, p. 467). However, in practice, legal tender status of foreign coin was not completely and finally removed until 1857 because of a perceived severe shortage of coins.

In spite of Thomas Paine's 1776 proclamation that 'No nation ought to be without a debt', for 'a national debt is a national bond', and in spite of Hamilton's earlier recognition of the desirability of national debt, in America, as Davies argues 'monetary quarrels have right from the start been deeply divisive and almost never ending' (Davies, 1997, p. 471) and have almost always been decided on the side of 'prudent finance', with a severe distrust of credit, banks and national debt. Thomas Jefferson advocated 'taking from the federal government the power of borrowing' (Stabile and Cantor, 1991, p. 29), while Andrew Jackson labelled the public debt 'a national curse', promising 'to pay off the national debt' (ibid., p. 37). And, indeed, Jackson accomplished this by January 1835, when 'for the first and only time, all of the government's interest bearing debt was paid off' (ibid.). A budget surplus continued for the next two years, which Secretary of the Treasury Levi Woodbury thought 'should be maintained as a fund to meet future deficits'. (Stabile and Cantor, 1991, p. 41) However, a deep recession began in 1837, and over the next three years the government issued $20 million in debt.

Even at the time, the Treasury understood the problem created by surpluses. Private banks held specie as reserves and payment of taxes drained coin from the banking system. When the government ran a surplus, by definition it was removing more coin than it was injecting through government spending.[42] The Treasury would then advocate retirement of outstanding debt, not only to eliminate the debt but also in full recognition that this would return specie to the banking system (generally, it was the Treasury's policy to pay interest and retire debt only with specie). However, it was frequently the case that there would be an insufficient quantity of government debt coming due. So the Treasury would seek special permission to purchase the debt on the open market; often the debt would be selling above par which meant that the Treasury had to buy it at a premium. For example in 1850, 'Secretary of the Treasury James Guthrie asked Congress for permission to buy government bonds on the open market' to 'put some of these funds [specie] back into circulation'; permission was granted and he paid as much as a 21 per cent premium 'to help avert a banking panic' (Stabile and Cantor, 1991, p. 46). In support of his policy, Guthrie testified that the Treasury had the potential to 'exercise a fatal control over the currency . . . whenever the revenue shall greatly exceed the expenditure' (ibid.).

Clearly, the Treasury was engaging in a 'central bank' open market operation to relieve pressure on the banking system. However, such an impact on private banks had long been recognized; Biddle had argued in 1832 that Treasury accumulation of specie in anticipation of debt retirement could destroy most state banks. Treasury Secretary Robert J. Walker had engaged in a 'repurchase' operation in 1847 to inject reserves, buying bonds and agreeing to resell them to their previous owners at the same price. In the 1850s as a new budget surplus developed, Treasury Secretary Charles Fairchild bought bonds, paying premiums as high as 29 per cent (Stabile and Cantor, 1991, p. 63). After the Civil War, surpluses were the norm, with large surpluses in the late 1880s leading to debt retirement and deep depression in the 1890s; the country would close out the century with persistent deficits.

We will skip over the tumultuous history of attempts to establish a national bank and national paper currency. By 1859, there were 9916 different kinds of banknotes as well as 5400 different counterfeit banknotes, circulating mainly at a discount from face value and requiring 'not only every banker but every trader of any importance' to 'make constant reference to one or other of a series of banknote guides' (Davies, 1997, pp.

480–1). However, the federal government was prevented from issuing paper money between the Revolution and the Civil War. This fact is often believed to be the source of the long-term stability of prices in the nineteenth century. However, in reality, it was the persistently 'tight' fiscal policy: except during war or deep recession, the budget was perennially in surplus, with the government taking in more specie than it paid out, exerting a deflationary influence on the economy.[43] The surpluses were only made possible by the deficits (and outstanding debt) run up during war and recession, which permitted the government to inject the coin back into the economy as it purchased its debt. Thus the US entered the twentieth century with prices similar to those that existed at the beginning of the nineteenth century and with total government debt of less than $2 billion (of which half was interest-paying and the remainder consisted of Treasury notes) (Stabile and Cantor, 1991, p. 65).

Civil War Period and After

Let us close this historical chapter with an examination of the Civil War, which offers a useful comparison of the financial outcomes of the two sides. The North was able to impose a significant tax liability and resorted to a much smaller extent to 'printing money' (deficit spending on the basis of issuing notes) than did the South, which was never able to impose and enforce taxes. In the North, for example, total spending on the war effort has been estimated at about $4 billion; taxes were equal to 21 per cent of expenditures and bond sales were equal to 62 per cent; only $450 million of 'greenbacks' were issued, and other sources were equal to 4 per cent of expenditures[44] (Lerner, 1954, p. 507). Inflation over the course of the war caused prices in the North to more than double. In contrast, prices in the South increased 28-fold. While it is true that the South was on the losing side, as we will discuss, much of the inflation appears more likely to have been a result of its inability to tax, rather than disappointments on the front.

The Confederate states faced a monumental task: how to create a currency and issue sufficient fiat money to prosecute the Civil War. While wars present unusual economic circumstances, it is possible that war finance can shed some light on the nature of state money. Like the colonies during the Revolutionary War, the Confederacy tried to impose taxes payable in kind. However, the taxes 'were avoided by the farmers and businessmen who sold their goods (or hid them) before collection time' (Lerner, 1954, p. 506). Further, '[n]either the right goods nor the right quantities of goods were collected, and the supplies that were obtained often rotted, became damaged, or were stolen before they could be transported to the areas where they were needed' (ibid.). All these problems should have been (and, indeed, were) expected with in-kind taxes. As a result, the Confederacy, 'like any government, purchased the bulk of its supplies'. (ibid., p. 507).

However, taxes equalled less than 5 per cent of the South's spending, which totalled about $2.7 billion, with bond sales equal to 30 per cent, notes issued by 'the printing press' equal to 60 per cent, and other revenue sources equal to 5 per cent of spending (ibid.). This is in contrast to the North's financial situation, discussed above. Christopher Memminger, Secretary of the Confederate Treasury, advocated higher tax receipts; however, the Congress argued for lower taxes, the Confederacy did not have the '[m]achinery for collecting large amounts of taxes' (ibid.), the Southern states strongly resisted centralized state power, and, at least initially, the South expected a speedy victory. Secretary Memminger

> saw two immediate and indispensable benefits from levying taxes payable in government notes. First, taxes created a demand for the paper issued by the government and gave it value. Since all taxpayers needed the paper, they were willing to exchange goods for it, and the notes circulated as money. Second, to the extent that taxation raised revenue, it reduced the number of new notes that had to be issued. Memminger's numerous public statements during the war show that he clearly realized that increasing a country's stock of money much faster than its real income leads to runaway prices. They also show that he believed a strong tax program lessens the possibility of inflation. (ibid., p. 508)

If taken out of context, this might appear to be no more than the belief that 'inflation is caused by too much money chasing too few goods', but it is clear that Memminger's understanding went far beyond this. He believed that if the state were merely to 'print up' notes to buy needed goods and services without creating sufficient demand for those notes, inflation would result. What was needed, therefore, was to impose sufficient tax liabilities to create a demand for the notes so that goods and services would be offered at relatively stable prices.

Memminger proposed to levy money taxes primarily on property whose future yield would depend on Southern victory, in order to make best use of 'patriotic' sentiment, and provided incentives for states to collect the taxes. Unfortunately, the states did not cooperate. Some merely confiscated the property owned by people in the North (counting the value as tax revenue), floated bonds and collected as taxes the money that would have gone as interest, or borrowed the amount required from state banks. This is partly to be explained by the feeling of citizens that they were already paying tremendous human costs to prosecute the war; thus there were strong local feelings against the taxes. However, given our understanding of the taxes-drive-money principle, it is clear that confiscating property of Northerners, or selling bonds to banks, cannot create demand for the currency. Throughout the war, Memminger would propose measures to increase tax revenues, only to find that Congress preferred to issue notes to 'finance' the war; even when tax rates were raised, it was easy to evade taxes, and the states tended to side with their citizens against the Confederate tax collectors.

As a result, Memminger was forced to rely on bond sales and note issues. Indeed, Memminger often issued bonds used by the Treasury as currency, forcing sellers to accept the bonds; however, he also allowed tax payments in the form of bonds – which means that bonds were essentially interest-paying currency. Memminger wrote to President Davis: 'When it is remembered that the circulation of all the Confederate States before the present war was less than 100 millions, it becomes obvious that the large quantity of money in circulation today must produce depreciation and final disaster' (Lerner, 1954, p. 520). By February 1864, well over $1.5 billion notes had been issued by the Confederacy.

Indeed, Memminger found that even with a staff of 262 in the note-signing bureau (each note was signed by hand in an effort to reduce counterfeiting) it was impossible to issue notes quickly enough to meet Treasury spending. When Congress refused to allow him to simply print a signature on notes (to increase speed of issue), he responded by recommending that the South resort to honouring counterfeits in an attempt to increase the money supply! Legislation to that effect was passed, which led banks openly to count as assets counterfeit notes held. Counterfeits could be turned over to the Treasury in return for a 6 per cent call certificate, whereupon the counterfeits would be stamped 'valued' by the Treasury, then reissued to finance government spending. (Lerner, 1954, pp. 120–21)

In light of our discussion above, the consequences of Confederate finance should not be difficult to guess. If a government determines the value of the currency by dictating the terms on which 'twintopt' may be obtained, and as well by ensuring that taxes are indeed paid, then the Confederacy set a low goalpost, indeed. Enforcement of taxes was virtually non-existent, while levies, even if enforced, were not even close to what would have been required to move needed resources to the government sector. Further, when Congress agreed to accept counterfeits, it essentially reduced the value of money to printing costs (the 'effort' involved in obtaining 'twintopt' was reduced to that associated with printing counterfeits).

Runaway inflation should have been the expected result, and, indeed, was the result expected by Memminger: 'The currency continues rapidly to grow in quantity. This increase causes a daily advance in prices . . . which if not arrested must result in consequences disastrous to the best interests of the country' (Lerner, 1954, p. 520). Inflation rose to 23 per cent per month by March 1864. Currency 'reform' in May 1864 repudiated the old currency and temporarily slowed inflation, but by 1 August $170 million of new notes had been issued while less than $10 million was collected in taxes, making renewed inflation inevitable. By November, the new Secretary Trenholm declared the currency reform a failure. The result, as they say, is history.

Certainly, wars present unusual economic circumstances (particularly when one is on the losing side!), and some inflation is just about inevitable given the probable gap between the quantity of goods and services the government requires and the taxes that can be imposed. One might also expect that even patriotic citizens might become less willing to accept currency (and government bonds) on negative news from the war front – thus the South's inflation might have resulted from doubts that it would win the war, since its currency surely would not be accepted if the North won. Surprisingly, Lerner reports that that was not the case: 'Strange as it may seem, military victories and defeats, to say nothing of changing political events, passed by without affecting the bond market' (Lerner, 1954, p. 518). Indeed, bond prices rose (interest rates fell) in both the North and the South throughout the war, with this trend reversing in the South only during 1864, when 'military supply lines had deteriorated so badly that General Lee's men were living from hand to mouth' (ibid.). Even then, only a small decline of bond prices resulted. Thus it seems unlikely that much of the inflation in the South was due to pessimism about its long-term prospects (which should have affected the demand for bonds even more than it would affect the demand for currency), but was due rather to its inability to enforce tax payments.

After the war, annual federal government spending fell from $1.3 billion in 1865 to an average of $365 billion for the rest of the century. The 1863 National Bank Act had set up charters for national banks, allowing them to issue notes against government bonds. During the war, the Treasury had built up from customs receipts a large gold reserve which was used after the war to retire greenbacks and bonds, becoming a 'sounder' reserve for the banking system. However, the Treasury found that the gold kept returning in the form of customs payments, and its redemption of bonds reduced the bonds available for use as reserves. As a result, few greenbacks were redeemed. In 1869 the Supreme Court ruled that they were not legal tender, but this ruling was reversed in 1870, and a ruling in 1884 declared that Congress generally had the authority to declare fiat money legal tender. Unlike the case with the 'Continentals', given the extremely tight fiscal policy that generated continual, large government surpluses, greenbacks remained 'as good as gold' during the following decades. Prices fell rapidly after the Civil War, and severe recessions of the 1870s and 1890s kept inflation at bay for the remainder of the century.

CONCLUSION

In this chapter we briefly examined the origins of money, finding them in debt contracts and more specifically in tax debt that is levied in money form. Similarly, we argued that coins were nothing more than tokens of the indebtedness of the Crown. Significantly, even though coins were long made of precious metal, it was only relatively recently that it came to be believed that the precious metal content determined the value of the coin. The gold standard attempted to stabilize gold prices in the belief that this would stabilize the value of money. However, we have argued that the relatively stable prices on the gold standard probably have more to do with the tight fiscal policy adopted. To some extent, a rigorously enforced gold standard would generate tight fiscal policy precisely because state spending would depend on the state's ability to obtain and coin gold. However, as we have shown, the temptation to go off the gold standard proved too great during war (and, indeed, during financial crisis). Thus at least in the case of the US, it was really the persistent state surpluses between wars that deflated the economy.

In truth, we can probably never discover the origins of money. Nor is this crucial for the purposes of this book, for we are most concerned with developing an understanding of modern money, that is, of the use of money in the modern economy. As we have discussed in the previous chapter, all modern economies do have a state money that is quite clearly defined by the state's 'acceptation' at 'public pay offices', even though our modern real-world government officials probably understand even less about money than did the colonial governors. In the next two chapters, we turn to an examination of modern fiscal and monetary policy.

NOTES

1. One need look no further than Paul Samuelson's famous textbook to find a relatively recent exposition that is in all essential aspects exactly like the 'fundamental theories' caricatured by Innes:

    Inconvenient as barter obviously is, it represents a great step forward from a state of self-sufficiency in which every man had to be a jack-of-all-trades and master of none. . . . If we were to construct history along hypothetical, logical lines, we should naturally follow the age of barter by the age of commodity money. Historically, a great variety of commodities has served at one time or another as a medium of exchange: . . . tobacco, leather and hides, furs, olive oil, beer or spirits, slaves or wives . . . huge rocks and landmarks and cigarette butts. The age of commodity money gives way to the age of paper money . . . Finally, along with the age of paper money, there is the age of bank money, or bank checking deposits. (Samuelson, 1973, pp. 274–6)

2. Davies (1997) also notes the 'ancient' origins of tallies and quotes Anthony Steel to the effect that 'English medieval finance was built upon the tally' (Davies, 1997, p. 147). The word tally seems to have come from the Latin *talea* which means a stick or a slip of wood; notches in sticks had long been used for recording messages of various kinds (Davies, 1997, p. 147). Note that one of the most common 'notches' was the score, which indicated 20 pounds; a one pound notch was a small groove the size of a barley grain – see the discussion below.

3. Some merchants may have brought goods to the market to use to settle accounts, with a retail trade developing from this practice. Admittedly, the view expounded by Innes is controversial and perhaps too extreme. What is important and surely correct, however, is his recognition of the importance of the clearing house trade to these fairs.

4. It is possible that the early Egyptian empires had taxes, debts and money; papyrus paper did not survive. It is fortunate that Mesopotamia was so rich in clay (and little else in the way of raw materials)!

5. It is true that there are coins of base metal with much lower nominal value, but it is difficult to explain why base metal was accepted in retail trade when the basis of money is supposed to be precious metal.

6. Even if there were institutions that published exchange rates for the myriad of coins (as in Amsterdam or Hamburg in the eighteenth century), it is difficult to believe that such information would have been at the fingertips of the typical market transactor.

7. Early coins did not normally have a stamped, nominal value but, rather, indicated the issuer. Not only would it be difficult to assess the real value of a coin, it would be difficult to assess the nominal value by looking at the coin.

8. However, it is possible that only in the case of seriously debased coin would floggings be required, which could be reconciled with the textbook story.

9. It is often asserted that coins were invented to facilitate long distance trade (as precious metal coins would have high value relative to weight). As Grierson notes 'The evidence, however, is against the earliest coins having been used to faciliate trade of such a kind, for the contents of hoards points overwhelmingly to their local circulation' (Grierson, 1977, p. 10).

10. As Grierson notes, it is frequently difficult to distinguish a coin from settons (or reckoning counters), tokens, medals and related objects (Grierson, 1975, p. 162).

11. Grierson also advances this thesis: 'The alternative view is that since coins were issued by governments – the supposed issue of the earliest coins by merchants is unproven and unlikely – it was administrative rather than economic needs they were intended to serve. Such needs would have included the payment of mercenaries . . .' (Grierson, 1977, p. 10).

12. Crawford suggests that '[c]oinage was probably invented in order that a large number of state payments might be made in a convenient form and there is no reason to suppose that it was ever issued by Rome for any other purpose than to enable the state to make payments . . .' (Crawford, 1970, p. 46). Further, '[o]nce issued, coinage was demanded back by the state in payment of taxes' (ibid.).

13. Recoining would be a strange activity if the value of the coin were determined by the value of the embodied precious metal. The modern equivalent is to call in the coins and knock three zeros off the reissue – an activity that is easy to explain in the case of a fiat money.

14. The wooden tallies were supplemented after the late 1670s by paper 'orders of the exchequer', which in turn were accepted in payment of taxes (Grierson, 1975, p. 34).

15. Davies similarly notes the importance of the tallies for payment of taxes and the development of a clearing system at the exchequer (Davies, 1997, pp. 146–8).

16. That is, even most private transactions took place on credit rather than through use of coin as a medium of exchange. McIntosh notes in a study of London of 1300–1600:

    > Any two people might build up a number of outstanding debts to each other. As long as goodwill between the individuals remained firm, the balances could go uncollected for years. When the parties chose to settle on an amicable basis, they normally named auditors who totaled all current unpaid debts or deliveries and determined the sum which had to be paid to clear the slate. (McIntosh, 1988, p. 561)

17. We do not have the space to examine the controversy over the possible use of money and possible existence of exchange and markets in traditional or tribal society. For a summary, see Wray (1993).

18. This is also the direction taken by Grierson, who argues 'I would insist on the test of money being a measure of value' (Grierson, 1977, p. 16), as well as by Keynes, who noted 'for most important social and economic purposes what matters is the money of account . . .' (Keynes, 1982, p. 252) and 'Money-Proper in the full sense of the term can only exist in relation to a Money-of-Account' (Keynes, 1976, p. 3).

19. In contrast, 'the currency grain of China was rice instead of wheat or barley' (Grierson, 1975, p. 56).

20. The *yuan* was 'both a unit of weight and a monetary demonination' in southern China (Grierson, 1975, p. 56).

21. There would be no point in doing this if the value of a coin was determined by the amount of precious metal contained therein.

22. For a modern example, we need look no further than the dollar in the US. It is still officially defined as 0.0231 ounces of gold, 'implying a gold price of $43.22 per ounce, about one-eighth of the free market price'. (Tobin, 1998. p. 27)

23. Confusion on this issue led to the debate over so called 'ghost monies'. See Wray (1993).

24. This appears far more likely as a source of a measure of monetary value than does the conventional story in which social consensus chooses a particular object as numeraire. As Grierson argues,

    > Units of value, like units of area, volume, and weight, could only be arrived at with great difficulty, in part because natural units are absent, in part because of the much greater diversity of commodities that had to be measured and the consequent difficulty of finding common standards in terms of which they could reasonably be compared . . . In any case, the generalized application of monetary values to commodities could scarcely have come about before the appearance of market economies, and monetary valuations were already in existence in what Sir John Hicks has felicitously christened 'customary' and 'command' pre-market societies. (Grierson, 1977, pp. 18–19)

    In other words, monetary units of account pre-existed market society so that it is quite unlikely that these came out of primitive barter exchange (if such ever existed).

25. Compensations were graduated down to injuries to one's pets and 'It would cost one four times as much to deprive a Russian of his moustache or beard as to cut off one of his fingers' (Grierson, 1977, p. 20).

26. These *wergeld* payments appear to be the source of some of our terminology. For example, the verb 'to pay' comes from *payer* and *pacare*, 'to pacify' or 'to make peace with'; 'the idea of appeasing your creditor lies in the more revealing *pacere*, to come to terms with the injured party'. (Grierson, 1975, p. 162) The word 'worth' comes from <u>Wert</u>, which when combined with <u>Geld</u> denotes the idea of measuring wealth and seems to have come from the practice of paying 'bride price' or 'bride wealth' compensation to a household for the loss of a daughter to marriage.

27. As such, it seems likely that the money of account first appears with the breakdown of traditional, tribal, forms of society that relied on reciprocity and with the rise of the temple or palace societies that could exact tribute. Grierson (1977) prefers to trace the origins of a money of account to either bride wealth or commerce in slaves, both of which grew out of the practice of wergeld. As discussed, the first of these does not appear to be the likely origin since payments of bride wealth would not require a universal equivalent. Grierson's argument in favour of commerce in slaves is more persuasive; however, it is based primarily on the case of the Germanic peoples. If it is true that the notion of valuation came from the practice of wergeld, then that practice must have been widespread. While Grierson argues 'the practice of wergeld, and the construction of related penalties, is a very widespread one', he admits that the existence of such systems is 'difficult to demonstrate in the case of past societies. It was only very exceptional circumstances that caused the European codes to be written down . . .' (Grierson, 1977, pp. 25–26). Indeed, if we are correct in supposing that writing, taxes and money evolved together (see below), then it will be very difficult to uncover any evidence of wergeld that predates money in the case of the granary empires of Egypt and Mesopotamia.

28. However, as Cook notes, iron 'could not have provided a currency until the Iron Age began about the eleventh century BC' (Cook, 1958, p 259). Thus other metals such as copper and bronze preceded iron.

29. So long as the tax was placed on the village, coins would not have been necessary. It would be relatively easy to record the tax debts on clay tablets held in the temples, and to record tax payments as they came in. However, later, when for example a king hired mercenaries and imposed individual head taxes, a large number of payments of similar size would have to be made, and coins would have greatly facilitated this process while eliminating the need for tedious book-keeping.

30. 'The function of witnessing requires the temple to overlook and – if necessary – enforce the obligations written in the contracts . . . This circumstance would provide an explanation for the name *Juno Moneta* – from *monere* = warn, induce, chastise: *admonitory* Juno – for the first recorded temple bank in Rome which minted its own money . . . from its function of reminding debtors of outstanding debts' (Heinsohn and Steiger, 1983, p. 19).

31. Here Innes may be exaggerating. There are many accounts of intentional debasement (see Grierson, 1975, for example); however, these do not appear to deal with the objections raised by Innes. Among other problems, one wonders how the population would recognize debasement as even modern numismatists have great difficulty in assessing the fineness of coins.

32. Medieval coins typically did not have a stamped face value, which is indicative of their 'token' nature.

33. For example, an old coin that had been worth a shilling in payment of taxes became worth only half a shilling; the new coins that were worth a shilling in payment of taxes would be worth two of the old coins. Sometimes 'a "cours volontaire", a voluntary rating, was given by the public to the coins, above their official value. In vain Kings expressed their royal displeasure in edicts which declared . . . that their coins should only circulate at their official value' (Innes, 1913, p. 387). This would be quite strange behaviour on the part of the public if it were true that debasement occurred because the king surreptitiously reduced gold content to obtain seigniorage!

34. Sometimes the government simultaneously adopted similar silver standards and silver prices, although this could lead to the 'two-price' problem – see below.

35. In non-monetary economies, ties of reciprocity, customary rights and obligations laid on individuals, and direction of labour through command ensured that labour remained fully employed. As Paul Davidson notes, '[R]eal economies that do not use money and money labour contracts to organize production (e.g., feudalism, slave economies, South Sea Islanders discovered by Margaret Mead, etc.) may . . . [face] an uncertain future – but there

is never an important involuntary unemployment problem' (Paul Davidson, PKT archives, quoted in Mosler 1997/1998, p. 167). Whether or not this causes a real hardship for the population depends on the degree to which it has become monetized; if there were still ample opportunity to satisfy wants outside of markets, then 'unemployment' would cause hardship only if individuals were unable to come up with the govs required for taxes.

36. Furness, almost certainly in error, called these 'stone currency' and imagined that they were used as some sort of primitive 'medium of exchange'; however, his description uncovers no evidence that there were any markets.

37. In early Greece, stones were used to mark the property of a farmer who had gone into debt. They were 'paid off' by the farmer providing labour to the debt holder. Thus much like the black crosses, the stones were sufficient to draw forth a labour supply.

38. As Neale and others emphasize, this was not always a happy, smooth process even when colonizers might have had good intentions.

39. A similar story could be told about the creation of a monetary economy out of the feudal European economy. While money and markets had existed for many centuries, the feudal economy of Europe was largely 'non-monetized', with most production done by peasants for their own consumption or to be provided as an in kind payment of rent to feudal lords. Just as in the case of the African colonies, taxation payable in money form (and imposition of rents in money form) induced production for markets and helped to destroy the traditional economy. (See Aston and Philpin, 1987, and Hoppe and Langton, 1994.)

40. The earliest paper money issued in America 'was a total of £7000 in units of between 5s. [shillings] and £5 issued by the Massachusetts Bay Colony to pay the soldiers on an expedition against Canada in 1690' (Grierson, 1975, p. 36).

41. The dollar was modelled on the Spanish dollar and was a pointed rejection of the British pound.

42. If, however, the Treasury purchased gold by minting new coins, this would replace coins drained by running budget surpluses. Gold purchases are not counted as government expenditures, but can compensate for the deflationary impacts of government surpluses by providing the means with which taxes can be paid.

43. Except in time of war, most revenue came from customs duties. The government typically received taxes in the form of specie and paid out specie. However, as mentioned above, foreign coins were accepted as legal tender until just before the Civil War. Thus importers needed specie to pay the duties, but could use foreign coins. As noted above, federal government purchases of gold also injected specie, partially offsetting the persistent surpluses.

44. Note that the North accepted state banknotes, greenbacks and specie in payment of taxes. Estimates of total spending by the North and South differ. Stabile and Cantor (1991, pp. 58–9) estimate total direct cost of the Civil War at $5.2 billion, with $3.2 billion for the North and $2 billion for the South. According to Stabile and Cantor, in the North taxes contributed 22 per cent of the cost, with borrowing at $2.8 billion.

4 Government Spending, Deficits and Money

According to the conventional view, tax revenue provides the income needed by the government to finance its spending. A government might be able to spend in excess of its revenue, at least temporarily, if it is able to issue debt that the public will hold. That is, the government might be able to borrow from the public to finance deficit spending. One method that is almost universally scorned is for the government to issue non-interest-bearing debt – currency – to finance deficits. This can either be done directly by the Treasury, or indirectly through the central bank. Because government deficits financed in this manner would directly cause the money supply to expand, many economists claim this would directly cause inflation.

If, instead, the government sold interest-earning bonds to finance (or 'fund'[1]) its deficit, the money supply would increase – according to most economists – only if the central bank 'accommodated' by increasing bank reserves.[2] So long as the central bank did not accommodate, there should be no direct impact on inflation.[3] Government borrowing is likely, according to a common view, to 'crowd out' private borrowing because government borrowing adds to the demand for loanable funds, driving up interest rates, and displacing interest-sensitive private spending (investment, housing, consumer durables). Crowding out can be partial, complete, or even more than complete, depending on assumptions.[4] Over the longer run, if crowding out does occur, this will depress aggregate supply and could thereby induce cost-push inflation.

Finally, while most economists recognize that at least under some situations government deficits are desirable (and that at times, benefits outweigh costs), most would argue that persistent deficits must be avoided. Even Keynesian economists generally argue that structural deficits should be avoided; that is, while a government should run deficits in recessions, these should be offset by surpluses during expansions. It is believed that permanent deficits must be avoided because no government can operate in such a manner as to generate the expectation that it will never be able to retire its debt, that is, the expectation that debt can only be 'rolled over'. While there may not be a specific dept-to-GDP or deficit-to-GDP ratio at which markets lose trust in the government, it is not doubted that such thresholds exist. Governments are thus believed to be subject to market forces that determine the quantity of debt the government can issue as well as the price (interest rate) of the debt. If the domestic population will not take up all the debt, the government is forced to sell bonds in international markets. International markets might even force the government to borrow in a foreign currency (issue foreign-currency-denominated debt) if the country's finances are questionable. Indeed, the government may be forced to impose austerity on its population in order to placate international markets before it will able to sell bonds internationally.

We do not intend to explore these positions in more detail. Rather, our analysis will demonstrate that this view completely misunderstands the nature of government spending, taxing, deficits and bond sales. As we claimed in the Introduction, permanent consolidated government deficits are the theoretical and practical norm in a modern economy. While it is certainly possible to run a surplus over a short period, as we will discuss, this has income and balance sheet effects that unleash strong deflationary forces.[5] Given usual private sector preferences regarding net saving, economic growth requires persistent government deficits. Further, government spending is always financed through creation of fiat money – rather than through tax revenues or bond sales. Indeed, taxes are required not to finance spending, but rather to maintain demand for government fiat money. Finally, bond sales are used to drain excess reserves in order to maintain positive overnight lending interest rates, rather than to finance government deficits. This leads to an entirely different view of the degree to which governments are 'forced' to respond to pressures coming from international markets. We will argue that most of the pressures that governments currently believe arise from international markets are actually self-imposed constraints that arise from a misunderstanding of the nature of government deficits.

Our view builds upon the Keynesian approach and is probably most closely related to Abba Lerner's functional finance approach. According to Lerner,

> The central idea is that government fiscal policy, its spending and taxing, its borrowing and repayment of loans, its issue of new money, and its withdrawal of money, shall all be undertaken with an eye only to the results of these actions on the economy and not to any established traditional doctrine about what is sound or unsound. (Lerner, 1943, p. 39)

He went on to list two 'laws' of functional finance:

> The first financial responsibility of the government (since nobody else can undertake that responsibility) is to keep the total rate of spending in the country on goods and services neither greater nor less than that rate which at the current prices would buy all the goods that it is possible to produce. (Ibid.)

When spending is too high, the government is to reduce spending and raise taxes; when spending is too low, the government should increase spending and lower taxes.

> An interesting corollary is that taxing is never to be undertaken merely because the government needs to make money payments . . . . Taxation should therefore be imposed only when it is desirable that the taxpayers shall have less money to spend. (Ibid., p. 40)

If the government is not to use taxes to 'make money payments', then how are these to be made? According to Lerner, the government should not turn to borrowing for the purposes of spending, because, 'The second law of Functional Finance is that the government should borrow money only if it is desirable that the public should have less money and more government bonds' (ibid.). In other words, the purpose of taxes and bonds is not really to finance spending as each serves a different purpose (taxes remove excessive private income while bonds offer an interest-earning alternative to money). Instead, the government should meet its needs 'by printing new money' whenever the first and second principles of functional finance dictate that neither taxes nor bond sales are required.

In summary, Lerner argued

> Functional Finance rejects completely the traditional doctrines of 'sound finance' and the principle of trying to balance the budget over a solar year or any other arbitrary period. In their place it prescribes: first, the adjustment of total spending (by everybody in the economy, including the government) in order to eliminate both unemployment and inflation, using government spending when total spending is too low and taxation when total spending is too high; second, the adjustment of public holdings of money and of government bonds, by government borrowing or debt repayment, in order to achieve the rate of interest which results in the most desirable level of investment; and third, the printing, hoarding or destruction of money as needed for carrying out the first two parts of the program. (Ibid. p. 41)

He concluded that functional finance 'is applicable to any society in which money is used as an important element in the economic mechanism' (ibid. p. 50).

What we are adding to Lerner's approach is (1) an explicit recognition of the role played by taxes in driving money (which, as noted in Chapter 2 above, was recognized by Lerner in another context); (2) an explicit examination of the impact on reserves of application of the second principle of functional finance (treated in more detail in Chapter 5 below); and (3) analysis of a government spending programme that will automatically generate full employment as recommended by Lerner (treated primarily in Chapter 6).

GOVERNMENT DEFICITS AND FIAT MONEY

As discussed in Chapter 1, all modern capitalist economies operate on the basis of a fiat money system. The fiat money is issued directly by the Treasury (as in the US, where the Treasury issues coins) or through the central bank (as in the US, where the Fed issues paper notes) as a non-convertible government liability. This fiat money generally functions as legal tender, that is, it is sanctioned by the courts as the money which fulfils 'all debts, public and private'. It is the only money that is ultimately accepted in payment of taxes.[6] It is also the money into which bank liabilities are convertible (either on demand or after some specified waiting period), and which is used for clearing among banks and between private banks and the central bank. It is the money used as the link between the public and private pay communities.[7] It is the money that sits at the top of the debt pyramid (or hierarchy), or the 'definitive' and 'valuta' money.[8] It is the most liquid liability used domestically – except in rare circumstances where a foreign currency is used domestically (as is the case in some of the formerly socialist countries today). The most important thing to understand is that in a normally functioning modern economy, the domestic fiat money is always accepted in exchange for domestic production; anything that is for sale with a dollar price can be had by delivering US currency (coins or notes).[9]

When a modern government spends, it issues a cheque drawn on the Treasury; its liabilities increase by the amount of the expenditure and its assets increase (in the case of a purchase) or some other liabilities are reduced (in the case of a social transfer, for example, social security payment liabilities are reduced by the amount of social security cheques issued). The recipient of the Treasury cheque will almost certainly 'cash' the cheque at a bank; either the recipient will withdraw currency, or, more commonly, the recipient's bank account will be credited. In the latter case, bank reserves are credited by the Fed in the amount of the increase of the deposit account. For our purposes, it is not important to distinguish between the Fed's and the Treasury's balance sheet. The bank reserves carried on books as the bank's asset and as the Fed's liability are nothing less than a claim on government fiat money – at any time, the bank can convert these to coins or paper notes, or use them in payments to the state. When the recipient 'cashes' a Treasury cheque, a bank will convert reserves to currency – which is always supplied on demand by the Fed, which acts as the Treasury's 'bank', converting one kind of Treasury liability (a cheque written to the public) to another kind (coins or an IOU to the Fed, offset by Fed issuance of paper notes).

The important thing to notice is that the Treasury spends before and without regard to either previous receipt of taxes or prior bond sales. In the US, taxes are received throughout the year (although not uniformly as receipts are concentrated around certain quarterly dates, as well as the 15 April deadline) mainly into special tax accounts held at private commercial banks. It is true that the Treasury transfers funds from the private banks to its account at the Fed when it wishes to 'spend', but this is really a reserve maintenance operation – when the Treasury spends, bank reserves increase by approximately the same amount so that the transfer from tax accounts is used to stabilize bank reserves. These additions to/subtractions from reserves need to be carefully monitored, with a central bank injection of reserves used to make up any shortfall (for example, if transfers from tax accounts exceed deposits of Treasury cheques) or a reserve drain used to remove excess reserves.

These central bank actions to offset the daily fluctuations that destabilize the overnight interest rate (called operating factors) will be taken up in detail in Chapter 5. The point is that the tax receipts cannot be spent. By consolidating the Fed and Treasury balance sheets, one sees that in reality, the Treasury cannot withdraw taxes from the economy before spending – any transfer of tax accounts from the private economy to the government's balance sheet must be exactly offset by government provision of an equivalent amount of 'fiat money' through use of the Fed's balance sheet. In any case, as government is the only supplier of fiat money, it cannot receive in taxes fiat money that it has not provided to private markets. The original source of all fiat money must be the (consolidated) government, and the coordination between the Treasury and central bank is required to maintain reserves. If it were not for the effect of government spending on bank reserves, there would be no need to tie spending to transfers from tax accounts; the coincident timing of tax 'receipts' and government spending (or central bank open market operations) is not an indication of a 'financing' operation but rather is required to maintain stability in the market for reserves. The implication is that tax payments do not 'finance' government spending but that they create a demand for currency and impact reserves.[10]

Starting from the aggregate level, it is easy to see that only the government can be a 'net' supplier of money. As shown in Chapter 5 below, every private creation of money held by someone is offset by creation of an equal private liability. For example, every time a bank creates a demand deposit (money), this is carried on the books of the depositor as an asset, but it is a liability of the bank. The deposit, in turn, is created by the bank as it purchases an asset – typically the IOU of a borrower. Bank money is an 'inside' money; while it is an asset of the holder (or depositor) it is offset by the bank liability and it can never be a net asset of the private sector.

Payments using bank money cause the bank money to shift pockets but leave it intact except (1) if a bank loan is repaid, or (2) if a bank cheque is presented for cash, or (3) if payments are made to the government. In all three cases, the bank money is destroyed; the latter two cases require an outside, government, money. When households use bank deposit money to pay taxes a clearing drain results so that banks cannot meet reserve requirements.[11] Overnight interest rates (in the US, the Fed funds rate) are driven up as banks desperately try to meet legal requirements; given excess demand for reserves and very nearly zero elasticity of demand (since requirements must be met) a market break would ensue (with a demand but no supply). The central bank would at this point have to step in to provide the fiat money reserves required. The most likely course would be to engage in open market purchases of government bonds. Clearly, this is not sustainable as an equilibrium solution, for the public (including banks) would eventually run out of government bonds to sell to the central bank.

The central bank at that point could offer to purchase other types of assets from the public. For example, central banks can, and do, purchase foreign currencies from the public, thereby injecting domestic fiat money reserves. Alternatively, the central bank could begin to buy domestic financial assets, or even domestic goods and services. Indeed, in countries which appear to run surplus budgets, some combination of these central bank policies is invariably used to provide the fiat money the public must have to pay taxes. In a sense, this is nothing more than an accounting gimmick – the government keeps two sets of books, the Treasury's book and the central bank's book, and runs a surplus on one and a deficit on the other.[12] It is only because the central bank's purchases of government bonds, private bonds, other private assets, foreign currencies, or even goods and services are not counted as part of government spending that it can appear that persistent government surpluses are possible. In conclusion, a persistent surplus is not feasible because households will run out of net money hoards; a surplus on the Treasury's account is possible so long as the central bank injects reserves through purchase of assets or through loans of reserves.[13]

When the government creates fiat money to purchase goods and services (or assets such as gold, or to reduce liabilities such as payments owed to social security recipients), this shows up on the books of the public as a credit of fiat money and a debit of goods and services sold to the government (or assets sold or claims on government). This is 'net money creation' because it is not offset by a private sector liability. This 'net money' (also called 'outside money') is available to pay taxes. When taxes are paid, the public can reduce its outstanding tax liability which is exactly equal to the reduction of its holding of 'net money' (government fiat money).

In principle, then, the government first spends fiat money (to purchase goods, services, and assets or to provide 'transfer payments', which retires a government liability). Once the government has spent, then that fiat money is available to be transferred to the government to meet tax liabilities. As a matter of logic, the public cannot pay fiat money to the government to meet tax liabilities until the government has paid out fiat money to the public. In a modern capitalist economy, it may appear more complex than this because most taxes are paid using cheques drawn on bank deposits, rather than currency. However, this amounts to the same thing since every payment of taxes generates a reserve clearing drain, or, a loss of reserves.[14] Thus taxes cannot be paid until actual coins or notes are injected into the economy, or bank reserves have been created. Government expenditure will generate coins, notes or bank reserves that are needed to 'pay taxes'.

Given these considerations, a balanced budget is the theoretical minimum that a government can run continuously. If the government were to attempt to run a surplus, the public would find that its 'net money' receipts of fiat money would be less than its tax liability, requiring households to dip into hoards of fiat money (accumulated from past government deficit spending and purchases of assets) to pay taxes. Eventually, of course, the hoards would be depleted. Finally, the public could present maturing government bonds for payment to obtain fiat money with which to pay taxes, but, again, this is limited to the portion of the outstanding debt stock that is maturing (itself a function of previous government deficits and the maturity structure of the debt). At this point, the only sources of fiat money to pay taxes are new government (deficit) spending or government purchases of assets.

DEFICITS AND SAVING

Fiscal policy or, more specifically, the expenditure decision, principally determines the amount of fiat money (coins, notes or reserves – which are always convertible on demand to coins and notes) available to pay taxes. While it is true that central bank net purchases (or lending) also supplies reserves (thus fiat money), this is small relative to government spending and taxing and is taken as a defensive action to add/drain reserves on a short term basis. Previously, we examined the reasons for public acceptance of fiat money. Briefly, the public would not give up goods and services to the government in return for otherwise worthless coins or notes unless there were good reason to do so. The primary reason the public accepts fiat money is because it has tax liabilities to the government. This should not be misinterpreted as an argument that people accept government money only because of the tax liability (which would be true only in the simplest version of our hypothetical colonial governor story). The tax liability is a sufficient but not necessary condition for the 'acceptation' (Knapp called it) of state money. We do claim, however, that if the tax system were removed, the government would eventually find that its fiat money would lose its ability to purchase good and services on the market.

Normally, taxes in the aggregate will have to be less than total government spending due to preferences of the public to hold some reserves of fiat money. Individuals also hold interest-earning bank deposits (inside money) and other private financial assets; however, as these can be converted on demand to fiat money, banks will hold some fiat money reserves – or will arrange to hold liquid assets (such as government bonds) that can be converted to fiat money reserves. In the modern economy, the banking system ensures that taxpayers can always exchange bank liabilities for fiat money; thus households have no need to hold currency for tax payments. Household hoards of currency are thus a function of uncertainty over the safety of banks, illegal activities, convenience and other idiosyncratic factors. In turn, bank holdings of fiat money are a function of required reserve ratios, which are effectively 'minimum balance' requirements. In a country without legally required reserves, if reserves do not earn interest, each bank tries to operate such that its reserve balance at the end of each day is zero; the implications are equivalent to requiring a minimum balance of zero.[15] In either case, the central bank must operate to ensure that minimum balances are met. Note also that some portion of private household and bank portfolios will be devoted to government bonds; these are little more than interest-earning government currency provided as part of monetary policy to drain excess reserves to allow the central bank to hit its interest rate target. Thus the government can safely run a deficit up to the point where it has provided the quantity of non-interest-earning fiat money and interest-earning bonds desired by the public.

Another way of looking at this issue is through a 'Keynesian' demand approach. At any point in time, the public desires to achieve some flow of saving – that is, to spend less than its income in order to accumulate nominal claims on wealth. The private sector cannot create net nominal wealth – every private financial asset is offset by a private financial liability. At the aggregate level, in a simple, closed economy without government, private investment exactly equals private saving – all saving is created by investment. To simplify, we can assume that it is the household sector which saves and the business sector which invests; the net (inside) indebtedness of the business sector is exactly offset by the net (inside) financial wealth of the household sector.[16] It is frequently the case that the household sector wishes to save more than the business sector wishes to invest. In our simple economy, this must exert deflationary pressures until household income falls sufficiently that its desired saving equals the investment undertaken by firms. This is the idea behind the 'paradox of thrift': investment determines saving so that given low investment by firms when households are excessively thrifty, income falls until the aggregate of saving decisions (as determined by income and the marginal propensity to save) is consistent with the aggregate of investment decisions.[17] Alternatively, aggregate saving cannot be increased by trying to save more, but only by investing more – which raises income and thus saving.

When we add a foreign sector, this complicates matters only slightly. One country, say Country A, can have an aggregate flow of saving over any particular time period which exceeds its aggregate flow of investment spending so long as another country, say Country B, has an aggregate flow of saving which is less than its aggregate investment flow. In this case, Country A can run a trade surplus while Country B runs a trade deficit; the financial counterpart is that Country A will accumulate net financial claims against Country B. Thus in our open economy (still without a government sector), a country's aggregate saving flow is equal to its aggregate investment flow plus its net export flow; saving can exceed investment when net exports are positive, but will fall short of investment when net exports are negative. The country running a trade surplus is able to net save (accumulate net outside wealth) in the form of the net liabilities of countries running trade deficits.

If we add a government, then its deficit spending allows net (outside) saving by the household sector (ignoring, again, the foreign sector). In this case, when the household sector desires to save more than the business sector wishes to invest, the government's spending can provide the extra income that households do not wish to spend. In this expanded economy, household saving equals business investment plus the government's deficit. Given a level of planned investment, and a level of government spending, then a reduction of taxes will increase the government's deficit and actual household saving. If the household sector was previously trying to save more than the sum of business investment and government deficit, the lower taxes which generate a larger deficit can allow the household sector to meet its desired level of saving. (To be complete, when we allow for a government sector in an open economy, then the flow of aggregate saving is identically equal to investment plus the government's deficit, plus net exports.)

If the private sector chronically desires to save more than it wants to invest, the government can fill the 'demand gap' by deficit spending and thus allow households to save as much as desired. If government lowers taxes and this generates more saving than desired, households can increase spending (consumption) until income and desired saving rise to equality with actual saving (generated by the deficit plus investment). Beyond some point, this is likely to cause inflation. That is, a deficit can be both too small (causing actual saving to fall short of desired saving) and too large (causing actual saving to exceed desired saving). The first case causes deflationary pressure while the second creates inflationary pressure; in both cases, nominal income adjusts until desired saving equals actual saving.

We can define saving less investment as 'net nominal saving' (or Sn) of the public, which in our closed economy is in the form of fiat money or government bonds but in the open economy can include liabilities of foreigners.[18] If the public desires to have positive net nominal saving, this can be realized only if the government runs a deficit and/or the economy runs a trade surplus. Ignoring the foreign sector, then, government deficits are necessary to allow the public to have positive net nominal saving. If the government runs a balanced budget, then the desires of the public cannot be realized, but will exert deflationary pressures on the economy until realized income is sufficiently low that desired and actual net nominal saving is zero.

However, there are two complications. First, unlike desired saving (S), it is not clear that desired net nominal saving (Sn) is a positive function of income. That is, as income declines, it is possible that desired net nominal saving (Sn) rises (for example, due to rising uncertainty in a recession, the public wishes to increase hoards of fiat money and banks wish to increase holdings of excess reserves). This means that when the deficit is too small, it can induce an unstable deflationary spiral that does not restore equilibrium between actual and desired net nominal saving – unless the government's deficit automatically grows in a countercyclical manner (for example, through automatic tax decreases and spending increases in recession).

On the other hand, as we have discussed, at least in the short run, the central bank can provide fiat money by purchasing assets or lending reserves at the discount window.[19] This tends to mitigate deflationary pressures of a deficit that is too small. Indeed, to some extent central bank provision of reserves would be automatic so that if the public wanted to hold more fiat money, the central bank would ensure that banks would be able to convert deposit money to fiat money. However, the central bank, in practice, imposes conditions for such loans on banks. For example, the central bank requires collateral (only lending against certain types of assets) and might force a borrowing bank to sell assets or at least to stop making new loans. This will then add to the deflationary pressure that results from a deficit that is too small.

Until full employment is reached, deficits can be increased to allow incomes to rise and generate more net saving. Once full employment is reached, additional deficit spending will generate additional income that is likely to cause inflationary pressures – except in the unlikely case that all additional income represents desired net saving. Beyond full employment, then, any further reduction of taxes or increase of government spending (increasing deficit spending) is likely to reduce the value of money as prices are bid up.

Involuntary unemployment is of significance only in modern, monetary, economies-that is, economies that use a chartal money. Traditional or tribal societies did not experience unemployment; even the command economies of feudal Europe or of medieval monasteries did not experience involuntary unemployment on a significant scale. However, all economies that operate with a chartal money do suffer from periodic, if not chronic, unemployment. As will be discussed in Chapter 6 below, unemployment is *de facto* evidence that the government's deficit is too low to provide the level of net saving desired. If the government were to increase its deficit, and thereby increase the supply of fiat money, actual household net saving would rise. At the same time, the additional deficit spending would increase incomes and generate additional spending, and thus additional employment. In a sense, unemployment results because the government has kept the supply of fiat money too scarce. An increase (through deficit spending) would stimulate the private sector so that it would create more jobs and reduce unemployment. Since the government is the sole supplier of fiat money, and since fiat money is essentially a resource that is potentially unlimited in supply, it makes little sense to restrict the supply of fiat money to the extent that this causes unemployment, unless unemployment serves a useful purpose. We will return to this issue in Chapter 6, however, it is important to note that there are no real resource constraints to prevent raising of the deficit until unemployment has been eliminated. Beyond that point, real constraints intervene so that additional deficits will run up against the inflation barrier.

This does not mean that government deficits can only be inflationary when the economy operates beyond full employment. If the tax system breaks down, the government's fiat money can become worthless – which is manifested as 'hyperinflation'. The government can print ever-increasing amounts of money, but find little for sale even as resources sit idle. Clearly, this does not require full employment; indeed, most hyperinflations occur with substantial unemployment. This is not surprising, because once the value of the fiat money collapses, it becomes virtually impossible to undertake 'money now for more money later' propositions (which is what most production involves). The only way a complete collapse of the economy can be avoided is if the private sector can write contracts in an alternative money with a relatively more stable value. For example, it is possible that a foreign fiat money might be used domestically for private contracts. Alternatively, sometimes transactors resort to barter when the domestic currency has lost value. Even in transactions where legal tender is required, private parties can agree to accept the domestic fiat money at the current exchange rate with the foreign currency of account. In any case, the belief that hyperinflations are caused by the government 'printing too much money', running the printing presses 'at full speed' captures only the effect, not the cause of the problem. It is usually the breakdown of the tax system, rather than the speed of the printing presses alone, which creates the hyperinflation. While it may be superficially accurate to call this a case of 'too much money chasing too few goods', this does not identify the source of the inflation.

BONDS AND INTEREST RATE POLICY

If government spending is 'financed' through creation of fiat money, and if taxes are designed to call forth things for sale to government – rather than to 'finance' government spending – then why does the government sell bonds? Of course, governments believe that they must sell bonds to borrow the funds necessary to financing spending. However, this is an illusion, as the spending must come first. As we will argue, bond sales (whether by the Treasury or by the central bank) function to drain excess reserves; they cannot finance or fund deficit spending. This view builds upon Lerner's second law of functional finance: 'the government should borrow money only if it is desirable that the public should have less money and more government bonds' (Lerner, 1943, p. 40). More specifically, bond sales are designed to substitute an interest-earning government liability for non-interest-earning government fiat money, and is properly thought of as a monetary policy operation rather than a fiscal policy operation. In this section we will briefly examine the nature of bond sales, while we will examine monetary policy in more detail in the next chapter.

As discussed above, all government spending is initially financed through issuance of fiat money; this normally takes the form of a Treasury cheque, deposited at a private bank, increasing bank reserves by the amount of the government spending. To avoid a situation of excess reserves, a simultaneous transfer is made from bank tax and loan accounts to the central bank. However, in the case of a government deficit, the amount of fiat money created exceeds the amount of bank reserves removed through tax payments. In a fractional reserve system, this necessarily creates an excess reserve position of the banking system. Some reserves will be withdrawn by the non-bank public, which holds some fiat money in the form of currency. However, most will remain as excess reserves.

Individual banks will offer excess reserves in wholesale markets – namely, the Fed funds market at the Fed funds rate – which can shift reserves around but cannot eliminate the excess. The excess supply will force the overnight rate to be bid down; at the limit it will be pushed to zero. While it is true that in the longer run banks can adjust to a position of excess reserves through normal growth of their loan and deposit portfolio (to increase required reserves), in the short run the only adjustment can be to the Fed funds rate. As a result, to prevent a Fed funds market break, with a zero per cent bid for reserves, the central bank and/or Treasury must drain the excess reserves. This is done through bond sales. Since, as discussed in Chapter 5 below, all modern central banks operate with an overnight interest rate target, excess reserves automatically trigger bond sales (typically, reverse repos or matched sale-purchase transactions) by the central bank. These prevent the overnight rate from falling, allowing the central bank to hit its target.

In the US, primary sales of bonds to drain reserves are undertaken by the Treasury, while the Fed uses repos and reverse repos to 'fine-tune' as it adds/drains reserves to offset daily operating factors. Primary bond sales 'mop up' excess reserves created by government deficits, providing interest-earning alternatives to non-interest-earning excess reserves held by banks and cash held by the public, while secondary sales in open market operations by the Fed are designed to offset daily 'operating factors' that can leave banks in an excess reserve situation.[20]

In order for the central bank to sell bonds, obviously, the Treasury must issue them. While central bank sales in secondary markets might on any day be a large portion of total sales, over the longer run most sales must be made by the Treasury in primary markets. These are then available to be purchased by the central bank when it needs temporarily to inject reserves into the system.

If a government were to decide to avoid sales of bonds in primary markets, the central bank would eventually drain all the reserves it could through sales of bonds and foreign currency; in the end it would also have engaged in all the reserve-absorbing behaviour it had at its disposal. At this point, if excess reserves still existed in the system, overnight rates would fall to zero. This reinforces the view that bond sales are part of monetary policy and not a financing operation to allow the government to run deficits. It also points out that beyond some volume of deficit spending, the 'natural rate' of interest is zero (at least, in the case of the Fed funds rate); rather than deficit spending raising interest rates, it actually causes overnight rates to fall to zero when it is at a level that generates excess reserves.

Government spending is never constrained by the quantity of bonds that markets are willing to purchase; rather, bond sales are undertaken to provide an interest-earning alternative to cash and excess reserves. Government spending is constrained only by private sector willingness to provide goods, services or assets to government in exchange for government money, which is ultimately derived from the public's desire for money with which to pay taxes and to hold as net saving. Anything which is for purchase in terms of the domestic currency can be had through government creation of fiat money.

Governments sometimes believe that they must sell bonds in international markets because domestic markets are already saturated with bonds and any further domestic sales would require higher interest rates. While this can be true, it has reversed the causation: the government does not 'need' to sell bonds at all; bond sales are by design an 'interest rate maintenance' operation. Thus while it might be true that at a higher interest rate, government might induce the public and banks to give up some fiat money (although as noted above this effect is probably quite small because the demand for fiat money is interest-inelastic), this is not an indication that the government is 'forced' to pay higher rates to 'finance' its deficit. Once domestic households and banks are content with their holdings of government bonds and non-interest-earning cash and reserves, then government need not drain any more reserves from the system – or, equivalently, it need not sell any more bonds.

What if government sells bonds to foreigners? So long as these bonds are denominated in the domestic fiat currency, they do not entail any 'risks' that domestically held bonds do not hold – and they serve exactly the same purpose, which is to provide an interest-earning alternative to non-interest-earning fiat money. Concern is often expressed that foreign-held bonds commit a country to paying interest to foreigners, which is said to 'burden' domestic taxpayers (see also the discussion of burden of the debt below). However, interest can always be paid through creation of fiat money – just as any other government spending is financed through creation of fiat money. Future bond sales will be undertaken to drain excess reserves, just as current bond sales drain reserves; again, this entails no 'burden'. And there is no possibility that government might find itself in a crisis because it is unable to sell or 'roll over' bonds – since the purpose of bond sales is nothing more than to offer interest-earning alternatives to fiat money. As Lerner argued, bonds should only be sold when the public has more non-interest-earning currency (and bank reserves) than desired.

Sometimes governments believe that the 'market' forces them to issue foreign-currency-denominated bonds. There is only one case in which this would be true – when the government wishes to purchase goods and services that are not for sale in terms of the domestic fiat money. In this case, the government cannot issue the currency desired by sellers. Nor can it dictate the price it will pay in terms of its own fiat money. Nor can it create the currency to be used in payment for the goods and services. In this one case, the government must sell something (or borrow – which is the sale of an IOU) to obtain the currency required by sellers of the goods and services it would like to obtain. Unlike the case of domestic-currency-denominated bonds, this can 'burden' an economy for now interest payments cannot be financed through creation of fiat money. The government may have little influence over the foreign-currency price at which the bonds will sell. It will have to obtain additional foreign currency in the future to service the debt. In some situations, markets might fear that a government will not be able to do this – which could lead to default – causing a rational run out of these bonds. As a result, the government may feel forced to impose austerity on its population to maintain a trade surplus to obtain the needed foreign currency. In this one case, the austerity can be at least partially blamed on 'market discipline'. However, it must be recognized that this is only because the government desired goods and services that were not for sale in the domestic currency. In all other cases, the government is not subject to 'market discipline', and any austerity and hardship is 'self-inflicted'.[21]

Since bond sales are nothing more than an interest rate maintenance operation, the government decides the interest rate it will pay – or, alternatively, the price of government bonds – in its monetary policy. Thus government deficit spending is never subject to 'market discipline' regarding either the quantity of bonds sold or the price at which they will be sold, so long as the bonds are issued in the domestic currency. When there are excess reserves, the market will 'demand' bonds at any interest rate above zero, for the alternative is non-earning excess reserves. There may be very good reasons for maintaining a significantly positive interest rate on government bonds, but it is never necessary to do so merely because the market would like a high interest rate. A high government borrowing rate is evidence that the government (Treasury plus central bank) has chosen a high interest rate – it tells us nothing about 'market forces' of supply and demand. The government can always have a lower interest rate merely by reducing the interest rate target. (More on this in the chapter that follows.)

Most of the time, governments do not appear to understand this, but there are exceptions. For example, during WWII, the US government was able to 'borrow' to finance 'massive deficits' (five times larger than President Reagan's deficits, relative to the size of the economy) at a short term interest rate of 3/8 of 1 per cent. Bond sales were not actually required to finance the deficits but were instead required to drain fiat money reserves (something the government probably did not understand). Bond sales were also designed to 'force' net saving by the public in order to ensure that goods and services would be released from consumption for the war effort (this was no doubt understood by the government). The public viewed the bonds as a patriotic (and interest-earning) means of accumulating financial wealth that would be used in the postwar period to support higher levels of consumption. Clearly, the government did understand that the price of bonds (and, therefore, the interest rate paid by government) was not determined by markets; it was set exogenously by government policy. The government also understood that many of the prices it paid for goods and services were not market determined – but, rather, were administratively set by the government. Similarly, government determined the price of labour – directly and indirectly – so that even as the economy operated well beyond 'full employment', prices of labour and of output purchased by the government were relatively stable. Most of the lessons that could have been learned from WWII finances were not learned or, at least, have been forgotten.

FUNCTIONAL FINANCE AND THE BURDEN OF THE DEBT

Indeed, they were quickly forgotten, at least by some politicians and economists. In his State of the Union message of 7 January 1960, President Eisenhower made a statement that could have been made by President Jackson (and perhaps by President Clinton): 'Personally, I do not feel that any amount can be properly called a surplus as long as the nation is in debt. I prefer to think of such an item as a reduction on our children's inherited mortgage' (President Eisenhower, quoted in Bowen, Davis and Kopf, 1960, p. 701). Bowen, et.al. then attempted to defend Eisenhower's belief that government debt represents a burden on future generations, arguing that future generations will have to reduce consumption in order to pay the taxes required to retire the outstanding debt. This was a pointed response to those who adopted the functional finance approach (and even to Paul Samuelson) who argued that any real burden of government deficit spending must be borne at the time the borrowed funds are spent. In brief, Bowen, et. al., argued that the functional finance approach ignores the eventual burden on the later generation (dubbed Generation II) when 'the government decides to retire the debt by levying a general tax in excess of current government spending and using the surplus to buy up the bonds that are now held by members of Generation II. The inevitable outcome of this decision is a reduction in the lifetime consumption of Generation II' (ibid. p. 701). While it is true that the taxes raised from Generation II are merely redistributed to bondholders in Generation II, there is still a net lifetime reduction of consumption of Generation II since these bondholders had to reduce consumption when they purchased bonds from 'Generation I'.

In a masterful response, Lerner (1961) addressed many of the errors of the Bowen, et. al., exposition:

> The 'red herring' nature of having the Lowells lend the money now (so that we can call them the present generation) and having the Thomases pay the taxes in the future (so that they can be called the future generation) jumps to the eye if we note that the shifting of the real burden of the project from the Lowells to the Thomases (or indeed of any other burden) could take place just as well at the time of the project (or at any other time) by simply taxing the Thomases instead of the Lowells (Lerner 1961, p. 139).[22]

The key to the Bowen, et. al., result is a series of misunderstandings and strange assumptions. For example, they presume that when Generation I reduces consumption to buy bonds that result from deficit spending, there is no flow of income that results from the government spending (money that is supposed to have been raised from the bond sales mysteriously disappears). In reality, deficit spending must (all else equal) create the same amount of aggregate saving (initially in the form of Treasury checks). Bond sales then merely allow households (and banks) to hold bonds rather than money. This does not mean that there is no burden associated with the government spending – presumably, real goods and services are moved from the private sector to the public sector[23] – but the burden is borne immediately and results whether or not the government sells bonds. Further, the supposed burden imposed in the future by taxing Generation II is really due to the government's decision to run a surplus (taxing more than it spends). No one who adopts the functional finance approach would deny that a government surplus (all else equal) reduces private sector income and net saving. When the government then retires bonds, it merely substitutes non-interest-earning government liabilities for interest-earning liabilities; this simply restores the fiat money removed when the government taxed more than it spent. The same result could be obtained if the government were to forego the budget surplus, but were to confiscate all outstanding government bonds. Yes, there is a real burden involved, but it has nothing to do with the method of 'financing' of government spending chosen. No government that understood the principles of functional finance would ever confiscate outstanding government debt (nor would it ever believe it must increase taxes to retire outstanding debt). The power to tax is the power to destroy (net private sector wealth, that is).

THE PROPOSED EMU AND GOVERNMENT DEFICITS

As we write, the European Union (EU) is implementing an Economic and Monetary Union (EMU) which creates a European Central Bank (ECB) that becomes responsible for the European System of Central Banks (ESCB), with existing national central banks becoming operating arms of the ESCB (see Arestis and Sawyer, 1998). Under the EMU, monetary policy is supposed to be divorced from fiscal policy, with a great degree of monetary policy independence in order to focus on the primary objective of price stability. Fiscal policy, in turn will be tightly constrained by criteria which dictate maximum deficit-to-GDP and dept-to-GDP ratios (3 percent and 60 percent, respectively). Most importantly, as Goodhart (1997) recognizes, this will be the world's first modern experiment on a wide scale that would attempt to break the link between a government and its currency. The EMU would have a single currency[24] and essentially a single monetary policy, but would (in theory) allow each country to operate independent fiscal (spending and taxing) policy (within the constraints mentioned). Most importantly, it is envisioned that this arrangement will forever cut off the possibility that a government can use monetary policy to bail-out errant fiscal policy, for example, by having the central bank 'print money' to finance excessive deficits. Fiscal policy will become subject to the Maastricht criteria (with penalties imposed for excessive deficits) and to the dictates of the market (since treasuries cannot turn to central banks to sell government bonds the private markets do not want).

It is sometimes claimed that the EMU simply follows the example of American integration, with a single currency used throughout the United

States (thereby reducing transactions costs and contributing to integration of the member states). Goodhart (1997) and Godley (1997) rightly question the analogy. In the United States, as we have discussed in this chapter, what are normally called monetary and fiscal policy are in fact closely intertwined. Government spending is financed through issue of currency, taxes generate demand for the currency that results in sales to government, bond sales merely substitute bonds for money, and central bank operations determine interest rates and defensively add or subtract reserves. The relation of member countries to the EMU is more similar to the relation of the treasuries of member states of the United States to the Fed than it is of the US Treasury to the Fed. In the US, states have no power to create currency; taxes really do 'finance' state spending and states really do have to borrow (sell bonds to markets) in order to spend in excess of tax receipts. Purchasers of state bonds do worry about the credit – worthiness of states, and the ability of states to run deficits depends at least in part on market perceptions of riskiness. As Goodhart (1997) points out, the US state with the very worst credit rating in 1994 was Louisiana, with a ratio of debt service to revenues of 11.5 percent. In contrast, Germany had a ratio of 17.8 percent, while Italy had a ratio of 50 percent – and presumably no one operating in private markets would believe that Louisiana was a better credit risk than Germany or even Italy. The reason, of course, is that markets recognize that the treasuries of sovereign nations do have the ability to issue currency while the individual US states do not.

While it is certainly true that Louisiana can fall back on US government help when required, it is not so clear that the individual countries of the EMU will be so fortunate. As currently designed, the EMU will have a central bank (the ECB) but it will not have any fiscal branch. This would be much like a US which operated with a Fed, but with only individual state treasuries. It will be as if each EMU member country were to attempt to operate fiscal policy in a foreign currency; deficit spending will require borrowing in that foreign currency according to the dictates of private markets:

> If a government does not have its own central bank on which it can draw cheques freely, its expenditure can be financed only by borrowing in the open market in competition with businesses, and this may prove excessively expensive or even impossible, particularly under 'conditions of extreme emergency'. . . The danger, then, is that the budgetary restraint to which governments are individually committed will impart a disinflationary bias that locks Europe as a whole into a depression it is powerless to lift (Godley, 1997, p. 2).

Kregel (1998b) has proposed a solution to the likely deflationary forces that will be created by the EMU. He would have the ECB offer to provide the *euro* (the new currency) to 'hire all workers who were willing and able to work, but could not find employment in the private sector, at a basic wage' (Kregel, 1998b, p. 10). This programme is much like our employer of last resort programme, outlined below in Chapter 6, with the ECB taking over the fiscal policy role. Whenever private markets in the individual member countries were depressed, the ECB would provide the deficit spending necessary to return to full employment; when private markets recover, the ECB's deficit would fall. In this case, rather than having the individual member countries follow the principles of functional finance, it would be the ECB's role to provide the spending required to reach full employment without regard to the principles of so-called 'sound finance'.

GOVERNMENT SPENDING AND EXOGENOUS PRICING

Government spending decisions affect the value of the currency or inflation and deflation. It is quite easy for the government to devalue the currency – all it need do is offer to pay ever-increasing prices for the things it purchases. Private buyers will have to compete with the government, which is willing to pay higher prices. It would be quite surprising if this did not generate inflation. On the other hand, the government could choose to help stabilize prices by refraining from paying rising prices – for example, by refusing to index the price it pays to inflation. The immediate result might be a refusal of private suppliers to produce for government. Government spending would fall, depressing the private economy. Tax payments would lead to a reserve drain, forcing the central bank to provide necessary reserves – but this would come at a cost of imposing ever-stricter conditions on borrowing banks, which would in turn impose ever-stricter conditions on private borrowers. This would reinforce the deflationary conditions. Eventually, the prices offered by government would not look so bad to private suppliers. Of course, the process is symmetric: if market prices are falling but government holds its prices constant, this will help to reduce deflationary pressures. There are two essential points: first, if the government stabilizes the price it offers, this will exert a stabilizing influence on market prices; and second, government does not have to pay market price.

In Chapter 7 we will present a simple model in which the government exogenously sets the price of those things it purchases. In theory, it is possible for the government to set the price of everything it buys, but this does not mean that we advocate such a policy. Indeed, in Chapter 6 we advocate that the government use a buffer stock policy to help stabilize prices. Here we will briefly summarize the argument.

The government would choose one important commodity to act as a buffer stock, fixing its price. It would then let the quantity of this commodity purchased 'float'; as a consequence, the government's budget deficit would also float. By fixing an important price, that is, the price of an item that enters as a major cost in the private sector, the government would impart some price stability to the economy. By allowing its deficit to float, it would help to close the demand gap created whenever private spending is too low, allowing the deficit to increase so that actual saving could rise to equality with desired saving (or fall to equality with desired saving if actual saving were too high).

As we will discuss, the best commodity to use in such a buffer stock policy is unskilled labour. By stabilizing the wage of unskilled labour, the government will help to stabilize private sector wages and thus costs and prices. At the same time, by letting quantity 'float', the government can increase its employment of labour when unemployment is high or reduce it when unemployment is low. In this way, the deficit will float countercyclically, filling the demand gap. All the government need do is offer to employ anyone who wants a job at some announced, fixed wage; labour not required by the private sector would then become part of the buffer stock programme. When the private sector desired more labour, it could hire it away from the government's buffer stock at a slight mark-up over the buffer stock wage. This programme automatically guarantees:

(a) full employment, defined as all those willing and able to work will be able to find a job;
(b) a counter-cyclical deficit that exactly fills the gap between actual and desired saving; and
(c) greater price stability than the current system.

These issues will be examined in detail in Chapter 6.

NOTES

1. Economists often use the term 'finance' to indicate use of money to purchase a good, service or asset. It usually means the money was borrowed short term. The term 'fund' is used to indicate long-term borrowing. Thus one might borrow short term temporarily to 'finance' a purchase, then use long-term borrowing to retire the short-term debt and 'fund' the purchase long term.
2. See Chapter 5 below for the theory of the relations among reserves, money supply and inflation.

3. The deficits still might be inflationary either due to 'bottle-necks' that lead to supply constraints and cost-push inflation, or due to excessive aggregate demand (causing demand-pull inflation) if the economy operates beyond full capacity.

4. It is even conceivable that 'crowding in' might occur – the government's borrowing actually increases the demand for private bonds – although most economists do not pay much attention to this theoretical possibility. Some economists recognize that some government spending (for example, that on public infrastructure investment) is likely to increase private sector productivity and reduce private sector costs, which might encourage private investment. See Aschauer (1998).

5. For all practical purposes, surpluses can be run only so long as deficits have been run in previous years. Recall Chapter 3 in which it was argued that in the nineteenth century the US typically ran large deficits during wars and then surpluses following the wars that eventually generated recessions and renewed deficits.

6. We say that fiat money is a government liability. For what is the government liable? To accept its money in payment of taxes.

7. These terms were defined in Chapter 2 above. In Chapter 5 we will argue that the fiat money created by government is 'leveraged' by the private pay community.

8. See Chapter 2.

9. In the case of some extremely large transactions, it is conceivable that due to obvious problems arising from dealing with large sums of currency, intermediaries must be used so that no actual currency changes hands. The sale thus leads to credits and debits on computerized balance sheets of intermediaries – which leads to reserve-clearing transfers on the balance sheet of the central bank – but this changes nothing of principle, and these credits could be exchanged for fiat money both in theory and in practice.

10. The necessary coordination between the Treasury and central bank is so complex that details will have to wait for Chapter 5.

11. We are assuming there are no undesired excess reserves in the banking system.

12. Perhaps it is too strong to call this a gimmick. When the Treasury spends, this is automatically treated as a current account expenditure regardless of what it buys. Even long-lived real assets are simply treated as current spending. When spending exceeds tax revenues, this is called a deficit. However, no matter what the central bank buys, this is treated as a purchase of an asset; thus all Fed liabilities are offset by assets and no deficit spending is possible, because accounting conventions do not call such purchases by the Fed deficit spending.

13. As discussed in Chapter 5, the Treasury can also keep its 'surplus' in private bank accounts in which case the reserves do not leave the banking system. Indeed, this is exactly what the US Treasury found necessary as it ran surpluses in the nineteenth century.

14. Unless the tax payment is offset by the Fed's injection of reserves as it purchases assets.

15. If interest rates are paid on reserves, positive reserve balances will be held even if not required. In this case, the reserves are effectively similar to an interest-earning government bond. See Chapter 5.

16. This is unrealistic because in the real world, most saving is done by firms; however, this changes nothing of substance.

17. This need not be a smooth process, as discussed below.

18. The late William Vickrey had a similar notion of net nominal saving. See Vickrey (1997).

19. This does not affect saving flows, but converts private inside wealth to fiat money (but not to net outside wealth). For example, when the Fed discounts private 'bonds' held by banks, bank reserves increase and the firm then owes the government rather than the bank. This is a temporary injection of fiat money since the created reserves will have to be used to retire the loan from the Fed (which requires outside money). Thus a discount by the Fed of a private liability does not create net outside wealth since the outside wealth held by the bank

is offset by a debt to the Fed.

20. See Chapter 5 for a discussion of alternative methods of absorbing excess reserves. Things are actually a bit more complicated than this.

21. This does not imply, however, that there can never be a run out of a country's currency, including a run out of its government debt – not due to fear of default by the government, but due, for example, to fear of a currency depreciation. It is also possible that a large government deficit could trigger such fears. So while we deny that a deficit by itself can generate a rational fear of default on domestic-currency-denominated government debt, we do recognize that deficits can impact expectations concerning the international value of a currency.

22. Bowen, Davis and Kopf replied to Lerner in Bowen, et. al., (1962), but missed the entire point of Lerner's critique. They simply repeated their exposition, but assumed that Generation I had died off before the taxes were raised to pay off the debt held by Generation II (on the belief that Lerner's criticism relied on a terminological dispute over the word 'generation').

23. But even this does not mean that private consumption was necessarily reduced, for these could have been goods and services that would not have been produced. In fairness, however, Bowen, et. al., had assumed full employment of all resources, although Lerner had argued the assumption was unrealistic given the then current level of unemployment.

24. 'On January 1, 1999 the euro is planned to be launched only for inter-bank/business transactions. The ECB will formally take charge of monetary policy from the European Monetary Institute. On January 1, 2002 notes and coins denominated in euro begin to circulate across the EU and national currencies are withdrawn' (Arestis and Sawyer 1998, p. 12).

5 Monetary Policy: Interest Rate Targets and the Non-Discretionary Nature of Reserves

In this chapter, we will argue that monetary policy directly sets a narrow range for the overnight interest rate – or the 'price' of money – which only very indirectly affects the quantity of money. Regardless of the Fed's stated intermediate target, the Fed funds rate is the primary operating target; that is, even when the Fed claims to adopt a reserve aggregate as a target, it in fact targets the Fed funds rate. Most central bank actions are defensive in nature, and are mainly undertaken to offset Treasury operations. Fed policy can never be independent of 'fiscal policy' – the Fed must coordinate its policy with fiscal policy to ensure that the correct amount of reserves is available to the banking system.

In the previous chapter, we examined government spending and taxing. As we argued, persistent government deficits are the theoretical and practical norm. These deficits are 'financed' through injections of fiat money, which are in the first instance credited to the banking system as bank reserves. The purpose of the sale of government bonds is to support the overnight interest rate because untaxed government spending (deficit spending) creates an equal amount of reserves in the banking system. Government borrowing is undertaken as a reserve drain, and the federal debt publicly held can be characterized as an interest rate maintenance account (IRMA). Thus it is fiscal policy that determines the amount of new money directly created by the federal government, rather than monetary policy, which really has to do with interest rate management. Monetary policy includes those Treasury and central bank operations that add or drain reserves as well as other operations that set the overnight interest rate target.

THE TEXTBOOK VIEW OF MONETARY POLICY

Traditionally, economists have thought that monetary policy uses tools (open market operations, discount rates) to hit operating targets (Fed funds rate, reserve aggregates) that are believed to be closely related to intermediate targets (short-term market interest rates, monetary aggregates) in order to achieve longer-run goals (low inflation, high employment, sufficient economic growth). Over time, a consensus developed according to which the central bank uses its tools to determine the quantity of bank reserves which then determines the quantity of money (through the 'money multiplier' – see below), whose impact (at least in the long run) is primarily on prices. This view is enshrined in all the 'money and banking' textbooks, and until recently it formed the basis for monetary policy formation.

Current monetary policy is in a quandary, however. There is no longer any consensus on the relation of the Fed's operating targets to some of its intermediate targets. In particular, the experience of the 1980s cast considerable doubt on the relation between reserve aggregates and monetary aggregates (because the 'money multiplier' became unstable). Over the past decade and a half, the Fed's ability to hit monetary targets appeared to be seriously impaired – even when the Fed continually adjusted its monetary targets to accord more favourably with recent experience it still failed to hit them. Indeed, the Fed was forced to drop M1 targets altogether in the 1980s, and has recently acknowledged that it pays little attention to monetary aggregate growth rates. Furthermore, the relations between monetary aggregates and inflation broke down in the 1980s. Still, many economists are reluctant to abandon the traditional belief that the Fed somehow determines the quantity of money and that this determines the rate of inflation. However, the textbook vision seems no longer to provide much guidance for policy formation.

As we will argue, the orthodox view seriously misunderstands what monetary policy is all about. The central bank never has controlled, nor could it ever control, the quantity of money; neither can it control the quantity of reserves in a discretionary manner. Indeed, the orthodox view fundamentally confuses fiscal policy with monetary policy; fiscal policy has more to do with the quantity of money and with the value of money, while monetary policy simply determines overnight interest rates. Working in conjunction with the Treasury, the central bank can also affect longer-term interest rates. However, any impact of monetary policy on money, prices, unemployment or growth rates is necessarily very indirect, with 'many a slip 'twixt cup and lip'.

BRIEF OVERVIEW OF THE FED AND ITS OPERATING PROCEDURE

In Chapter 3 we examined the 'history of money', with some discussion of pre-twentieth-century US monetary history. In this chapter, we briefly review the history of US monetary policy from the creation of the Federal

Reserve System (our first permanent central bank).[1] As stated in the preamble to the Federal Reserve Act of 1913, the Fed was created 'to furnish an elastic currency, to afford the means of rediscounting commercial paper, to establish a more effective supervision of banking in the United States, and for other purposes' (Meulendyke, 1989, p. 18). For many years thereafter, the guiding principle of the Fed was the 'Real Bills Doctrine' under which the Fed was to 'rediscount' eligible paper (thus make loans of reserves to member banks) to meet the needs of trade. Note that the original Act did not provide for open market operations, but, in any case, the outstanding government debt stock was very small.

During WWI, a significant amount of government debt became available, much of it purchased by the Fed as a means of obtaining interest-earning assets. It was not until the 1920s that the effect of open market operations on interest rates and bank reserves was noticed. It was also at this time that the 'deposit multiplier' was discovered:[2] an open market purchase would create reserves that would support a multiple expansion of deposits (Meulendyke, 1989). This led to the first attempt in 1924 to use open market operations countercyclically, in the belief that the Fed could loosen policy in the recession and cause banks to increase lending. However, many analysts at the time found that the open market purchases did not increase reserves because banks chose to retire loans at the discount window. This was the first of many times that the Fed learned the lesson that it could not 'push on a string': reserves and loans (and, thus, the money supply) are demand determined and cannot be increased directly through monetary policy. Symmetrically, analysts at the time noticed that open market sales merely forced banks to the discount window to replace the lost reserves. As Meulendyke grudgingly acknowledges, 'Some people interpreted this pattern to mean that open market operations had no effect on reserve availability or on a bank's ability to lend' (ibid., p. 24). Unfortunately, such lessons were quickly forgotten and doomed to be repeated.

The Great Depression led to significant changes of policy and philosophy at the Fed. Interpretations of the Fed's policy during the Great Depression range from the Monetarist claim that the Fed reduced the money supply, causing the financial crisis and Great Depression, to the more common belief that the Fed's inaction probably made things worse. Actually, the Fed intervened immediately and forcefully, buying $125 million of Treasury securities on the day of the stock market crash, five times the maximum weekly amount it was authorized to purchase – nearly doubling Fed holdings in one day. The New York Fed also opened its discount window to New York banks that were helping correspondent banks. During the early months of the crisis, the Fed continued to meet currency demand (although aggregate reserves of banks did fall – loans and deposits were shrinking) and used open market operations to stabilize money market rates. However, by autumn 1931, gold outflows had become significant, leading the Fed to raise discount rates to stem the flow to protect its gold reserves (the only alternative would be to abandon gold). The money supply (and reserves) was shrinking not because this was the policy of the Fed, but rather because banks could not find worthy borrowers. Thus while there certainly was confusion[3] and while mistakes were certainly made, the Fed does not deserve all the blame.

As discussed in Chapter 4, WWII generated huge deficits and bond issues. The Fed agreed in 1942 to peg the 3-month Treasury bill rate at 3/8 of 1 per cent throughout the war; longer-term bonds were informally pegged at higher rates. The record expansion of government deficits generated reserves, drained through bond sales, and the long-term legacy of the war was the large debt stock that enabled the Fed to rely on open market purchases rather than discount window borrowing. After the war, the Fed was concerned with the potential for inflation. In 1947, the Treasury agreed to loosen the reins on the Fed, which raised interest rates. Postwar fiscal surpluses, combined with the tighter monetary policy, helped to cause a recession in 1949. The Fed continued to lobby for greater freedom to pursue activist monetary policy, resulting in the 1951 Accord in which the Fed abandoned its commitment to maintain low interest costs for the government. The Fed would henceforth manipulate the interest rate to implement countercyclical monetary policy.

During this period, the Fed also began to focus on the short end of the market, with only occasional forays into the long end. It also increasingly relied on repurchase agreements and reverse repos rather than outright purchases and sales in order more finely to tune market conditions. When banks were short of reserves, they would sell government bills, pushing up bill rates. The Fed would then intervene to prevent the rates from exceeding targets. For political reasons, the Fed did not announce interest rate targets – its newly won 'independence' from the Treasury required that it proclaim it was not pegging rates. However, it is clear that the Fed was targeting bill rates until the mid-1960s, when it switched to a Fed funds target because the Fed funds market had become the primary market for adjustment by individual banks to reserve requirements. Any aggregate deficit of reserves would immediately place pressure on the Fed funds rate, inducing Fed intervention. Not only did the Fed funds rate serve as an almost immediate indicator of reserve positions, a Fed funds target did not have the political baggage that accompanied a bills rate target. Of course, the two rates would be inextricably linked, but it was easier for the Fed to increase the Fed funds rate than it would be to explicitly raise government interest costs.

The notion that the Fed could influence reserve and monetary aggregates had been around for quite some time – as indicated above. However, the Fed did not adopt formal monetary targets until 1970, with the express purpose of bringing down inflation by reducing money growth. Still, during most of the 1970s, the Fed explicitly adopted the Fed funds rate as the operating target used to hit intermediate money targets; if the rate of growth of the money supply was above the Fed's target, it would raise the Fed funds target. In 1972, the Fed adopted the money multiplier model and briefly tried to hit reserve targets as a way to allow it to hit M1 targets. The results foreshadowed those of the 1980s: the Fed proceeded to miss the reserve targets. However, during the 1970s, the Fed became quite adept at hitting Fed funds targets; as markets came to expect that the Fed would indeed hit targets, banks would 'trade funds in a way that tended to keep the rate on target' (Meulendyke, 1989, p. 43).

In October 1979, the new Chairman, Paul Volcker, announced a major change of policy: the Fed would use the growth rate of M1 as its intermediate target and would allow the Fed funds rate to rise as high as necessary to allow achievement of this goal. The Fed would calculate the total reserves consistent with its money target, then subtract existing borrowed reserves to obtain a non-borrowed reserve operating target. If the Fed did not provide sufficient reserves in open market operations (as it hit its non-borrowed reserve target), banks would simply turn to the discount window, causing borrowed reserves to rise (and, in turn, cause the Fed to miss its total reserve target). Because required reserves are always calculated with a lag (see below), the Fed could not refuse to provide needed reserves at the discount window. Thus the Fed found it could not control reserves. Further, the rate of growth of M1 actually exploded beyond targets in spite of persistently tight monetary policy. Apparently, the Fed could not hit money targets, either. The attempt to target non-borrowed reserves effectively ended in 1982 (after a very deep recession); the attempt to hit M1 growth targets was abandoned in 1986; and the attempt to target growth of broader money aggregates finally came to an official end in 1993.

We turn now to a detailed analysis of the reasons for the Fed's inability to control the quantity of reserves. Every attempt to target reserves this century has met with failure; the Fed has learned and re-learned the lesson that bank reserves are not a discretionary variable from the standpoint of policy. We will then discuss the reasons for the Fed's inability to hit money targets. While the following discussion is a bit technical, it is necessary to understand some of the details in order to remove the mystery that surrounds central bank operations in order to dispense with the common, but incorrect, notion that monetary policy determines the quantity of money.

THE INELASTICITY OF THE RESERVE MARKET: LAGGED AND CONTEMPORANEOUS ACCOUNTING[4]

In the US, banks must hold reserves as a fraction of certain kinds of deposits.[5] The Fed defines the method that banks are required to use in computing deposits and reserve requirements. The period during which a depository institution's average daily reserves must meet or exceed its specified required reserves is called the reserve maintenance period. The period in which the deposits on which reserves are based is the reserve computation period or base period. The reserve accounting method is occasionally changed, but this does not affect the Fed's role in the market for reserves.

Before 1968, banks were required to meet reserve requirements contemporaneously: reserves for a week had to equal the required percentage for that week. Banks estimated what their average deposits would be for the week and applied the appropriate required reserve ratio to determine their reserve requirement. Bank reserves and deposits, of course, continually change as funds are deposited and withdrawn, which confounded each bank manager's task of managing reserve balances. Neither the average deposits for a week nor the average amount of required reserves could be known with any degree of certainty until after the close of the last day. Under such a system, banks would be sure to have sufficient reserves only if they held substantial excess reserves as a buffer; as reserves do not earn interest, they would do this only if the penalty for missing reserve requirements were high. In any case, when a bank came up short, as there was no way to change deposits after the fact, the Fed had to supply any deficient reserves – implying that reserves had to be supplied on demand (albeit at penalty rates).

In September 1968, lagged reserve accounting (LRA) replaced contemporaneous reserve accounting (CRA). Under LRA the reserve maintenance period was seven days, ending each Wednesday. Required reserves for a maintenance period were based on the average daily reservable deposits in the reserve computation period ending on a Wednesday two weeks earlier. The total amount of required reserves for each bank and for the banking system as a whole was known in advance, but as the deposits were 'history', there was nothing banks could do to alter their reserve requirement to bring it into line with actual reserves. The Fed had to make up any difference. By the early 1980s, Fed officials, economists, and bankers debated whether shortening the reserve accounting lag could give the Fed control of reserve balances. This had become important because of the ostensible change of Fed policy to a reserve aggregate target (see above). It was decided that moving to a CRA system would allow the Fed freedom to refuse to accommodate the demand for reserves.

In 1984 a form of CRA was reinstated. Since 1984, required reserves have been calculated based on net deposits (excluding cash items in the process of collection and balances due from domestic banks). The reserve accounting period is now two two-week periods, one for time deposits and the other for demand deposits (beginning two weeks after the close of the period for time deposits). The base period is thus about six weeks; the settlement period (over which reserves are calculated) also lasts about six weeks, with overlapping of the two periods consisting of all but the first two days and the final two days. In other words, a bank comes to the end of the base period with a calculation of its average time deposits (held a month ago) and of its average demand deposits (held over the previous two weeks), and then calculates its reserve requirement. Actual reserves are calculated by totalling average vault cash held during the base period for time deposits, while reserves held at the Fed about two weeks later are counted. The bank finally has two days to make up any deficiency, with reserves on the last day of the accounting period equal to 1/14 of the total to be averaged. (For example, if a bank borrowed $7 billion reserves for one day it would currently add 1/14 of $7 billion, or $500 million, to the average level of reserves for the maintenance period.)

Although this system is called contemporaneous it is, in practice, a lagged system because there is still a two-day lag: reserve periods end on Wednesday but deposit periods end on the preceding Monday. Banks for all practical purposes cannot change their current reserve requirements (based on previously held deposits). If banks were left on their own to obtain more reserves no amount of interbank lending would be able to create the necessary reserves. For example, suppose the total reserve requirement for the banking system were $60 billion at the close of business today but only $55 billion of reserves were held by the entire banking system. Unless the Fed provides the additional $5 billion in reserves, at least one bank will fail to meet its reserve requirement. Since deposits are always 'history' from the standpoint of calculating reserve requirements, the Fed would have to supply reserves on demand or force banks to hold inadequate levels of reserves.[6]

On the other hand, if banks are faced with an aggregate excess reserve position, inter-bank lending cannot eliminate the excess reserves. Only the government can drain these through sales of bonds. If it refuses, overnight rates immediately fall toward zero – as we will discuss below.

Alternatively, the central bank could try to use other methods to absorb excess reserves. One method is to raise required reserve ratios. However, as reserves do not earn interest (in the US), this necessarily reduces bank profitability and so would be unpopular. It would also be difficult to implement this in a sufficiently timely manner. The central bank can also sell gold, limited to the quantity of gold held in reserve.[7] It could lower its target overnight rate, which might increase voluntary excess reserve holdings as well as non-bank holdings of fiat money (since the opportunity cost of holding non-earning fiat money is then lower), but these effects are very minor since it is unlikely that cash holdings and desired excess reserves are very interest sensitive and, in any case, they require time before bank preferences might change. If lower interest rates stimulate aggregate demand, this also might increase bank lending and deposits, thus increasing required reserve levels; however, again, this process requires time so would do almost nothing to absorb excess reserves during the reserve settlement period. It could also drain reserves through sales of foreign currencies; this would be limited by the central bank's holdings of foreign reserves (quite small in relation to government spending for many countries). However, none of these methods is typically used so that, when all is said and done, bond sales are the primary tool used to drain reserves and have the advantage of an immediate effect on the quantity of excess reserves (while most other methods – except gold or foreign currency sales) would take time, during which the Fed funds rate would approach zero.

WHAT IF RESERVES ARE NOT LEGALLY REQUIRED?

Some readers will legitimately wonder whether these arguments hold in the absence of legally required reserves. There are two further reasons why reserves are not discretionary from the point of view of the central bank, even if there are no legal requirements. The first has to do with interest rate targets and the second with par clearing.

As mentioned, banks need reserves for clearing among banks and for clearing with the central bank (for example, when taxes are paid by cheque) and vault cash for withdrawals. On the other hand, because reserves do not pay interest, banks want to minimize holdings. At a point in time, each bank will have some level of desired reserve holdings.[8] When a bank finds itself with excess reserves, it lends them in overnight markets, and when it is short it borrows overnight funds. When there is an aggregate reserve surplus this immediately places downward pressure on the overnight rate; conversely, in an aggregate deficit situation there is immediate pressure on overnight rates.[9]

The central bank will thus obtain immediate information concerning the aggregate reserve situation of the system through fluctuations of the overnight rate. Unless the central bank wants the overnight rate to move, it must intervene to supply reserves or to drain them in order to hold the interest rate at its target. While it is always true that the central bank could choose to move its target, the point is that an interest rate target necessarily forces the central bank to respond. Still, one could argue that the central bank could hold fast in a situation of deficient reserves, allowing interest rates to rise as high as necessary to force banks to economize and perhaps even shrink their balance sheets by selling assets. Note, however, that sales of assets cannot actually increase aggregate reserves (except in the unlikely event that households use cash hoards to buy bank assets) and that the demand for reserves is interest-inelastic. Thus the impact on overnight rates could be very great and a high degree of instability would have to be accepted as the consequence of central bank refusal of reserves.

There remains the question of reserve clearing. When a bank's depositor writes a cheque that is deposited either at another bank or into the Treasury's account at the central bank, the bank loses reserves. The central bank typically handles the clearing among banks, although private clearing houses can also be used. In all modern economies, cheques clear at par. If a cheque were presented to the clearing house against a bank which did not have sufficient reserves, it could not be cleared at par. Thus the only possibilities would be either not to clear the cheque at par or to lend needed reserves to the bank. In fact, because par clearing is typically guaranteed, there is no choice but to lend the reserves to the deficient bank. In reality, then, the central bank cannot stand firm and refuse to provide reserves that are needed by the system; as the private banking system cannot create reserves and as all banking systems operate with a fractional reserve system, banks that are deficient are automatically loaned reserves. Indeed, once a state accepts bank money in payment of taxes, par clearing and provision of reserves on demand are necessary consequences.

For these reasons, it makes no significant difference whether reserves are required. As an example, we can look to the case of Canada, which dropped reserve requirements.[10] The Canadian central bank (Bank of Canada) requires direct clearing banks to hold balances with the central bank for clearing purposes. They earn interest of 50 basis points below the overnight bank rate (equivalent to the discount rate in the US) on positive balances, and are charged the bank rate on deficits. The Bank of Canada sets a target range for the overnight market rate, which has a ceiling of the bank rate and a floor equal to the bank rate less 50 basis points. The reserve target is for bank settlement balances to equal zero on average (positive balances of some banks are to be offset by deficits of others). A presettlement period of half an hour before closing is supposed to allow each direct clearer time to lend or borrow reserves to reach a zero settlement balance by the end of each business day.

The Bank of Canada then attempts to set the net supply of settlement balances at zero. At any overnight market rate that is more than 50 basis points below the bank rate, the demand for reserves (positive settlement balances) is infinite (since direct clearers can earn bank rate less 50 basis points on positive balances), while at any overnight rate above the bank rate the demand for negative settlement balances is infinite (since the penalty for negative balances is only the bank rate). The Bank of Canada then operates on reserves to keep the market rate within the band.

The main instrument used to adjust the aggregate supply of settlement balances is the transfer of government deposits (tax accounts) between the Bank of Canada and the direct clearers. An increase of settlement balances due to government spending not balanced by tax payments places downward pressure on the market rate, which would fall to the bottom of the target band (50 basis points below bank rate). The Bank of Canada then absorbs the excess balances by reducing the supply of government deposits auctioned to banks, through sale and repurchase agreements or through outright sales of Treasury securities to banks. This brings the settlement balances back to zero and the market rate to within the target band. On the other hand, if tax payments exceed government expenditures, negative clearing balances drive the overnight market rate up (demand but no suppliers) above the target. Negative clearing balances are made up through increased supply of government deposits auctioned, special purchase and resale agreements or outright Treasury security purchases. This increases the supply of settlement balances and brings the market rate back to the target band.

If the Bank of Canada were instead to refuse to supply settlement balances in the case of an aggregate deficiency, it would force negative settlement balances on some individual direct clearers. Because cheques among banks and between banks and the Bank of Canada must be cleared, negative settlement balances must be made up by a loan of reserves from the Bank of Canada at the bank rate. In other words, any 'fail' must automatically be booked as an overdraft or loan. The only other possibility would be to prevent cheque clearing. In the case of positive aggregate settlement balances, overnight market rates fall to the bottom of the target range, with the Bank of Canada paying bank rate less 50 basis points on the settlement balances (the rate cannot be driven lower as demand is infinite at any lower rate). To reduce its interest payments, the Bank of Canada must eliminate the excess settlement balances.

Thus it makes little difference whether reserves are required. Indeed, in some respects, the Canadian system makes central bank operations more transparent – reserves are not a lever to be used to control the money supply. The Bank of Canada intervenes to keep net settlement balances at zero, an operation that by its very nature must be defensive.

THE MYTH OF THE MONEY MULTIPLIER[11]

Money and banking textbooks invariably use the concept of the money multiplier to demonstrate the determination of the quantity of money. The multiplier links a change in the monetary base (reserves plus currency – what we have been calling fiat money) to a change in the money supply, where the money supply equals the base times a multiplier.[12] In the simplest models, the multiplier equals the inverse of the required reserve ratio. No matter what the legally required reserve ratio was, the standard example always assumed 10 per cent so that the maths was simple enough for college students to calculate a money multiplier equal to 10. On 12 April 1992, the Fed, for the first time, set the required reserve ratio on demand deposits at the magical 10 per cent, making theory coincident with reality. Given the simplicity of the money multiplier, it is a shame that the myth must be laid to rest.

In the real world banks make loans independent of reserve positions, then borrow reserves to meet requirements. Bank managers generally neither know nor care about the aggregate level of reserves in the banking system. Certainly, no loan officer ever checks the bank's reserve position before approving a loan. Bank lending decisions are affected by the price of reserves and expected returns, not by reserve positions. If the spread between the rate of return on an asset and the Fed funds rate is wide enough, even a bank that is already deficient in reserves will purchase the asset and cover the reserves needed by purchasing (borrowing) reserves in the Fed funds market.

The money multiplier concept reverses the direction of causation: changes in the money supply cause changes in bank reserves and the monetary base, not vice versa. The various empirical studies that purport to show a high correlation between changes of reserves and changes of the money supply are really proof of Fed accommodation. Because the Fed has no 'exogenous' control over the aggregate quantity of reserves, it can never use a 'stable money multiplier' relation to hit a monetary aggregate target. Rather, reserves must be supplied on demand, so that when reserves are growing at a rate in excess of what the Fed believes would be consistent with achieving a money growth rate target, it must cause the overnight interest rate to rise (rather than refusing to provide needed reserves) in the hope that this will eventually slow money growth (and thus reserve growth). However, higher interest rates increase the 'reserve tax' (since banks do not earn interest on reserves), inducing innovations to reduce reserve requirements (so they can increase the money supply without increasing required reserves). Further, demand for finance is very inelastic so that even if the Fed succeeds in slowing reserve growth, and even as banks economize on reserves, the money supply will continue to grow so long as there is a demand for finance even if the interest rate rises dramatically. This, in turn, causes the 'money multiplier' to become unstable – leading to a breakdown of the money – reserve relation. This follows from 'Goodhart's Law': any attempt to use an empirically stable relation to formulate policy will lead to a breakdown of that relation.

According to the textbook money multiplier model, the Fed can increase the money supply by injecting reserves through an open market purchase. However, this fails to recognize that the added reserves in excess of required reserves would immediately drive the Fed funds rate to zero, since reserve requirements do not change until the following accounting period. That would force the Fed to sell securities, draining the excess reserves just added, to maintain the funds rate above zero. On the other hand, if the Fed wants to reduce the money supply by taking reserves out of the system when there are no excess reserves, this simply guarantees that some banks cannot meet their reserve requirements. The Fed would have no choice but to add reserves back into the banking system to keep the funds rate from going, theoretically, to infinity. In either case, the money supply remains unchanged by the Fed's action. Changes in the money supply cause changes in the monetary base, not vice versa.[13]

HORIZONTALISM: THE BUSINESS OF BANKING

In most textbooks, banks are presented as intermediaries that take in deposits, hold a small fraction of these on reserve, then lend out the remainder: 'deposits make loans'. Each bank loans only the amount of its excess reserves, while aggregate lending expands through the 'deposit multiplier' as discussed above. Profitable loan opportunities are foregone if reserves are not available. Some allowance is made for discretion: the deposit multiplier is a function of interest rates and interest rate differentials, bank preferences regarding excess reserve holdings, and public preferences regarding cash, time deposit and demand deposit ratios. But, as Brunner (1968) 'demonstrated', these factors are of only minor importance. Because the central bank supposedly controls the quantity of reserves, it is able to control the money supply. Money is said to be 'exogenous' in the control sense, determined by the central bank. This has been called the 'verticalist' approach, because in most textbooks the money supply is presented as 'vertical' (perfectly inelastic with respect to interest rates).

In reality, the business of banking is complicated and is in some respects not much different from that of other profit-seeking firms. Banks, like other firms, take positions in assets by issuing liabilities on the expectation of making profits. As we argue below, much bank activity can be analysed as a 'leveraging' of fiat money – but many other firms engage in similar activity. For our purposes, however, the main difference between banks and other types of firms involves the nature of the liabilities. Banks 'make loans' by purchasing IOUs of 'borrowers'; this results in a bank liability – usually a demand deposit, at least initially – that shows up as an asset ('money') of the borrower.[14] Thus the 'creditors' of a bank are created simultaneously with the 'debtors' to the bank. The creditors will almost immediately exercise their right to use the created demand deposit as a medium of exchange; bank liabilities are the money used by non-banks. The government accepts some bank liabilities in payment of taxes, and it guarantees that many bank liabilities will be redeemable at par against fiat money.[15]

In turn, reserves are the 'money' used as means of payment (or interbank settlement) among banks and for payments made to the central bank; as bank 'creditors' draw down demand deposits, this causes a clearing drain for the individual bank. The bank may then operate either on its asset side (selling an asset) or on its liability side (borrowing reserves) to cover the loss of reserves. In the aggregate, however, such activities only shift reserves from bank to bank. Aggregate excess or deficiencies have to be rectified by the central bank. Ultimately, then, reserves are not discretionary in the short run; the central bank can determine the price of reserves – admittedly, within some constraints – but then must provide reserves more or less on demand to hit its 'price' target (the Fed funds rate).

The approach outlined in this section has been called the 'horizontalist' approach, in the sense that the supply of bank money is determined 'endogenously' by the demand for bank loans, rather than 'exogenously' (Moore, 1988). According to those who adopt the horizontalist approach, any impact of monetary policy on the quantity of money is very indirect and operates primarily through interest rate effects. Rather, it is mainly the private demand for loans, plus the willingness of banks to lend, that determines the quantity of loans, and thus of deposits, created. The demand for loans, in turn, is determined by spending decisions of private economic agents (including decisions regarding asset purchases); these can be affected, but only very indirectly, by the loan rate of interest. The supply of loans is then never independent of the demand; banks supply loans only because someone is willing to 'borrow' bank money by issuing an IOU to banks. One can think of the supply of bank money as 'horizontal' at the loan rate of interest, with banks supplying loans on demand.

This does not indicate that banks are merely passive, fully accommodating all demand for loans. Clearly, large segments of the population are 'quantity rationed' in the sense that banks do not meet their demand for loans even though they are willing to borrow at the going interest rate. There can be several reasons for such rationing.[16] Banks might worry about default risk of borrowers, but might not be able to raise interest rates sufficiently to cover default risk – so that quantity rationing is superior to price rationing. Often, banks probably have better information than do borrowers about such risks; for example, the borrower who wishes to open a new restaurant might not have good access to information about bankruptcy rates in the industry or might simply be overly optimistic. On the other hand, banks can never know the future, so must operate on the basis of rules of thumb (for example, informal rules that restrict loan size). Some quantity rationing can even be irrational – perhaps discriminatory – because banks have traditionally forgone certain kinds of loans. We will not dwell on such issues; the point is that the supply of loans does not simply and fully accommodate the demand at some interest rate. However, the analogy with a horizontal supply curve is useful to emphasize that the supply of bank money depends on the supply of loans which is not under the control of the government as in the verticalist story.

Another conclusion that follows from such an analysis is that the interest rate cannot be determined by the 'supply and demand' of loans if supply and demand are not independent. Rather, banks can be characterized as price-setters in short-term retail loan markets; they then meet the demand for loans – with some quantity rationing – at that price.[17] Short-term retail interest rates can be taken as a mark-up over short-term wholesale interest rates. Exactly what determines the mark-up (and whether it is variable) is controversial, but not important to our analysis here (see Moore, 1988, and Wray, 1990). Wholesale interest rates, finally, are under the influence of central bank policy. Individual banks use wholesale markets to rectify a mismatch between retail loans and deposits. Most banks will not be able to match exactly their retail loans and deposits; some banks will be able to make more retail loans than they can retain in deposits (suffering a clearing drain), while others will find fewer loan customers than depositors (resulting in a surplus reserve position). Banks then use wholesale markets to either 'purchase' reserves by issuing wholesale liabilities (for example, negotiable, large denomination CDs or by borrowing Fed funds), while surplus banks will sell Fed funds. As discussed above, the central bank sets the overnight interbank rate. This rate then determines other short-term wholesale rates (mainly as a mark-up, but also as a mark-down) through arbitrage. Thus another tenet of the horizontalist approach is that the central bank determines the short-term wholesale interest rate directly, and the short-term retail lending rate indirectly (as the wholesale rate is marked up). In conclusion, the supply of money is determined endogenously while the price of money (short-term interest rate) is determined exogenously as a result of central bank policy.

HORIZONTAL AND VERTICAL: AN INTEGRATION

In some sense, the verticalists and the horizontalists have each captured some elements of the money supply process. One can conceive of a vertical component of the money supply process that consists of the government supply of fiat money; money drops vertically to the private sector from government through government purchases of goods and services (and occasionally assets) as well as central bank purchases of assets (such as gold and foreign currency, and also through discounting of assets held by banks). (See Mosler and Forstater, 1998, for a similar analysis.) Recall from our discussion above and in previous chapters that the private sector is willing to accept government fiat money because the government has previously imposed tax liabilities on the private sector. Tax payments (which discharge the liability) then drain fiat money, which can be pictured as a vertical movement from the private sector to government (and, hence, 'down the drain' as the money is literally burned, or simply wiped off the liability side of the central bank's balance sheet – see Figure 5.1). The net difference between these two vertical flows (deficit spending) leads to accumulation of fiat money hoards (currency in the hands of the public plus bank reserves). The government can also offer to vertically exchange interest-earning bonds for non-interest-earning cash and reserves.[18]

On the other hand, the bank-money-supply process is horizontal; it can be thought of as a type of 'leveraging' of the hoarded vertical fiat money. Clearly, bank money is only one type of leveraging of the fiat money. A partial list of other types of leveraging would include commercial paper, private bonds, all types of bank liabilities, indeed, all IOUs denominated in the fiat money of account. All of these private IOUs share three characteristics: they are denominated in the fiat money of account, they

Figure 5.1: Horizontal and Vertical Components of Money Supply

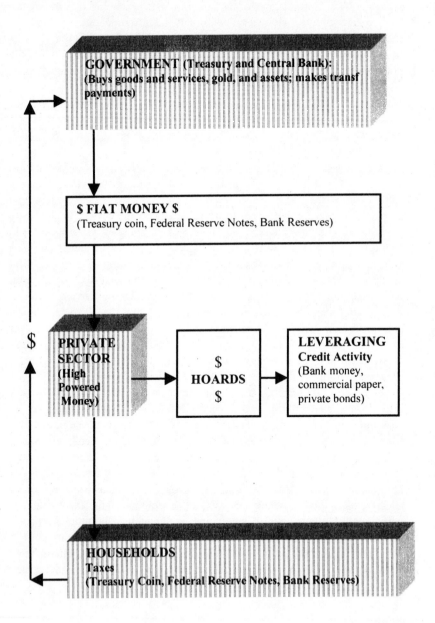

consist of long and short positions, and they are 'inside' debt such that the longs and shorts net to zero. A bank deposit can be thought of as a long position in fiat money, while the bank's borrowers have short positions, betting that they will be able to obtain money for delivery later.[19]

A reduction of government spending can generate a 'short squeeze', where the borrowers of banks are not able to obtain sufficient money to make payments on loans. When there is a short squeeze, the shorts cannot obtain the money required through an increase of the horizontal money supply because longs and shorts net exactly to zero.[20] If the longs were willing to spend their deposits or if others were willing to come into the market to take new short positions (lending to those squeezed), then the short squeeze could be relieved by operations in the horizontal section. The vertical portion is the only net supplier of money to relieve a short squeeze. If it does not react to the short squeeze, the bank borrowers are forced to try to sell assets, roll-over loans or try to obtain new loans. This can lead to a deflation of the prices of assets, which could degenerate to a general debt deflation. On the other hand, this can be avoided if the central bank enters as lender of last resort (discounting assets or buying assets held by the private sector) or if the Treasury increases its deficits.

In some respects, then, money is like any other commodity with both horizontal and vertical sections. For example, the soybean market also has vertical and horizontal components. The vertical component is the commodity market for physical delivery, with the supply coming from farms and the demand coming from households; consumption of soybeans is equivalent to tax payments, while soybeans that are stored are equivalent to fiat money hoards. Production in excess of consumption (net production) adds to hoards while consumption in excess of production depletes hoards (just as government spending in excess of taxation creates fiat money hoards and taxation greater than spending depletes hoards). Note that it is impossible for households to consume soybeans before any are produced, just as it is impossible for households to pay taxes until they have received money. Production is the only source of 'net' soybeans, which are then 'leveraged' in the horizontal component – the futures market which consists of longs (those agreeing to buy) and shorts (those agreeing to sell) which necessarily net to zero. Note that the longs (or shorts) far exceed the inventory of soybeans – exactly analogous to the relation between fiat money and bank money.

If there is a crop failure, a squeeze on shorts can result that may not be resolved in the horizontal component. Prices rise and those with short positions lose their bets, unless new shorts come into the market to take positions of the shorts, or the longs liquidate (sell their contracts for soybean delivery).

What is the money equivalent to a crop failure? If the government reduces its deficit spending on goods and services, the flow supply of money into hoards to be leveraged declines (unless offset by an increase of central bank purchases of assets). We can relate this to the discussion in the previous chapter: when government reduces the deficit, desired net nominal saving (*Sn* from Chapter 4) is likely to exceed actual or available net nominal saving (which has fallen) so that any particular household can obtain its desired hoards only at the expense of another. Bank borrowers (as well as others with short positions) find it increasingly hard to obtain money in order to make loan payments to banks and to pay taxes, for example, through sales of produced goods and services or through sales of assets. They may be forced to lower prices on goods, services and assets in order to make sales. If prices fall too much, they are not able to make their loan payments (resulting in defaults on loans) or to pay taxes. Banks find that their own income flows may be below their own payment commitments (for example, interest promised on liabilities); as their loans go into default, their capital is eroded.

If things become sufficiently bad, banks become insolvent, with asset values below the value of liabilities. If the depositors with long positions 'liquidate' (demand fiat money instead of bank deposits), banks are forced to the discount window to borrow reserves. Beyond some point, as bank balance sheets deteriorate, they will not have sufficient capital (net worth) to obtain discount window loans, requiring the deposit insurer to step in to 'resolve' the bank. As prices fall, borrowers default, and banks fail, the private economy will almost certainly suffer a recession (or worse), lowering government tax receipts and perhaps raising government spending (through automatic stabilizers) – which increases the government deficit (and available net saving).

The 'vertical' component of money differs from the 'vertical' component of soybeans in several key ways. First, soybeans actually have to be produced by farmers, and this depends on technology, weather and seasonal factors. Fiat money can be created by government at any time without delay. Further, while fiat money is mainly provided in exchange for goods and services, government can create it as necessary to buy assets or make loans. In the case of an insolvent bank, government might create money during the resolution – simply providing it to depositors even when the assets of the bank are worthless. This is really nothing more than deficit spending although it might not be treated as such. There is thus greater room for resolving a short squeeze in money than a short squeeze in soybeans. A short squeeze in soybeans, leading to rising prices, will provide a greater incentive to produce them, but this will require time so that prices may rise steeply. However, in the case of a short squeeze on money, the 'price' of money (that is, its relative price in terms of what it can buy) need not rise much (meaning deflation of other prices) before the government steps in to relieve the pressure. This would be similar to a situation in which the farmer had vast stores of soybeans which could be lent to those who are short. Another difference is that the government is the single vertical supplier of fiat money, while the soybean market is far from monopolized. While no individual soybean farmer can set the terms (or price) on which soybeans will be provided, the government as monopoly supplier of fiat money is able to do so. This does not mean that it does so, nor that it should. However, as we discuss in Chapter 6, this monopoly power to set price can be used in a buffer stock policy to stabilize prices.

COORDINATION BETWEEN THE CENTRAL BANK AND THE TREASURY[21]

Most 'money and banking' textbooks contain a section that analyses coordination between the central bank and the Treasury, without recognizing the implications for monetary and fiscal policy. The important point is that tax payments would lead to a reserve drain while Treasury spending would lead to a reserve infusion; in order to minimize impacts on bank reserves, the Fed and the Treasury have developed a quite complicated operating procedure. Careful analysis clearly shows that reserves cannot be discretionary from the point of view of monetary policy; rather, Fed actions with regard to quantities of reserves are necessarily defensive. The only discretion the Fed has is in interest rate determination.

Assume for a moment that the Treasury uses only the Fed as its banker, writing cheques on its Fed account when it spends, and receiving money into its accounts when taxes are paid.[22] If the Treasury ran a daily balanced budget, there would be no net effect on bank reserves. Reserves are affected when the government's budget is not balanced daily – both because it typically runs an annual deficit and because spending tends to be spread throughout the year while tax receipts are bunched around quarterly receipts (and around 15 April!).

One of the methods used to reduce the impact on reserves resulting from tax payments is to allow the Treasury to hold tax receipts in special 'tax and loan accounts' at specific private banks (general depositories and special depositories).[23] In this case, tax payments merely move reserves within the banking system. On the other hand, when the Treasury spends, this (almost always) takes the form of a cheque written on its account at the Fed. Obviously, if nothing else were done, this would increase bank reserves by the amount of the Treasury's spending (except for the drain from banks to cash holding of the public). In order to prevent this, the Treasury transfers funds from its tax and loan accounts to its account at the Fed simultaneously as it spends. While it might appear that the Treasury 'needs' the tax revenue so that it can spend, that is clearly a superficial view. The simultaneity of the transfer from tax and loan accounts and Treasury spending is due to the necessity of stabilizing bank reserves. The government certainly does not need to have its own IOU returned before it can spend; rather, the public needs the government's IOU before it can pay taxes. More accurately, banks must have reserves before these can be eliminated through a transfer from tax and loan accounts, and the reserves must have come initially from government.

Perhaps this would be clearer if we were to examine a counterfactual example. Suppose the Treasury were to 'write a cheque' on the Fed but had no 'money in the bank', so that the Fed 'bounced' the cheque – returning it to the Treasury unpaid. The implication would be that the Treasury had either obtained goods and services from the private sector without paying for them, or that the Treasury had not paid some bill that had come due (for example, a social security payment). The seller in the private sector (or the social security recipient) would have a legal claim on the government. Of course, it would never come to this. The Fed would, as a matter of course, offer an overdraft to the Treasury, essentially lending reserves as necessary (the Fed's balance sheet would expand by the amount of the Treasury spending, increasing bank reserves as a liability and holding the Treasury's IOU as an asset). This is obviously nothing more than an internal accounting procedure, with the real result that the Treasury would have spent by creating fiat money.

The manipulations of tax and loan accounts are, then, designed to minimize impacts on bank reserves and do not provide the Treasury with deposits it can spend. In practice, the Treasury tries to manipulate its accounts so as to maintain a closing balance of $5 billion at the Fed each day. Only net changes to the Treasury's account will affect bank reserves, so maintenance of a constant balance of $5 billion would neutralize the Treasury's impact on banks. Thus if the Treasury spends more on a particular day than it receives in tax receipts to its account at the Fed, it will have to transfer deposits from tax and loan accounts to the Fed at the end of the day (to maintain its $5 billion balance). If it did not, its 'deficit' for that day would increase bank reserves by an equivalent amount.

There are two further considerations, one longer-term and the other short-term. The first concerns primary bond sales. Since government deficits increase reserves over the course of the year, it is not possible for transfers from tax and loan accounts to neutralize the impact of Treasury spending on bank reserves. Unless the reservable portion of bank balance sheets grows in step, the result would be system-wide excess reserves. As we have discussed above, excess reserves place immediate pressure on overnight interest rates that can be relieved only by monetary policy (banks cannot engage in reserve-absorbing activities quickly enough). The excess reserves thus need to be drained through monetary policy, which takes the form of bond sales. In the case of a temporary excess (due, for example, to imperfect coordination of taxing and spending), this is done through Fed repurchase agreements or outright sales. However, in the case of a 'chronic' flow of excess reserves (that is, persistent Treasury expenditures in excess of tax receipts), only primary market sales by the Treasury can drain the excess. These sales of government bonds simply replace non-interest-earning excess reserves with interest-earning government bonds. In a sense, this is nothing more than a transfer from one kind of account at the Fed (reserves) to another kind of account (bonds). The purpose of this transfer is to defend the target overnight rate. For this reason, the whole operation should be called an 'interest rate maintenance operation'. It is not a 'borrowing' operation. The Treasury does not 'need' to borrow in order to deficit-spend. After all, what it is doing when it 'sells bonds' is to create an 'interest rate maintenance account' to prevent non-earning excess reserves from arising. This transformation does not provide the Treasury with anything it 'needs' in order to spend; indeed, the bond sale is required only because the Treasury has already spent in excess of tax receipts – the existence of the excess reserves is proof that the bond sale takes place after the Treasury has 'deficit-spent'. Indeed, if the Treasury were to try to sell the bonds first, it would be draining required reserves rather than excess reserves. (We will return to that in a minute.) Over the longer run, then, the Treasury maintains a constant balance at the Fed, even as it deficit-spends, through the sale of government bonds that removes reserves from the banking system (restoring the Treasury's balance at the Fed).

The second consideration is that in reality it is impossible for the Treasury accurately to predict the timing of tax receipts and expenditures on a short-term basis. Even if the Treasury were to plan its spending carefully, it cannot know exactly when its cheques will be deposited in banks. Furthermore, it cannot (and indeed does not even try to) time its sales of bonds to coincide exactly with daily excess reserve positions of banks. Thus it has developed complicated procedures that are used to minimize its impacts on reserves, and cooperates closely with the Fed. For example, when the Treasury anticipates that its closing balance will exceed $5 billion on a particular day, it will try to place deposits into tax and loan accounts. However, it may find that banks are unable or unwilling to take the full amount of deposits offered – either because they cannot meet collateral requirements or because they do not want to pay the interest rate that must be paid on the Treasury's deposits. In this case, the Fed will cooperate with the Treasury, engaging in an open market purchase (or in a repurchase agreement). If, on the other hand, the Fed were to predict that banks would have excess reserves at the close of business, it might ask the Treasury to accumulate deposits in excess of $5 billion in its Fed account.

In addition, the Treasury allows banks with tax and loan accounts to purchase bonds without losing reserves. When new government debt is auctioned, the Treasury often designates a portion of the auction as being eligible for purchase through credit by special depositories. In this case, the special depository obtains the bond as an asset by issuing a deposit in the name of the Treasury.[24] This eliminates unintended impacts on bank reserves. The Treasury can see whether its closing balance at the Fed is near to its $5 billion target; if it is too low, it places a 'call' for the created deposits in tax and loan accounts, draining reserves as necessary.[25] Again, it is clear that such bond sales are not required to obtain money in order to allow the Treasury to spend in excess of tax receipts; the bond sales actually create the deposits in tax and loan accounts that can then be drained whenever desired to remove excess reserves from the banking system. The purpose of such operations is to avoid undue impacts on reserves from Treasury actions, in order to maintain interest rates at target levels.

CONCLUSIONS

In this chapter, we have examined the non-discretionary nature of reserves. We have argued that the conventional view of a 'deposit multiplier' has reversed the direction of causation: banks do not wait for excess reserves before making loans and creating deposits. Rather, if faced with a credit-worthy customer and a demand for a loan, a bank makes the loan. It then operates to obtain reserves as necessary to meet legal requirements. If banks in the aggregate are short of required reserves, the central bank must supply them either through open market purchases or at the discount window; trying to restrict reserves through fewer open market purchases merely forces banks to the window. In practice, discount window borrowing is entirely at the discretion of borrowers – in spite of rhetoric about Fed policy to discourage such borrowing. If a bank fails to meet legal requirements, this is booked as a loan of reserves. It is simply impossible for the Fed to refuse to supply the reserves needed by the system. Further, this result is not dependent on either CRA or LRA, nor does it depend on a legal reserve ratio. Instead, it depends on the existence of a mono-reserve (supplied only by the government), pyramiding of reserves (or 'fractional reserve system'), par clearance, and typical non-marketability of bank assets (so they cannot shrink balance sheets quickly).

The Fed's policy variable is the overnight lending rate for reserves – now, the Fed funds rate is the targeted overnight rate. The Fed is able to hit its target without error. In spite of announced reserve (or other) targets, it is this overnight lending rate that is always the instrument of discretionary policy. Arbitrage then determines the wholesale short-term interest rate; the retail rate is set (perhaps rather complexly) as a mark-up over the wholesale rate. This view can be summarized as 'the short-term interest rate is exogenously set by central bank policy'.

The central bank has no direct control – and very little indirect influence – over the quantity of bank money. The quantity of bank money is actually determined by the quantity of bank loans. Obviously an increase of bank money must be matched by an increase of bank loans (simply due to accounting); our argument is that the decision to increase loans is the result of private negotiation between banker and borrower. Because the demand for loans is inelastic, at least in the short run, interest rate changes play a secondary role in the decision to borrow/lend. More importantly, it is the decision to spend that influences the quantity of bank money created. This view can be summarized fairly accurately as 'planned spending determines the demand for loans, the supply of loans substantially accommodates the demand, and this then determines the quantity of bank money created'; more succinctly, 'loans create deposits'. Thus the horizontal money supply is endogenously determined, while the short-term interest rate is exogenously determined.

Finally, close examination of coordination of Treasury and Fed actions demonstrates that the Treasury does not need tax receipts or receipts from bond sales in order to spend since spending only depends on the Treasury's ability to issue fiat money that the public accepts. Rather, manipulation of its tax and loan accounts is part of monetary policy – that is, to ensure that Treasury operations do not make it impossible to hit interest rate targets by creating positions of insufficient reserves or excess reserves in the banking system.

NOTES

1. In Chapter 3 we showed that for much of the nineteenth century, the Treasury performed central bank functions; during their brief periods of existence, central bank functions were also performed by the First and Second Banks of the US.

2. Actually, the multiplier was *re*-discovered, as it had been familiar to Marx and other classical economists.

3. For example, the Fed was concerned with inflation for most of the years of the Great Depression even though massive deflation was actually occurring – one could find interesting parallels between this episode and Chairman Greenspan's Fed of the mid-1990s.

4. Much of the discussion of this section draws on Mosler (1995) and on Wray (1990, Chapters 7 and 9). The author would like to thank Warren Mosler for permission to use some of his arguments here.

5. In some countries (such as the UK and Canada – see below), there is no legal reserve requirement but we will argue that nothing of substance is changed. Legal reserves can be thought of as nothing more than a minimum balance requirement; the US has a 10 per cent minimum balance requirement, while Canada has a minimum balance requirement of zero. Whatever the requirement, it must be met.

6. This would force banks to fail to meet legal requirements – something the Fed cannot do; we will return to this below.

7. Sale of anything by the government will absorb reserves since payments to government must be made in fiat money.

8. Desired reserves would be a function of a number of factors, including typical cash withdrawals, 'redeposit' ratios – itself partially a function of local market share – tax payments by depositors, total deposits issued, composition of deposits, degree of development of interbank lending, and so on.

9. Note that these effects exist regardless of the reserve ratio desired – any excess reserves will place downward pressure on the overnight rate and any shortage will place upward pressure. While reserve holdings desired will respond somewhat to changes of the rates (a higher rate would cause banks to economize while a lower rate would increase desired reserve holdings), this effect would be quite small because banks have an incentive to minimize holdings.

10. For analysis of Bank of Canada operating procedures, see Clinton (1997), Bank of Canada (1997) and Montador (1995).

11. This section draws heavily, again, on Mosler (1995) and Wray (1990).

12. This is usually written as $M = m \times B$, where M is money supply, m is the multiplier, and B is the base. Note that money supply would be defined as currency in the hands of the non-bank public, plus demand deposits – that is, close to the real-world definition of M1 – although nothing of substance would be changed by defining it somewhat more broadly, for example, as M2 or M3 (which would only affect the size of the multiplier).

13. The money multiplier is more accurately thought of as a divisor ($B = M/m$) or, simply, as the ratio of money to base – a ratio of no theoretical significance.

14. In Chapter 2 we examined the theories of Smith and Minsky, who held views very similar to those expounded here; in Chapter 3 we presented some of the ideas of Innes, who also had a similar view of banking.

15. Further, the government regulates banks in a manner different from the way in which it regulates other firms. And banks cannot declare bankruptcy (although they can, and do, become insolvent and sometimes require resolution).

16. There is a large literature on credit rationing. See Calomiris et al. (1986), Blinder and Stiglitz (1983), Stiglitz and Weiss (1981) and Bernanke (1981) for examples of the asymmetric information, adverse incentive and adverse selection approaches. See Papadimitriou et al. (1993) for discussion of rationing due to discrimination.

17. Actually, the interest rate on loans is usually administered, typically after negotiation between the bank and borrower.

18. Or, the Fed can do the opposite, exchanging reserves for bonds in open market purchases, simply restoring reserves that had previously been exchanged for interest-earning bonds.

19. Why do banks and borrowers do this? To obtain profits.

20. In many ways, the financial crisis is East Asia in the late 1990s can be thought of as a dollar short squeeze brought on, in part, by elimination of the US government deficit. See Mayer (1998) and Kregel (1998a).

21. This section draws heavily on Bell (1998).

22. As discussed below, things are actually more complicated because tax receipts are frequently held in private banks.

23. General depositories are also called remittance-option banks (ROBS), and special depositories are called note-option banks (NOBS). ROBS can hold funds in tax and loan accounts for one day only (and pay no interest on them), while NOBS can move Treasury funds from their tax and loan accounts after one day to note accounts (on which they must pay interest). The Treasury decides how much it would like to leave in note accounts; however, it can sometimes offer funds that NOBS are either unwilling or unable to take. NOBS have collateral requirements and size limits. About two-thirds of business tax payments go to NOBS and one-third to ROBS (Bell, 1998).

24. There is no reserve requirement against Treasury deposits in special depositories.

25. If the Treasury has injected reserves by running its balance below $5 billion, the Fed will immediately operate (for example, implement an open market sale) to drain the excess. The Treasury's call will restore its balance *ex post*, allowing the Fed to restore its balance sheet position (buying back the bonds).

6 Employment Policy and the Value of the Currency

Since WWII, it has been the stated policy of the US government to simultaneously pursue high employment and stable prices. These two goals have even been the subject of two laws, the 1946 Employment Act and the 1978 Humphrey–Hawkins Act; the latter Act strengthened the government's commitment to employment by setting a goal of 'full employment', with an interim goal of an adult unemployment rate of 3 per cent (or 4 per cent overall). Paradoxically, neither accepted theory nor practical experience appears to indicate that high or full employment is even possible with stable prices. As a result, for at least the past two or three decades, monetary policy generally has been geared toward raising the unemployment rate as a means to achieving stable prices; unemployment is perceived as the inevitable cost of price stability.[1] Many, perhaps most, economists doubt that it is even possible to achieve anything close to a 3 per cent unemployment rate without at the same time inducing accelerating inflation. For this reason, there has been discussion of repealing the above-mentioned Acts and even a movement to replace them with a new Act that would mandate only one goal for monetary policy – stable prices.

In this chapter, we will argue that stable prices and truly full employment are possible and, indeed, are complements. In fact, the Humphrey–Hawkins Act sets the goalpost too low; we will argue that the government can guarantee a zero unemployment rate, meaning that all who are ready, willing and able to work at the going wage will be able to find a job – only those unwilling (or unable) to work at the going wage would be left without work (and these are not normally counted as unemployed[2]). At the same time, by setting this 'going wage', the government will provide a price anchor to impart greater price stability to the system. We do not claim that this policy would cause any particular price index to remain constant over time (and indeed would not favour any policy that would attempt to achieve this result). The proposed policy would still allow market (and other) forces to affect both nominal and relative prices. However, the point is that the proposed full employment policy would not generate the sort of inflationary pressures that many economists believe must result from high employment. Thus 'inflation' – defined as persistent increase of some price index – could certainly coexist with our proposed full employment policy, but would not be caused by the policy. Whether or not absence of inflation, so defined, is desirable is beyond the scope of this chapter. However, we will show that a true full employment policy is not, in itself, 'inflationary' and indeed would almost certainly reduce inflationary pressures. Further, the full employment policy would help to reduce economic fluctuations (the 'business cycle') through a powerful built-in automatic stabilizer feature (although we make no claim that this would be sufficient to eliminate business fluctuations, nor are we certain that such would be desirable).

Before proceeding, it is necessary to admit that our proposed policy could lead to an increase of government spending; indeed, a persistent government deficit could result. However, it should be clear from the analysis in previous chapters (especially that of Chapter 4) that we do not view this result with horror – as would many economists. Some 'liberal' economists and policymakers would be willing to accept more government spending and larger deficits if these could achieve full employment without causing accelerating inflation – even while they believe that bigger government and larger deficits necessarily negatively affect the private economy, they would be willing to accept this 'trade-off' if full employment could be achieved. Others would reject this argument, arguing that the negative impacts of larger deficits outweigh any benefits of full employment. Our line of argument is different. We take the position that there is nothing inherently wrong with big deficits – these do not necessarily cause 'crowding out', they do not 'burden' future generations, and they cannot lead to 'financial ruin' of the government – indeed, persistent deficits are the expected norm for reasons previously discussed.[3]

In our view, fear of deficit spending is irrational and should never stand in the way of the spending that may be required to generate full employment. This is not to say that deficits cannot be too large. Once an economy is operating beyond full employment, any increase of aggregate demand (whether by government or by the private sector) might be inflationary. This has (but only rarely) been the case; a good example is the US situation during WWII, when the government purchased up to 60 per cent of the nation's output. During WWII, inflationary pressures would surely have arisen because with the government's deficit, aggregate demand would have exceeded potential output (in part because non-defence industries could not add capacity). However, a combination of patriotism, rationing and wage and price controls allowed the economy to operate well beyond full employment without generating substantial inflation. This package of policies was developed to allow the economy to operate at the level necessary to prosecute the war.

There is no need to exaggerate the problems facing the US today; they certainly are not as serious as those faced in 1940. However, as we will argue, there are conditions today that make it easier to pursue a policy of full employment with price stability than those that existed in 1940. Most important, the universal abandonment of the gold standard by all of the large economies has eliminated all rational barriers to deficit spending as a means to hire all the unemployed. Fortunately, full employment can be achieved, now, without wartime controls such as rationing and wage and price controls that would excessively reduce the level of freedom that is expected by the public during normal, peacetime, periods.

In the next two sections, we turn to the two primary components of the proposal: the government would

(a) act as employer of last resort, and
(b) exogenously set the 'marginal' price of labour.

In later sections, we will examine the general theoretical background and other implications of the proposal.

Before presenting the proposal, however, we will first list some caveats:[4]

(a) The programme is designed to offer a job to anyone who is ready, willing and able to work. It could be called a job opportunity programme, or a modified job guarantee programme (see below). Those who are not ready, willing and able to work are not the intended targets of this programme.

(b) ELR is not slavery; involuntary servitude is illegal in the US. No one will be forced by government to work in ELR. The programme is only for those who are willing to participate. Of course, in any capitalist economy, there is some degree of economic coercion that induces most people to work in order to obtain the means of livelihood. Thus out of economic necessity, some individuals may feel forced to accept an ELR job because the alternatives available do not provide sufficient income.

(c) ELR is not meant to be a form of 'workfare'. In the US today, there is a move to force welfare recipients to work to obtain welfare benefits. Presumably, there is a lot of political support to continue in this direction. However, as we envision it, ELR can supplement any sort of welfare safety net that is politically acceptable. We emphasize again that ELR is designed for those who are ready, willing and able to work. We do believe that many of those currently on welfare would voluntarily leave welfare to accept ELR employment. ELR provides greater freedom of choice. However, other programmes will still be required for those who are not ready, willing, and able to work.

(d) ELR workers can be fired, with restrictions placed on re-hiring.[5] Thus it provides a guaranteed opportunity to work but with performance standards. Those who do not measure up to required standards will be fired; they should be given a second or third chance, but after some point they will have to rely on the social safety net. ELR is only for those who are ready, willing, and able to work.

(e) The envisioned ELR wage will be a substantial improvement over the average package of welfare and unemployment benefits received in the US; in other countries with more generous safety nets, the improvement may be less significant. As a start, we recommend setting the ELR wage in the US at the minimum wage level that exists at the time ELR is implemented. In other countries it may be better to choose some other method for determining the appropriate ELR wage. In any case, we intend our recommendation as only a starting point for the purpose of analysis and discussion. The following discussion should make it clear that the essentials of our analysis hold regardless of the initial setting of the ELR wage.

(f) We recognize that ELR alone cannot resolve all employment, unemployment, underemployment, low income, and disability problems. We do believe that it offers a major improvement over the current situation. However, other social programmes will be required to deal with many social problems that will remain even after ELR is put into place.

We apologize for the repetition; however, we have found as a result of previous presentations that most objections raised to the ELR programme have centred around confusion over the issues listed above. Thus it may help to lay out as clearly as possible the target population of the ELR proposal: those who are ready, willing and able to work at the ELR wage (presumed to be $6.25 per hour for the purposes of our analysis).

GOVERNMENT AS EMPLOYER OF LAST RESORT

The first component of the proposal is relatively simple: the government acts as the employer of last resort, hiring all the labour that cannot find private sector employment.[6] As Hyman Minsky said

> The policy problem is to develop a strategy for full employment that does not lead to instability, inflation, and unemployment. The main instrument of such a policy is the creation of an infinitely elastic demand for labor at a floor or minimum wage that does not depend upon long-run and short-run profit expectations of business. Since only government can divorce the offering of employment from the profitability of hiring workers, the infinitely elastic demand for labor must be created by government. (Minsky, 1986, p. 308)

We will call this the employer of last resort (ELR) policy.[7] As will be discussed in the next section, the government simply announces the wage at which it will hire anyone who wants to work in the public sector, and then hires all who seek employment at that wage. We will call this the basic public sector employment (BPSE) at the basic public sector wage (BPSW). Of course, there will still remain many (non-BPSE) jobs in the public sector that are not a component of the ELR and that could pay wages above the BPSW. It is also important to emphasize that ELR policy is not meant to substitute for current public sector employment (BPSE workers should not displace current public employees).[8]

The implications for wages and prices, in general, will be explored below. Here we only discuss the implications for employment and the government's budget. For the sake of our discussion in this section, we will assume that the government's announced wage (BPSW) is $6.25 per hour or $12500 per year for full-time (BPSE) employment. We will also assume that this is a 'living' wage, and that it is the legal minimum wage that exists at the time the ELR programme is implemented.[9] As we briefly discuss below, careful analysis should be undertaken before establishing the BPSW. There is no reason why some individuals might not be allowed to work part-time. However, we will assume throughout that employment is full-time to simplify calculations.

This policy will as a matter of logic eliminate all unemployment, defined as workers willing to work at the going wage but unable to find a job even after looking. Certainly there will still exist many individuals – even those in the labour force – who will be voluntarily unemployed: there will be those who are unwilling to work for the government (perhaps at any wage!), those who are unwilling to work for the government's announced wage, those who are between jobs and who would prefer to look for a better job while unemployed, and so on. For well-known reasons, it is not optimal (either socially or individually) for each individual to be fully employed – voluntary unemployment can be rational. Thus our only concern is to ensure that all those ready, willing and able to work at the BPSW wage will be able to obtain a job at that wage. We define this as a state of full employment or zero unemployment.

One implication of the ELR is that much social spending that is currently targeted to the unemployed might be reduced or eliminated. For example, unemployment compensation currently provides some income replacement for those who are unemployed. The programme has only partial coverage (many of the unemployed are not covered), limited benefits (determined in part by income earned while employed), and time limits, and pays people for not working (generating obvious incentive problems). If, instead, unemployment compensation were replaced with government employment, all the disadvantages of unemployment compensation would be eliminated: coverage would potentially be universal (obviously, some unemployed would opt out of the programme), there would be no time limits, no one would be paid for not working, and pay would be equalized (for the BPSE jobs).

A less extreme change would allow newly unemployed workers the option of engaging in full-time job search in the ELR programme for a specific period of time, for example, for a period of six weeks.[10] If a job were not found within this time frame, the individual would undergo counselling and assessment to determine whether continued full-time search were warranted; alternatively, retraining or education might be indicated (for example, if the individual's skills did not match job opportunities). In this case, the individual might be placed into a full-time BPSE job to obtain on-the-job training; or the individual might be enrolled in a part-time or full-time educational programme.[11] Again, there could be time limits for such programmes; at some point the individual would be placed into an appropriate BPSE job. As the primary goal of BPSE is to prepare workers for employment in non-BPSE jobs (whether public or private employment), all BPSE jobs should contain at least some training. Thus ELR could provide something similar to 'unemployment compensation', but would differ from the current programme in three significant ways. First, coverage could be universal (for example, all newly unemployed would qualify, regardless of the reason for unemployment); second, the job search would be more closely monitored and assisted (for example, each ELR worker in the job search programme would be expected to devote a full eight hours each workday to job search – phoning for interviews, developing a cv, completing applications, and attending interviews); and third, the 'unemployment compensation' would be equalized (each would receive $6.25 per hour).[12] Clearly, some newly unemployed workers will 'opt out' of the ELR programme, either because they have negotiated sufficient privately supplied unemployment benefits (or severance pay), or because they have amassed sufficient savings to enable them to pursue full-time job search. We are concerned only with those who would voluntarily choose to participate in the ELR programme.

In addition, at least some spending on other types of social programmes could be reduced, such as general assistance (state-run programmes for indigents), aid to families with dependent children (AFDC), and food stamps.[13] Obviously, the ELR policy is not a substitute for these programmes – many individuals currently receiving such assistance are not (and probably could not be) in the labour force. Exactly who would be forced out of these current programmes and into the ELR programme is a subject of social policy but is beyond the scope of this chapter. As we stated above, the political currents in the US are moving away from welfare and toward workfare. However, we emphasize again that our concern is with those who are ready, willing and able to work. ELR will also eliminate the need for a statutory minimum wage, as the BPSW will become an effective minimum wage. Indeed, it will have complete coverage, unlike the current minimum wage law, as any worker can always choose to accept BPSE. (As Hyman Minsky always argued, if there is any unemployment, the effective minimum wage is zero; minimum wage laws are effective only at full employment.) The implication of ELR and the BPSW for the private sector wage is the subject of the next section.[14]

We will provide a rough calculation of programme costs; however, we note that the nominal cost of the programme is not important as an economic issue. When an economy is operating below full employment, the direct economic cost of putting unemployed resources to work is zero. There might, however, be indirect costs, such as environmental costs or induced inflation (the latter of which we take up below). If we assume that in the current economic environment, 8 million unemployed workers (not all of whom would be officially counted as unemployed) would be willing to accept the BPSW in BPSE jobs, the total wage cost to the government would be $100 billion.[15] However, there would be reductions of other kinds of spending partially to offset this cost. In 1996, for example, the government spent about $50 billion on unemployment compensation, $15 billion on AFDC, and more than $20 billion on food stamps; in addition, state governments spent billions on general assistance and many other billions were spent on programmes that provided assistance to the poor (housing allowances, medical care, disability payments, the earned income tax credit, and so on). The ELR could potentially eliminate all of the unemployment compensation and at least some of the other social spending (particularly on the assumption that the BPSW is a 'living' wage).

In addition, in 1996 millions of full-time workers earned less than $12 500 per year in private (and public) employment; many of these would leave their jobs to accept BPSE at the BPSW. Of course, private and public employers would respond with higher wages in an attempt to retain these workers. These higher wages, in turn, could reduce social spending on privately (and even publicly) employed workers (such as for food stamps, which currently go to more than 10 per cent of the population, and the earned income tax credit – which is essentially a negative income tax linked to low income), which are required because so many jobs currently pay less than a living wage. Still, the net effect would probably be some gain of BPSE so that total BPSE would rise somewhat above 8 million.[16] It seems reasonable to assume that the net cost of ELR to the government would fall between $25 billion and $50 billion (total expenses in excess of $100 billion, with savings in excess of $50 billion).[17]

Note that we are not including a variety of possible social and private benefits associated with lowering unemployment rates. For example, it is widely recognized that long-term unemployment contributes to crime, child abuse, divorce, loss of human capital, and other social and private degradation (including insecurity even of the employed) that may be hard to value economically.[18] Certainly unemployment is only one of the factors that contribute to such problems; however, there should be no doubt that substantial economic benefits should be generated from elimination of involuntary unemployment. Because these are so difficult to calculate, we will ignore them here. We will assume that the deficit would rise by a net $50 billion, with the ELR programme employing 8.5 million workers in BPSE at the BPSW. This is a 'back of the envelope' calculation, but nothing of substance would change in our analysis even if costs were two or three times greater (or half as much) – economically it would not matter, although it might matter politically.

Obviously, the budgetary effects of the ELR are quite small, relative to the size of the Federal budget, to the size of the Reagan or Bush deficit, and to the size of GDP. We will not provide a detailed rejoinder to the 'deficit-busting' arguments of those who advocate balanced budgets, as our analysis in previous chapters has made it clear that persistent deficits are the expected norm given positive desired net nominal savings. However, we have admitted that deficits can be too large. Thus an important question concerns the impact this programme would have on aggregate demand: is full employment going to increase aggregate demand sufficiently that accelerating demand-pull inflation would follow? Alternatively, is desired net nominal saving sufficiently high to absorb the additional government deficit spending without generating accelerating inflation?[19] The answer is easy to obtain. If in the absence of ELR, public plus private sector spending provides a level of employment that leaves 8 million workers involuntarily unemployed, this must be evidence that the desired net nominal saving position of the population is higher than the actual net nominal saving position generated by the government's deficit. For if the desired net nominal saving position were lower, the population would be spending more and creating more jobs for the unemployed.[20]

Indeed, existence of involuntarily unemployed workers is *de facto* evidence that desired net nominal saving exceeds actual net nominal saving. This means that the government can safely increase its deficit spending, lowering involuntary unemployment, to satisfy the excess desired net nominal saving of the population. So long as additional government deficit spending does increase employment, this must be evidence that desired net nominal saving still exceeds actual net nominal saving. ELR is designed to ensure that the deficit will rise only to the point that all involuntary employment is eliminated; once there are no workers willing to accept BPSE at the BPSW, the deficit will not be increased further.[21] Thus the design of the ELR guarantees that the deficit will not become 'excessive', that is, will not exceed desired net nominal saving.[22]

It might be objected that as the government implements ELR and begins employing some of the 8 million unemployed, this will raise aggregate demand and thus increase private sector employment. This is true and is desired as it will ultimately reduce the amount of BPSE required. By stimulating demand (through the 'spending multiplier'), ELR may find that only 4 million workers will eventually accept BPSE. Still, ELR automatically operates to ensure that the deficit spending attributable to ELR is at the correct level to equate desired and actual net nominal saving, since every private sector job created automatically reduces BPSE by approximately one job and the deficit by at least the cost of an ELR job (and probably more as tax revenues rise and government spending falls).

This should eliminate the fear that a full employment policy must necessarily generate excessive dem-and-pull inflation. Of course, it can still be objected that full employment and the BPSW will generate cost-push inflation by placing pressure on wages and thus costs and prices. In the next section we will examine the second part of the proposal: exogenous wage setting by the government.

THE BPSW AND EXOGENOUS PRICING

The size of the deficit spending necessitated by the ELR intervention will be 'market determined' by the desired net nominal saving position of the public. However, the price paid by the government for BPSE will be exogenously set – for the purposes of our exposition, at \$12 500 per year per worker. Thus while the quantity 'floats', the price is fixed. This could be called the fixed price, floating deficit alternative.[23] What are the implications for prices and wages?

With a fixed price, the government's BPSW is perfectly stable and sets a benchmark price for labour. Some jobs might still pay a wage below the BPSW if they are particularly desirable (for example, because the work is pleasurable, or where large wage increases are possible for a lucky few – as in sports or the arts). However, low-wage jobs which pay at or below the BPSW before the ELR is implemented will experience a one-time increase of wages (or will disappear altogether).[24] Employers will then be forced to cover these higher costs through a combination of higher product prices, greater labour productivity and lower realized profits. Thus some product prices should also experience a one-time jump as the ELR programme is implemented. If the BPSW is set at the statutory minimum wage, and if this minimum wage had universal coverage before ELR, then low-wage private sector jobs will experience only minimal impacts – private wages need rise only sufficiently to make private sector employment preferable to BPSE.[25] In short, at the low end of the wage scale, implementation of ELR might cause wages and the prices of products produced by these workers to experience a one-time increase. However, this one-time jump – no matter how large it is – is not inflation nor can it be accelerating inflation as these terms are normally defined by economists (since inflation is defined as a continuously rising price level).

Still, it can be argued that other wages are likely also to rise because by achieving full employment of labour, the threat of unemployment is removed, emboldening workers to demand higher wages – this is essentially the old Marxist 'reserve army of the unemployed' argument. Workers who might have previously earned $13 000 per year now demand $13 500, knowing that, in the worst case, they might be fired if they are too obstinate – but this would then lead to a BPSE job at a loss of only $500. By extrapolation, all workers might harden their positions, causing wages to jump upward. Prices would move upward to the extent that higher labour productivity and lower profits could not absorb the entire increase of wages. However, again, this is a one-time jump that is not defined as inflation, unless it can be argued that all workers above the $12 500 threshold continuously raise wage demands over time (generating a 'wage-price spiral'). This appears unlikely. The marginal $13 000 a year worker who decides to demand $13 500 per year on the calculation that this is worth the risk of losing her job and $500 per year pay (to take the BPSE job) will not face the same decision once she is a $13 500 per year worker demanding $14 000 – for now the loss is $1000 per year in the worst case. It is hard to see how the guaranteed $12 500 per year job will cause any individual worker to continually increase her wage demand through time, because as she gets further from the $12 500 benchmark, her potential loss due to obstinacy rises.

It is possible that the aforementioned $13 500 per year worker might calculate that if her wage demands are not met, she will fall back to a $13000 per year job rather than the BPSE – displacing some $13 000 per year worker to the BPSE – in which case the expected loss is again only $500 per year. In this way, it might be supposed that continuous wage pressure is applied as workers move up the wage ladder, expecting to fall back only one rung rather than all the way to the BPSW. However, if we can assume that wages and jobs can be loosely sorted by labour productivity, then this is not likely. Essentially, the government's BPSW determines the wage for the lowest productivity group – the pool of unskilled and semi-skilled workers during periods of normal demand. Those workers whose productivity is substantially above $12 500 per year will find jobs in the private sector; those with lower productivity will find BPSE. When private demand is below normal, the government will find the average productivity of its BPSE pool rising as workers are laid off in the private sector; when private demand is above normal, workers whose productivity was formerly too low to induce private hiring will leave the BPSE pool, lowering average productivity of this pool. At normal levels of private demand, then, workers in the private sector have a productivity that is above that warranted by a salary of $12 500.

Given that the relation between wages and productivity is loose, some ratcheting upward of individual wages after the ELR policy is adopted is possible. However, just as workers have the alternative of BPSE, so do employers have the opportunity of hiring from the BPSE pool. This is the primary 'price stabilization' feature of the ELR programme. If the wage demands of workers in the private sector exceed by too great a margin the employer's calculations of their productivity, the alternative is to obtain BPSE workers at a mark-up over the BPSW. This will help to offset the wage pressures caused by elimination of the fear of unemployment. The ELR pool will operate as a 'buffer stock', and just as a buffer stock of any commodity can be used to stabilize its price, the government's labour 'buffer stock' will help to stabilize the price of non-BPSE labour to the extent that workers in the ELR pool are substitutes for non-BPSE labour.[26]

It must be remembered that the BPSE workers are not 'lost' as a reserve army of potential employees; rather, they can always be obtained at a mark-up over $12 500 per year. In the absence of ELR, these workers can be obtained at a mark-up over the value of the package of social spending and private income obtained when unemployed (unemployment compensation, food stamps, under-the-table work, handouts, and so on); this mark-up, however, is likely to be higher than the mark-up over $12 500 since it must be sufficient to make employment preferable to unemployment (and recall that those in the ELR pool have demonstrated that they are ready, willing and able to work). Further, recent work has tended to place a high rate of 'depreciation' on idle human capital; the productivity of workers falls quickly when they are unemployed, and beyond some point, they probably become unemployable (due, for example, to loss of the 'work habit'). With an ELR policy, however, those who are not employed in the private sector continue to work; thus they will not depreciate so quickly. Indeed, social policy could actually be geared toward enhancing human capital of the BPSE pool. This would reduce the productivity-adjusted cost of hiring BPSE workers relative to unemployed workers, and thereby diminish inflationary pressures.

Indeed, it is hard to imagine that true full employment with an ELR programme would be more inflationary than the current system. The current system relies on unemployed labour and excess capacity to try to dampen wage and price increases; however, it pays unemployed labour for not working, and allows that labour to depreciate and in some cases to develop behaviours that act as barriers to private sector employment.[27] Social spending on the unemployed prevents aggregate demand from falling excessively, but little is done to promote aggregate supply (or growth of potential output). With ELR in place, however, labour is paid for working, which can lead to production of publicly supplied goods and services, can promote efficiency of the private sector (if, for example, BPSE generates productivity-enhancing public infrastructure) and reduce private sector costs (for example, by reducing crime), and can increase the education and skills of ELR workers (compared with education and skill levels of the unemployed). Thus ELR might increase aggregate supply (or potential output) and thereby place downward pressure on prices, rather than causing inflation.

This appears to be an unusual claim: full employment might be deflationary? Recall that we have argued that the primary determinant of the value of the currency is the 'effort' required to obtain the money that is required to pay taxes. ELR raises the 'stakes' involved because it requires that one must at least show up, ready to work, in order to obtain money; this requires greater effort than that required to obtain 'welfare'. We also expect that those who do show up for ELR work will become more employable, and thus operate as a better 'reserve army' buffer stock than do the unemployed. Further, much private and social spending associated with crime will be reduced (reducing the production of security systems, lowering the number of private security jobs, reducing the number of new prisons required), which will lower overall aggregate demand. Thus it is possible that rather than generating inflationary pressures, ELR will generate significant deflationary pressures. These can be mitigated by reducing taxes and/or increasing non-ELR government spending. In other words, once ELR is in place, we can probably 'afford' greater government stimulation and indeed might require it to avoid deflation.

The buffer stock aspects of ELR generate 'loose' labour markets even as they ensure full employment. This stands in stark contrast with 'Keynesian' demand management policies that were designed to 'prime the pump' with aggregate government spending that would increase private demand sufficiently to lower unemployment to the 'full employment' level. The danger was that this would lead to 'tight' labour markets due to bottlenecks in rapidly advancing or high-productivity sectors that would drag up the entire wage structure so that inflation would be generated long before full employment could be reached.[28] Indeed, most economists today believe that Keynesian policy proved to be a 'failure' precisely because the tight labour markets did generate unacceptable levels of inflation.[29] ELR is not subject to the same criticism, for it allows loose labour markets even at full employment. If the ELR pool shrinks too much in an expansion so that it cannot act as a buffer stock, the government can either raise taxes or reduce non-ELR spending to replenish the buffer stock. This allows the private economy to grow at its non-inflationary rate, but without requiring unemployment since any labour shed by the private sector is absorbed in the ELR pool. Thus aggregate 'fine-tuning' would operate through increases or decreases of the buffer stock, rather than by causing unemployment.

There are thus two conclusions that follow. If ELR is put in place, it is unlikely that this will be inflationary in the sense of generating continuous pressure on wages and prices. Wages might experience a one-time increase because the $12 500 plus mark-up that is required to hire workers of the lowest productivity rank might exceed the value of the social spending package plus mark-up that is required to hire unemployed workers in the absence of ELR. Workers of higher productivity might become more obstinate in their wage demands so that other wages also ratchet upward. However, against this tendency is the likelihood that BPSE will reduce loss of human capital, and even the possibility that BPSE will increase human capital of workers who are temporarily not needed in the private sector. When demand for private output rises sufficiently that they are needed, the somewhat higher cost of BPSE workers under ELR relative to the cost of unemployed workers in the absence of ELR is offset by higher productivity – reducing any pressures on prices. Further, because unemployment compensation would no longer be needed, there would be no need for experience-rated unemployment insurance taxes on firms. This means that those firms that typically have volatile demand for labour (those subject to seasonal or cyclical demand) would experience a reduction of overall labour costs – which would again tend to offset some of the higher wage costs. Finally, an ELR programme could increase potential output (or 'aggregate supply') by providing higher-skilled labour and greater public infrastructure. Thus even the one-time jump of wages and prices might be quite small. And if we are correct in our prediction, the overall impact of ELR will be to create deflationary pressures such that taxes will have to be reduced, or other spending raised.

ELR AS A BUFFER STOCK PROGRAMME

Some economists (including Keynes) have noted that there really is no labour market; labour is not like other commodities because it cannot be owned, it cannot be stored, and it is not nearly so mobile as other 'factors of production' typically are (see Galbraith, 1997). In addition, there are considerable 'information costs' and uncertainty involved in hiring workers. The ELR programme will resolve or reduce some of these difficulties. In a sense, the BPSE allows 'storage' of labour – when it is not needed by private employers (and non-ELR public employers), it can be 'stored' in the ELR buffer stock pool.[30] ELR employees will at a minimum be able to provide employment records to potential employers; if ELR is well administered they will also have records of education, formal training and on-the-job training obtained in BPSE. In a sense, the government will act as a 'market-maker', creating a market in labour by standing ready to 'buy' unemployed labour at a fixed price, or to 'sell' (provide it to non-ELR employers) at a mark-up over the BPSW. As is the case in all buffer stock schemes, that commodity used as a buffer stock is always fully employed.[31] It also always has a very stable price, which cannot deviate much from the range established by the government's announced 'buy' or 'sell' price. What we are proposing to do is to 'make a market in labour' by establishing a 'buffer stock of labour'. This is the 'trick' that allows us to obtain full employment and stable prices.

From time to time, there will be pressure for an upward revision of the BPSW. As the overall price level will not be held constant, and as there may be substantial forces in modern capitalist economies that generate trend increases of the price level, it is possible for the 'real' (inflation-adjusted) BPSW to fall over time – generating a need for an adjustment. In addition, there will be obvious pressures by labour to raise the BPSW – just as there are pressures currently to increase the minimum wage. When the government raises the BPSW, this in effect devalues the currency by redefining the amount of services that must be provided to the government to obtain the means of paying taxes. For example, an increase of the hourly wage from $6.25 per hour to $7.50 per hour reflects a 20 per cent devaluation of the currency. Again, other wages (and prices) will also adjust upward to reflect the devaluation – but there is no reason to suppose that this will be 'inflationary'. Rather than 'causing inflation', the devaluation will merely take account of inflation that results from factors that have little to do with the ELR policy.

This would be similar to a devaluation of the currency under a gold standard. Under a gold standard the government could act as a 'market-maker' for gold, utilizing a gold buffer stock. The government would set the value of the currency relative to gold 'exogenously', then make a market in gold; the government's 'price' (for example, $32 per ounce of gold) would be 'fixed', while its 'spending' on gold would be 'market determined' (as it bought all gold offered for sale at that price).[32] It has long been argued that a gold standard imparts some stability to prices; however, even on a gold standard, prices may rise and might induce the government to devalue (raise the money price of gold).[33] The analogy with ELR should be clear – 'devaluing' the currency by raising the price of gold or of ELR workers can simply be a response to inflation arising from other sources.

Note also that just as a gold standard ensures that gold is always 'fully employed' ('idle' gold can always be sold to government at the fixed price if it is not desired as a hoard), the ELR 'labour' standard ensures full employment of labour. Under ELR, the government would 'monetize' labour just as it 'monetizes' gold under the gold standard. The question is: do we prefer to have gold 'fully employed', or is it preferable to have labour 'fully employed'? Should we attempt to stabilize prices by re-establishing the gold standard, or should we move to a BPSW standard? Or should we simply continue on the present path, which requires unemployment of labour to try to minimize inflation?

This is not the place for an evaluation of alternative methods of obtaining 'price stability'. We only wanted to counter the belief that any policy designed to achieve high or full employment must generate accelerating inflation. As we have shown, the ELR will achieve what most economists would call zero unemployment (well beyond what they would call full employment) without creating inflationary pressures. The government will define the currency by setting the price of standard labour. This might initially devalue the currency – and periodic redefinition is likely.[34] The government would make no attempt to stabilize other prices – for example, the price of high skilled workers, or the prices of output of the private sector – under our scheme. We believe that the ELR policy would result in greater price stability than is currently the case – but that is not a primary claim of this chapter. We need only show that truly full employment can be achieved without generating more inflation pressures than exist under the current system.[35]

In conclusion, the ELR policy is not likely to induce inflation – much less to cause accelerating inflation – even if it does cause prices to rise when implemented and each time the BPSW is raised. However, the magnitude of the pressure on prices is attenuated by the likelihood that ELR will preserve and even increase productivity of the 'reserve army' BPSE workers who would have been unemployed in the absence of ELR.[36] Further, other private and social costs of unemployment will be reduced. Finally, the 'price anchor' of the BPSW may impart a greater degree of stability to wages by setting a well-known wage for homogeneous, 'standard' 'buffer stock' labour that can always be used by private employers as an alternative to higher-skilled workers with 'market determined' wages.

THE ELR, MODERN MONEY, AND GOVERNMENT DEFICITS

All modern economies have abandoned a gold standard and adopted a 'fiat money' standard in which the liabilities of the government (in the US, Treasury coin and Fed notes and bank reserves) serve as the 'ultimate' money. In all modern economies, the government 'spends' by issuing fiat money, which ends up in the hands of the public as cash holdings and in the banking system as bank reserves. If a government can create at will the money that the public willingly offers goods and services (especially labour services, for our purposes here) to obtain, then the government's spending is never constrained by narrow 'financing' decisions. The government can offer to hire all unemployed workers at any price it chooses, allowing the government deficit to float as high as necessary to ensure that unemployment is eliminated. Nor is there any significant problem experienced should the government decide to raise the BPSW (which will not only increase the cost per worker, but is likely to increase BPSE), and thereby increase the deficit. So long as the money is a fiat money, the government faces no narrow 'financial' constraint.[37]

Above, we linked the existence of unemployment to a desire for net nominal saving that exceeded the government's deficit. The government can safely increase its spending, while holding taxes constant, up to the point where the deficit equals desired net nominal saving at an equilibrium with zero unemployment.[38] If, for example, desired net nominal saving exceeded actual net nominal saving and the deficit, this would be reflected in a deflationary reduction of private spending and employment, causing the deficit to rise (through ELR spending), and increasing actual net nominal saving until it had risen to equality with desired net nominal saving. If, however, desired net nominal saving were less than actual net nominal saving, private spending and employment would rise, reducing BPSE and ELR spending, causing the deficit and actual net nominal saving to fall until it equalled desired net nominal saving. The ELR programme thus imparts a great deal of stability to aggregate spending and employment by acting as a powerful automatic stabilizer – much more powerful than previous programmes such as unemployment compensation or AFDC spending, which were not designed to allow government spending to 'float' sufficiently to eliminate all involuntary unemployment.

Still, ELR will not eliminate the business cycle. When private expectations are low, desired net nominal saving rises, and $40 000 per year workers lose their jobs. These jobs are replaced by BPSE at $12 500 per year. The deficit increases but not by so much as the private spending that is lost. The combination of a rising deficit (thus raising actual net nominal saving) and falling aggregate income (which might lower desired net nominal saving, if it is linked to income) restores an equilibrium (desired net nominal saving = actual net nominal saving) without unemployment – but at a lower level of aggregate activity. When private demand expands (or desired net nominal saving falls), leading to creation of high-wage private sector jobs, these replace BPSE, raising aggregate income. Equilibrium is restored at zero unemployment, a lower deficit, lower actual and desired net nominal savings, and a higher level of aggregate demand. Thus the business cycle persists, but with smaller amplitude.

There is another consideration that is related to the arguments of the previous section. If the currency issued by the government were 'backed by' and made convertible into a precious metal (or anything else) of relatively fixed supply, then the ELR proposal would become impossible to implement during times of crisis. The government would fear that if it were to hire all the unemployed and allow its deficit to float, then there could always be a run on its currency as the public attempted to convert government money to, say, gold. Even though the government could try to supplement its gold reserves (for example, by raising interest rates in an attempt to cause a positive flow of gold from foreign sources), any level of backing less than 100 per cent would still expose it to the danger of a run. Alternatively, the government might devalue the currency by reducing the conversion rate – however, this would be more likely to generate a run due to expectations of further devaluation than to prevent a run. Thus a gold standard (or any other standard which involves a promise to convert money on demand to a relatively scarce reserve) is not compatible with an ELR. Indeed, the ELR would expose the government to the greatest risk precisely when it was most needed, that is, during a collapse of the private sector of the economy.[39] The US abandoned convertibility during the Great Depression, although it was restored internationally after WWII. However, at the end of the 1960s and the beginning of the 1970s, fear of a run on the dollar led the government finally to abandon convertibility. Since that date, gold reserves could never again constrain deficit spending. There is no longer any major (real, as opposed to perceived) barrier to implementation of a full employment policy.

DISCRETIONARY ELR AND 'FINE-TUNING'

With an ELR programme, government fixes the wage but allows its spending to be 'endogenously' determined. It could, however, try to react in a discretionary manner. For example, if the ELR pool grew a great deal, the government could cut taxes or increase spending on other programmes to shrink the ELR pool; when the pool shrinks beyond some point, the government could increase taxes or reduce non-ELR spending to increase the size of the pool. Such activity could attempt to achieve a degree of stability that non-discretionary ELR policy alone could not achieve.

In a sense, the 'real' value of the currency will also will be constantly changing as the average productivity of the pool of BPSE workers changes. The pool will tend to contain the least productive workers. When private demand rises, the average productivity of the workers obtained by the government through the ELR programme will fall as private employers bid away the most productive BPSE workers; when private demand falls, the average productivity of the BPSE workers rises. Thus the quality of workers obtained by the government for the BPSW (for example, $12 500 per year) will continually fluctuate at the margin, causing the average quality to fluctuate. In this sense, the exchange rate between the dollar and the quality-adjusted labour available to the government (and to private employers) will vary over the course of the business cycle. From the perspective of firms, when aggregate demand is low, high-quality labour can be obtained from the BPSE pool at a mark-up over the BPSW; on the other hand, when aggregate demand is high, the marginal BPSE worker will have relatively low productivity. It is this fluctuating 'marginal productivity' of BPSE workers that helps to act as an automatic stabilizer because hiring is encouraged when demand is low and discouraged when demand is high.

Another way of looking at it is to argue that when aggregate demand is low, the value of the currency is high because quality-adjusted labour is cheap; when demand is high, the value of the currency is low because productivity of the marginal BPSE worker is low. It is possible that aggregate demand could become so high that the only workers left in the ELR pool are those whose productivity is zero or even negative (that is, the net cost is higher to put them to work than it would be to pay them the BPSW to stay at home). In this case, on the margin the value of the currency approaches zero in terms of the value of the workers that can be employed. Long before this point, the government should reduce non-ELR spending and/or increase taxes to replenish the pool and stabilize the value of the currency.

Note how existence of ELR will allow the government to react in a sensible manner to the threat of unemployment caused by 'downsizing', labour-saving technological advancement, or labour-displacing imports. Currently, when labour is displaced through any of these mechanisms, there is pressure on government to step in to try to prevent unemployment. For example, the government might be asked to make it more difficult for firms to lay off employees (whether due to technological advance or foreign competition). However, once ELR is in place, displaced workers can always find BPSE jobs, so the ELR pool grows as workers are displaced.

Of course, it is likely that ELR jobs pay less than the lost jobs. On the one hand, it can be argued that the social benefits of technological advance (or cheap imports) must exceed the private costs of moving from private sector employment to BPSE. On the other, one could argue that this ignores the social cost of loss of aggregate demand (as discussed above, replacing a $40 000 a year job with a $12500 a year job lowers aggregate demand), which could exert deflationary pressure on the economy. However, the government can react to this through discretionary tax cuts and non-ELR spending increases to shrink the pool. This means that the population as a whole benefits twice: first from technological advance or cheaper imports, and second from tax cuts or spending increases.

Perhaps 'free trade' and the possibility of trade deficits would not be perceived as so detrimental once ELR is implemented: a trade deficit would merely indicate that the population could enjoy 'Toyotas' in exchange for pieces of paper, and could get a tax cut on top of that. It would be hoped, of course, that the tax cut and/or spending increase would then encourage the private sector to create new jobs to replace those lost to foreign imports. If that is the case, and if ELR employment can prepare displaced workers for those new jobs, then it need not be the case that even the displaced workers would be worse off.[40]

OTHER ISSUES

Before concluding this chapter, let us examine several objections that have been raised to the ELR programme.

It will be impossible to administer the programme due to incompetence, corruption, racism, and opposition. Clearly, this is a significant problem; are there administrators today as capable as those who administered the New Deal?[41] There is a real danger that ELR jobs will be allocated in a discriminatory manner, with females and minorities allocated to the least desirable jobs. On the other hand, there is no reason to believe that the current social welfare system is free of corruption and discrimination. A civilized society must face up to and deal with these problems. We can suggest several possibilities. First, the existing unemployment programme administration might be used to administer an ELR programme. Alternatively, administration could 'devolve' to the state and local government level. The federal government would simply provide as much funding as necessary to let every state and local government hire as many new employees as they desired, with only two constraints: these jobs could not replace current employment, and they could pay only the BPSW (or, at least, the federal government would reimburse wages only at the BPSW rate). Finally, a similar offer could be made to qualifying non-governmental non-profit organizations, such as AmeriCorps, VISTA, the Student Community Service Program, the National Senior Service Corps, the Peace Corps, the National Health Service Corps, school districts, and Meals on Wheels.

ELR employment will consist of nothing but 'make-work' jobs, like the Works Progress Administration (WPA) before it. As we move farther from the 1930s, Americans seem to have forgotten the contributions made by WPA. WPA workers

> not only built or reconstructed 617,000 miles of roads, 124,000 bridges and viaducts, and 120,000 public buildings; they also left the nation with thousands of new parks, playgrounds, and athletic fields. Moreover, they drained malarial swamps, exterminated rats in slums, organized nursery schools, and taught illiterate adults to read and write. Unemployed actors set up theaters throughout the land, often performing in remote towns and backwoods areas. WPA orchestras gave 6,000 live concerts. WPA artists produced murals, sculptures, and paintings that still adorn our public buildings. Even though it was a means-tested relief program, WPA helped sustain the talent of artists like Jackson Pollock, Ben Shahn, and Willem de Kooning, and of writers like Saul Bellow, Studs Terkel, and Richard Wright – as well as the dignity of millions of other

people who would otherwise have been forced to remain idle (Ginsburg 1983, p. 11).

On one hand, it can be argued that the 1930s were special because so many talented people were unemployed; on the other, there is no reason to suppose that there are no Studs Terkels or Hyman Minskys (another WPA employee, who estimated Cobb-Douglas production functions on the government payroll) among today's unemployed. Further, ELR is specifically designed such that the most talented and productive will work their way out of ELR. It is through productive activity that the talented will prove to potential employers that they are indeed productive. Finally, in the worst case, ELR workers must at least 'sell' their time in exchange for dollars, which many Americans might find preferable to 'welfare'. We can attempt, however, to describe some of the jobs that ELR workers might undertake; to minimize impacts on the private sector, we probably would want to undertake activities that are not currently undertaken by profit-seeking firms, nor would we want to take job prospects away from the currently employed. Possible ELR jobs include:

- *Companion*   ELR workers could serve as companions to the elderly, engaging in conversation, playing games, and perhaps helping with light chores. Each companion would also attend classes or seminars in care-giving, and perhaps also attend daily group discussions with other ELR companions. Their training would make them employable in a wide variety of private sector jobs that provide care. Companions could also be assigned to non-elderly people: orphans, the bedridden, and the mentally or physically disabled.

- *Public school classroom assistant*   ELR workers could be assigned to public school classrooms (and also to Headstart and preschool programmes), acting as reading, writing, and maths tutors, and to help in recreational and artistic activities. ELR workers could be very valuable in classrooms with children whose first language is not English. In addition, ELR workers could take classes and seminars, earning high school diplomas and advanced degrees to better prepare them for the workplace.

- *Safety monitor*   ELR workers could be assigned to public school grounds, areas surrounding schools, and perhaps other areas (such as playgrounds, subway stations, street intersections, or shopping centres) to help maintain safety through video monitoring, and by serving as crossing guards and hallway monitors.

- *Neighbourhood cleanup/Highway cleanup engineers* ELR workers could help to clean-up playgrounds, parks, sidewalks, squares, streets, and abandoned property.

- *Low-income housing restoration engineers* ELR workers could engage in 'Habitat for Humanity' type low-income housing restoration.

- *Day care assistants for children of ELR workers* To promote welfare to work programmes, a tremendous increase in the number of low-cost day care centres will be required. ELR workers can be assigned to such centres; some ELR workers might want to start their own centres.

- *Library assistants* ELR workers could help in libraries, perhaps alleviating the pressure to reduce hours and services offered. New programmes could be started by ELR workers, such as 'story time', musical performances, and arts and crafts activities for children.

- *Environmental safety monitors* There are a wide variety of tasks in the environmental safety area that could be assigned to ELR workers. For example, ELR workers could test for lead paint in low-income communities; they could be trained to test water safety (public water supply, public beaches, public swimming pools); they could help in removal of some types of environmental contamination; and they could help in fire detection and prevention (for example, in national parks).

- *ELR artist or musician* Just as the WPA employed artists and musicians, the existence of the ELR programme would be a good way to directly and to indirectly promote the 'arts'. ELR artists could paint murals, participate in community art projects celebrating local people, culture and traditions; or they could perform in ELR bands.

- *Community or cultural historian* ELR workers could record elders' stories, collect historical records, and write histories of communities.

Obviously, this list is not meant to be definitive, but is only to suggest that there are many jobs that could be done by ELR workers. We have not listed the more 'obvious' jobs, such as restoration of public infrastructure (patching holes in city streets, repairing dangerous bridges), provision of new infrastructure (highway construction, new sewage treatment plants), and expansion of public services (new recycling programmes) that should be carefully considered because they might reduce private costs and increase private profitability. These are types of social spending that should be done even without an ELR programme, and that might be better accomplished by non-ELR (including unionized) workers. However, it should be noted that WPA employees did indeed engage in this sort of work.

States are already implementing welfare to work programmes; why is ELR needed?   State governments cannot run continuous deficits; most state constitutions prevent deficits, and only the federal government can 'create money' to finance deficits. When an economy is expanding so that state tax revenues are rising and unemployment levels are falling, welfare to work can meet with at least some success (although states like Wisconsin admit that 'work' costs the state *more* than 'welfare' does). However, when the economy heads into a recession, and, thus, precisely when ELR is most needed, states will find unemployment rates rising, welfare rolls rising, and tax revenues falling. They will not be able to expand spending as it is required to provide jobs for the newly unemployed. Only the federal government can finance an ELR programme in the worst of times. Many of the other benefits arising from a nationwide ELR programme that were discussed in this chapter are not likely to be generated by current state programmes. For example, the ELR programme provides a pool of workers who are available for private hire at a mark-up over the known BPSW; state programmes often subsidize private employment and can generate obvious incentive problems (firms use subsidized labour to displace current employees; firms lay off employees as soon as subsidies run out). As state programmes vary, there is no uniform 'package' of wages and benefits received by those in the welfare to work programmes. Further, states have no intention of offering a permanent job to those leaving welfare; they deny any longterm responsibility for taking care of the indigent – indeed, that is nearly a guiding principle of the welfare to work experiment. The ELR programme would offer the promise that in the worst case scenario, one could have a life-time of ELR work. While it is not a goal of ELR to retain any employee for life, there is the possibility that some individuals will never obtain private employment, and, at the very least, ELR will force them to sell their time to obtain income. However, none of this precludes *administration* at the local level.

What can be done with belligerent/anti-social/lazy ELR workers?   ELR will require that one show up for work more or less on time; beyond that, requirements would have to be made almost on a case-by-case arrangement. Some workers may be difficult: they could be racist or sexist; they could be lazy; they could refuse to follow directions; and they might be emotionally unstable. Anti-social workers can be given jobs that require a minimal amount of interaction; in extreme cases, some workers might work alone at home (sorting envelopes; working on a computer). Discipline would be maintained *primarily* by the promise of promotion to more desirable ELR jobs, and, eventually, to private sector employment. In the worst case, some workers might be so irresponsible that their employment would be day-by-day, or even hour-by-hour with a cash payment for a specified amount of time spent on the job. Again, in extreme cases it is likely that 'narrow economic efficiency' would dictate that it would be more efficient to simply provide hand-outs; however, some efficiency might be sacrificed to the principle that income should come from work. As discussed, ELR workers could be fired from their jobs for just cause; there could be conditions placed on re-hiring (for example, the fired worker might have to wait for 3 days – without pay – before re-hiring; the penalty could be increased for subsequent firings). In extreme cases, some individuals may not be allowed to work in a BPSE job; BPSE cannot provide income for all the needy.

What about people who are unable to work? ELR cannot replace all social spending. Leaving aside those who are unable to work due to disabilities, some will not be able to work due to family responsibilities, low skills, or other such reasons. As a society, we might decide that single mothers with young children should be able to choose to stay home; their ELR 'job' would be to care for their children. More generally, it might make sense to train (or retrain) some workers rather than to put them into unskilled jobs; their ELR 'job' would be to attend school or an apprenticeship programme. Some individuals, as mentioned above, might not be employable because of behavioural problems.

What effect will ELR have on unions? In general, the effect of ELR on union workers should not be clearly positive or negative. On one hand, ELR removes the fear or threat of unemployment, which is often said to be an important disciplinary method used by firms against workers. It also establishes a true, universal minimum wage – below which wages will not fall. It still permits unions to negotiate benefits with employers – such as unemployment compensation (so that although there might not be any federal unemployment compensation, workers could still negotiate privately -supplied benefits). ELR could include a package of benefits, including health care. This would then set the lowest standard (and could, for example, lead to universal health care). On the other hand, the ELR pool will also dampen wage (and benefit) demands of non-ELR workers as employers will have the alternative of hiring from the ELR pool. Thus, it is not clear that ELR is biased in favour of workers or employers.

Will participation in BPSE lead to stigmatization? If ELR takes only those workers the private sector 'doesn't want', then participation in BPSE might be seen as a negative indication of character, education, or skill level, much as participation in 'welfare' stigmatizes a person. This is a danger, but the danger can be reduced through creative action. For example, ELR can be promoted as a universal 'AmeriCorps' service, open to all who would like to perform community service (unlike the current AmeriCorps programme, which limits the number of participants). We could institute a national service requirement, much as many countries require military service or national service. Alternatively, we can rely on persuasion: universities could favour applications from prospective students who have served for a year in an ELR position; or they might offer 'junior year programmes' in ELR as an alternative to 'junior year abroad' programmes. Corporations could allow leaves of absence to professionals and executives to work in the ELR programme as a community service. Retired executives, professionals, and politicians could serve in the ELR programme (much as they now serve with President Carter in Habitat for Humanity). ELR might even provide for some part-time positions (perhaps even unpaid) for volunteers who would like to perform community service without giving up other employment. It is possible that ELR service could come to be seen as an advantage on the résumé, rather than as a stigma.

What if the Fed or financial markets react negatively?   Implementation of an ELR programme might cause a reaction by financial markets because they come to expect that the deficit will crowd out investment and cause inflation, or, more likely, because they expect the Fed to react by raising interest rates. Note that if the Fed did raise interest rates and if this slowed the private sector, this would only increase ELR employment. In other words, the Fed would no longer be able to fight fiscal policy by causing unemployment, but would only be able to reduce private sector employment and raise government sector employment. In response, the appropriate fiscal policy would be to increase non-ELR spending or to reduce taxes. While it would be far preferable to coordinate monetary and fiscal policy, at least with ELR in place, the Fed could not raise unemployment. It would be hoped that the private sector would place pressure on the Fed to relax policy because it would be obvious that the tight monetary policy only hurts the private sector and increases the size of government.

Why worry now, when US unemployment is lower than it has been for a generation?   Many pundits have proclaimed that we have entered a 'new age' with the 'new economy'; it is claimed that things 'have never been better'. If true, this means that the best that can be expected is a situation in which six and a half million are unemployed and millions more work fewer hours than desired or are forced to patch together several jobs. It also means that welfare to work programmes are doomed to fail because the best that can be done is to redistribute jobs, still leaving millions unemployed. Finally, it means that price stability can only be obtained at the cost of millions of unemployed and many millions more out of the labour force.[42]

Indeed, as shown in Pigeon and Wray (1998), even after the long Clinton-era expansion in the US, there has been very little improvement in job opportunities for the half of the population that has not attended college.[43] Between 1992 and mid 1998, for example, of the 11.6 million net jobs created, 10.9 million of them went to workers with at least some college education – leaving only 700,000 new jobs for the bottom half of the population that did not attend college. In other words, economic expansions promote 'hiring off the top' and do little to increase opportunities for those at the bottom unless demand is so great that it induces wage inflation for the highly skilled sufficient to cause employers to 'hire off the bottom'. This is why economic expansions are likely to cause inflation before full employment is reached.

The Pigeon and Wray study also shows that the official unemployment rate does not give a good indication of the degree of labour market tightness, especially for the bottom half of the population, because flows among employment, unemployment and out-of-the-labour-force categories are large. Even at the business cycle peak, the labour force participation rates of those who did not attend college are significantly lower than participation rates of those who attended college.[44] Indeed, if all educational attainment groups were to achieve the labour force participation rate achieved by college graduates, more than 26 million additional workers over age 24 would be in the labour market. The ELR programme will 'hire off the bottom', taking those the private sector does not want to hire. It will then provide them with work experience and training that will make at least some of them attractive to the private sector. This is why ELR can achieve full employment without inflation, and, indeed, is likely to reduce inflationary pressures. As we have discussed previously, it is difficult to estimate how many will accept ELR employment, but we suspect that many ELR workers will come from among the more than 26 million identified in the Wray and Pigeon study as 'potentially employable' – the vast majority of whom have not attended college and are currently out of the labour force.

CONCLUSION

The main issues examined in this chapter concern the desirability and feasibility of an ELR programme. The ELR programme is desired because (1) a more or less free market system does not, and perhaps cannot, continuously generate true full employment; (2) no civilized, and wealthy, society can allow a portion of its population to go without adequate food, clothing and shelter; and (3) our society places a high value on work as the means through which most individuals should obtain a livelihood. ELR policy cannot resolve all social problems. ELR cannot even replace all transfer spending. Some individuals will not be able to work in an ELR programme. Some individuals will not be willing to work. However, ELR will ensure that all of those willing and able to work at the BPSW will be able to obtain a job by selling their time to the government at the BPSW.

Indeed, 'ability' should be defined as broadly as possible to include virtually all those who are willing to work. There is no reason to impose a narrow 'efficiency' standard to ensure 'productivity' above the BPSW. Any production will normally be better than no production;[45] if one begins with the belief that even the unproductive must be supported, then the state will have to provide income whether or not they work. Generally, it will be better to have someone working. In many cases, the 'net product' may well be negative from a narrow economic standpoint because supervision, capital investments and personal services required to put some people to work (for example, to employ severely disabled people) could greatly exceed the economic value of output. However, a rich society can afford inefficiencies, and the non-economic benefits of work can offset at least some of the economic costs.

ELR intervention is feasible. The modern government does not face 'financial constraints' because anything for sale in terms of the domestic currency can be had by delivering fiat money. Neither taxes nor bonds 'finance' spending. However, the government faces 'real' constraints to the extent that it can purchase only that which is for sale. Involuntarily unemployed labour is, by definition, for sale.

Finally, we have argued that ELR operates like a buffer stock to stabilize prices. As we argued in previous chapters, government can use its monopoly over currency issue exogenously to set the price of anything it buys. In this chapter, we have outlined an exogenous pricing scheme in which government stabilizes the price of that commodity used in its buffer stock scheme. Indeed, we can view zero unemployment as a consequence of a buffer stock price stabilization scheme. Just as the gold standard generated full employment of gold, a labour 'standard' or buffer stock programme will generate full employment of labour.

NOTES

1. Most economists and policymakers do acknowledge the possibility that 'NAIRU' (the 'non-accelerating inflation rate of unemployment') can be variable. But, as Gregory Mankiw insists, 'Life is full of tradeoffs. Consumers trade off spending today against saving for tomorrow. Congress trades off tax cuts against deficit reduction. And the Federal Reserve trades off inflation against unemployment' (Mankiw, 1977, p. 36).

2. Below we will note that 'zero unemployment' does not mean that all who would like to work are indeed working. For example, there could still be 'frictional' unemployment, with some choosing to remain unemployed as they search for better-paying jobs; there would also be many who would like to work, but are not willing to work for the 'going wage' they are able to obtain.

3. See Cavanaugh (1996) for an examination of the 'myths' associated with government deficit spending.

4. Most of these topics are dealt with in more detail below, or in Wray (1997).

5. For example, any ELR employer could dismiss a worker for cause; after the second such dismissal, the worker would have to wait three days before being rehired, with the wait increasing for each subsequent firing. After some point, say, the fifth dismissal, the worker would become ineligible for ELR employment and would have to rely on another income source. ELR employers would have available to them any and all disciplinary methods legally available to private sector employees, including the right to fire employees.

6. It is legitimate to wonder whether government can handle the task of employing perhaps as many as 8 million persons in an ELR programme. As discussed below and in Wray (1997), it is only necessary that the federal government provide the funding, and not the administration, for the programme. The programme could be highly decentralized, with the federal government providing funding to allow all local and state governments to hire (and administer, equip and supervise) as many ELR workers as desired; this arrangement could be extended to not-for-profit organizations as well. Duties at the federal government level might be kept to record-keeping and some programme evaluation. It must be noted, in any case, that the current unemployment compensation programme requires administration (much of which is decentralized to some degree) which could be diverted to the ELR programme.

7. We will retain Minsky's terminology, calling this the employer of last resort policy. In some respects this may not be the best title for such a programme, as calling it 'last resort' will perpetuate the notion that there is something wrong with workers in the programme. A better, and perhaps more accurate, term would be 'buffer stock employment' – as discussed below, ELR will operate much like any buffer stock programme. However, again, workers in the programme would probably not enjoy being viewed as a buffer stock. When the time comes to write up this proposal for purposes of legislation, it will probably be best to come up with a better name for the programme, such as 'basic public sector employment (BPSE)', 'inflation-fighting employment programme (IFEP)', 'currency stabilization jobs programme (CSJP)' or the 'full employment and price stability programme (FEAPS)'.

8. The preferred strategy is to prohibit use of the ELR programme as a means of replacing existing workers, many of whom receive a wage above the likely BPSW. An alternative would be to allow replacement; this would reduce the costs associated with providing government services (which some would find desirable), but would also generate deflationary pressures on the economy (since higher-paying jobs would be replaced with BPSW-paid workers). This could be compensated by a tax cut or spending increase (to try to 'reflate' the economy). It is probably more politically feasible to prohibit replacement of existing workers. We are purposely avoiding political issues in this book. As discussed below and in Wray (1997) it is not clear that an ELR programme strengthens the hand of labour at the expense of employers, nor vice versa. On one hand, workers obtain greater security because unemployment is eliminated, but on the other, employers can always hire

from the ELR pool. Wage pressures may be reduced; however, an effective, universal, minimum wage is put into place. Finally, depending on the political consensus, ELR could provide a path to universal health care and child care since private firms would have to match the benefits package provided in ELR employment. See Wray (1997) and the discussion below.

9.   It is probable that neither of these assumptions will be correct, of course. It is difficult to expect that people will work full-time for less than a 'living wage'; however, the current US minimum wage is probably below a 'living wage' for most minimum wage workers. The current minimum wage must be supplemented with food stamps, other social spending, private charity, tax breaks (such as the earned income tax credit) or a second job. If the BPSW is set equal to the minimum wage, then 'disruptions' to the private sector caused by ELR might be reduced – see below. If we are to be serious about replacing 'welfare' with 'work', then the minimum wage (and the BPSW) must be a 'living wage', and should be supplemented with the requisite benefits (health care, child care and retirement).

10.   In contrast to the current 'unemployment compensation' system (which might encourage at least some of the unemployed to 'take a vacation at the government's expense'), ELR can require that the six weeks will be spent doing specific full-time search activities (reporting to an office to make phone calls, prepare a 'cv', attend job interviews, obtain job search training, and so on). An even less extreme change would be to retain the current unemployment compensation programme and to supplement it with ELR. Thus those not covered by unemployment benefits (more than half the officially unemployed typically do not qualify) could immediately find work in the ELR programme (which could include a period of job search), while those covered by unemployment compensation could receive unemployment benefits while searching, but could at any point choose to join the ELR programme.

11.   While the finance of the ELR programme must come from the federal government, administration can be decentralized. It is possible that some parts of the programme, such as the job training elements, might be subcontracted to private firms. Other parts could be run by not-for-profit charities (for example, BPSE jobs that refurbish low-income housing could be administered by Habitat for Humanity). Still others could be administered by state and local government. See Wray (1997). Note that in this chapter we will not attempt to provide a detailed discussion of the types of jobs that might be included in ELR. (Again, see Wray, 1997.) These matters are of secondary consideration. As Keynes remarked in 'Can Lloyd George Do It?' in response to those who argued that there were not enough things to do to find places for all the unemployed after WWI, 'As soon as we have a new atmosphere of *doing things*, instead of one of smothering negation, everybody's brains will get busy, and there will be masses of claimants for attention, the precise character of which it would be impossible to specify beforehand' (Keynes, 1972, p. 99).

12.   Currently, unemployment compensation is based on earnings before job loss. We propose that under ELR, all workers receive the same wage. We believe this is justified for several reasons. First, highly paid workers who lose their jobs have had greater opportunity to accumulate savings and net wealth. Second, eight hours of job search should be 'worth' the same amount, regardless of the previous income. And most importantly – as discussed below – the strength of our proposal is the price stability imparted by the 'pool' of ELR workers who can be obtained at a fixed, known, wage. When private markets are depressed, highly productive workers can be obtained from the ELR pool at a mark-up over the BPSW – encouraging private employment and thereby stimulating demand. If highly productive workers were paid higher BPSW, they would become more costly to the private sector, depressing the incentive to hire them out of the pool. See below.

13.   The Personal Responsibility and Work Opportunity Reconciliation Act of 1996 replaced AFDC with increased work requirements ('workfare') and imposed strict time limits. In addition, time limits and work requirements were imposed on the food stamp program. Thus, it is now much more difficult to obtain 'welfare' without working. Note, also, that the US

has never had a program titled 'welfare'; rather, this term applies to a variety of federal programs (AFDC, Medicaid, food stamps, unemployment compensation – most of which also involved state administration and funding) and state programs (general assistance) that have varying requirements.

14. An ELR programme could also provide a path to de facto universal health care coverage. If the BPSE compensation included health care benefits, then private sector jobs would also have to provide health care benefits (or a salary sufficient to induce workers to forego such coverage). ELR does not have to include such benefits, and our calculations below will not include costs of such benefits, but this would be one way to induce firms to provide health care benefits without actually mandating that they do so. Note that adding health care benefits to ELR will probably not generate much additional federal spending as it will reduce spending on other federal programmes such as Medicaid and Medicare. As the sick are generally treated (one way or another) anyway, adding health care benefits to all jobs probably will not increase the portion of US GDP devoted to health care (which is already the highest in the world). However, there are expensive ways and cheaper ways to provide health care, and it is beyond the scope of this chapter to examine such issues.

15. It is difficult to calculate how many individuals would be willing to accept BPSE; in addition to those who are currently counted as unemployed, many people now out of the labour force would accept a job. In addition, many part-time workers (and probably some individuals who hold more than one job) would accept a full-time BPSE job. Immigrants (including illegal immigrants) as well as individuals currently working in the underground economy might also add to the supply seeking ELR work. We have included only wage costs for the estimated 8 million workers. In addition, as discussed above, ELR might include health care costs or other benefits; this would add to costs (health care benefits could nearly double programme costs), but would also substantially reduce health care costs of current programmes, such as Medicare and Medicaid. There would also be administrative costs of the programme; on the other hand, if ELR replaces unemployment compensation, we should include savings of administrative costs of the unemployment insurance programme. Furthermore, if administration is highly decentralized, costs to the federal government would be reduced. For example, if the federal government allows all non-profit organizations to hire as many ELR workers as desired (with the government paying wages of $6.25 per hour), these would then be expected to cover any associated administrative costs. Finally, there would be 'capital' costs – ELR workers would need equipment, office supplies, uniforms, and so on. Of course, spending on such items would increase private demand through the multiplier, increasing private sector employment and reducing the number of BPSE jobs.

16. Of course, ELR should also have a 'multiplier effect' because BPSE income would raise aggregate demand and stimulate private employment. This, in turn, would raise tax revenues and lower government spending (the effect on non-ELR government spending might be quite small once ELR is in place since there would be fewer on social assistance who might be induced into the labour force; however, ELR spending would decline since BPSE would fall almost on a one-for-one basis as private jobs are created).

17. This is calculated as 8 million employed in ELR at $12 500 each ($100 billion) minus savings of $50 billion in unemployment compensation and savings of up to $25 billion for AFDC, food stamps, EITC and other 'welfare' programmes. Gordon (1997) has proposed a similar ELR-type programme and estimated the net cost at $39–$41 billion. He also assumed that the programme would employ 8 million. The $39 billion figure was obtained by assuming workers would be paid $4.75 per hour (leading to a total cost of $79 billion), but then subtracting $40 billion of unemployment compensation. The $41 billion figure was obtained by assuming each ELR family earned an income equal to the poverty threshold (adjusting the wage by the number of family members, and compensating for number of family members in the labour force); again, the only savings presumed were the $40 billion of unemployment compensation. Harvey (1989) had calculated the cost of a job guarantee

programme for 1986 at $28.6 billion.

18. A recent study has found that gang violence is more highly correlated with unemployment rates than with other variables commonly thought to be linked to crime, such as age, race, education level or single parent families. As Epstein (1997) reports, nearly 1 out of 50 men of working age are currently in prison (a total of 1.5 million people are in prison, most of whom are men). The unemployment rate for male high school dropouts has risen from 5 per cent in 1973 to 11 per cent in 1996; at the same time their labour force participation rate has fallen from 86 per cent to 74 per cent. High unemployment rates and low labour force participation rates probably result at least in part from actual or perceived diminished job opportunities for this group; if nothing else, 'idleness' creates an environment that might encourage crime. If all the costs of unemployment could be calculated (including social and private costs), it is likely that an ELR programme could 'pay for itself' by reducing these costs.

19. Where net nominal saving (*Sn*) is defined as in Chapter 4 as accumulation of 'outside' financial wealth (government or foreign debt) – or is defined as saving which remains after netting the increase of private sector financial liabilities from private sector financial assets. Note that the late Nobel Prize winner William Vickrey had a similar argument, and a similar definition of net nominal saving. He believed that the excessive desired net nominal saving of the population of modern capitalist economies prevents movement toward full employment of resources. He argued that the deficit must be increased precisely because the private sector desired to save too much, and the deficit would provide the 'wherewithall' for private sector savings (see Vickrey (1997)).

20. This would result in higher net nominal saving of firms, in the form of profits, since saving cannot be reduced by increasing consumption.

21. Of course, this presumes that other types of government spending are not excessively increased – as would be likely in the event of a major war. During a war as large as WWII, BPSE would fall toward zero, but deficit spending on the war effort could be so large as to push the economy well beyond full employment, causing accelerating inflation. Other policies might be required to prevent inflation in this case, just as they were during WWII.

22. It is possible that in an economy comprised of monopolistic or oligopolistic market structure, any increase of demand enables monopolists and oligopolists to increase their prices even before full employment is reached. Thus if ELR raises aggregate demand, some price increase (or inflation) follows. In this case, however, inflation results not because ELR has driven the economy beyond full employment (or increased the deficit beyond the level of desired net saving) but rather because the existing market structure allows firms to increase prices when demand increases regardless of the degree of excess capacity. The question in this case is what sort of programme can raise employment and aggregate demand with the smallest potential for generating inflation. Note also that the government can attempt to avoid contributing to bottlenecks through countercyclical spending on capital (tools, equipment, uniforms) for ELR workers, selectively increasing such orders when private demand is low (and, if necessary, stockpiling the capital) and reducing spending when private demand is high. As Forstater (1998) argues, the government can also alter the capital/labour ratio as necessary to reduce bottlenecks – using a high capital/labour ratio when private demand for output of the capital goods sector is low, or labour-intensive techniques when private demand for capital goods is high. To give an example, when private sector orders for trash collection equipment are high, the government favours labour-intensive methods of roadway clean-up.

23. We do not mean to imply that government can arbitrarily set the BPSW anywhere it likes. It must consider existing wages, including the minimum wage, existing welfare benefits, and an estimate of the living wage. It must also weigh political factors, such as relative strength of unions. Finally, it must consider its exchange-rate-adjusted relative wage (although global competitiveness will have played a role in determining wages and/or exchange rates before implementation of ELR). If the government sets the BPSW too high relative to the

exchange-rate-adjusted employment costs of its foreign competitors, there are likely to be impacts on the exchange rate.

24. Exactly how big the jump will be will depend on the setting of the BPSW. If this is set at a living wage, the jump, in turn, will depend on the current gap between a living wage and low wages actually paid. 'Living wage' will in turn depend on circumstances: the living wage of a single parent with children is much higher than is that of a young worker who lives with her parents. Gordon (1997) has outlined an ELR-type programme that allows for differential incomes, depending on family size. We do not support that feature as it reduces the price-stabilizing aspects of the programme.

25. If BPSE includes benefits, such as health care, that low-wage private sector jobs normally do not include, then impacts will be larger as employers will have to increase private sector benefits to 'compete' with the BPSE.

26. Of course, workers in the ELR pool are not 'perfect substitutes' for non-BPSE workers; they might have to be trained and still may never reach the same skill level. Workers who are 'unique' (due to particular skills or knowledge; for example, Barry Bonds) may not face a realistic threat of replacement by ELR workers; these enjoy a monopsonistic bargaining position (just as they do before implementation of ELR). In other cases, imperfect substitution can be partially alleviated through capital substitution (an ELR worker plus capital investment might be more cost-effective than paying higher wages to an existing worker). In cases where ELR workers are perfect substitutes, then non-BPSE wages will approximate the BPSW unless public policy or bargaining agreements establish higher wages.

27. In any case, some recent literature suggests that wages are determined by the employed, while the unemployed are 'outsiders' who have little influence over wages. With an ELR in place, however, those in the pool become 'insiders' who provide an effective means of influencing wage determination.

28. One could say that Keynesian policies tend to induce hiring 'off the top', by stimulating private demand sufficiently that firms will try to hire the most qualified workers. As aggregate demand is stimulated, firms attempt to bid employed workers away from other firms, as well as attempting to induce unemployed workers into the labour force. It is not surprising that very high levels of aggregate demand are required to induce firms to hire the least skilled and otherwise least desirable workers, and that this is accomplished only after wages of more desirable workers have been bid up. On the other hand, ELR attains full employment by hiring 'off the bottom' – taking those workers who are not desired by private employers – and then trying to make these workers more desirable to the private sector (as they gain experience and training).

29. We do not necessarily endorse this view, at least for the case of the US – which almost never operated so close to full capacity that labour markets would have been sufficiently tight to induce inflation.

30. See Mitchell (1997) for presentation of an ELR style proposal as a buffer stock programme.

31. For all commodities other than labour, it is more accurate to say that it is owned. Thus if the government operates a buffer stock programme for a commodity (say wheat), anyone with undesired inventory can always sell it to the government at a fixed price. Note also that we are referring only to government buffer stock schemes; any private scheme is undertaken on the expectation of making profit, usually by cornering the market to reap gains from rising prices.

32. Note that under a gold standard, the money price of gold is generally set above its value in alternative uses; this is to ensure that it remains monetized, rather than being melted for alternative use. This does not mean, however, that all gold would flow to government, for hoards of gold protected hoarders against the possibility of debasement of the currency (raising the money value of gold).

33. As we argued in Chapter 3 above, however, it was primarily the tight fiscal policy during the nineteenth century that stabilized prices, and not the gold standard.

34. However, it would be possible to appreciate the currency by setting the BPSW below the current cost of hiring unemployed labour – say at $5000 per year, and it is possible that BPSE could increase potential output sufficiently that the currency would be revalued even if the BPSW were set at the prevailing minimum wage.

35. If we are correct in arguing that the ELR pool operates much like a buffer stock policy (for example, a gold standard), then the claims for the price-stabilizing feature of this proposal are strengthened.

36. We emphasize, again, the possibility that an ELR policy might raise productivity and 'aggregate supply' sufficiently that no price increase occurs; even as BPSW is raised over time, so long as this only keeps pace with productivity increases, prices may not rise.

37. This does not mean there is no 'real' constraint: any government is constrained by the potential output (of course, in an open economy, a government is not constrained by domestic potential output, unless its currency is unacceptable abroad).

38. Defined, as above, as a situation in which anyone willing, ready and able to work at the BPSW has a job.

39. This could be restated as a 'two-price problem': if the government tries to fix both the BPSW and the price of gold, market forces can cause the relative price of gold and ELR workers to change. It is difficult simultaneously to pursue a 'gold standard' and an 'ELR standard' (or even a silver standard, as the US discovered while on a bi-metal standard). While a government can maintain two buffer stocks simultaneously, it cannot simultaneously peg the value of its currency to two standards unless their relative prices remain fixed.

40. Admittedly, it is impossible to guarantee that this would be the case. We must weigh the benefits received by the vast majority of the population against the losses incurred by the relatively small number of displaced workers; other policies can be targeted to these workers to minimize their loss.

41. No case of fraud in administration of the New Deal's work programs was ever uncovered.

42. Pundits are revising downward estimates of the number of unemployed required to maintain price stability; not long ago, it was believed that NAIRU was well over 6 percent, perhaps even 7 percent, meaning that perhaps 10 million unemployed might be necessary to achieve price stability. However, because unemployment has dipped below 5 percent – with no acceleration of inflation – some now believe that we can accept a situation in which perhaps 6.5 million are officially unemployed.

43. In the US, of the 25 years and older population, 25 percent has graduated from college, another 25 percent has attended (but not graduated from) college, 33 percent has graduated from high school (but not attended college), and 17 percent has not completed high school.

44. The employment-to-population ratio in mid 1998 was 79 percent for college graduates, 72 percent for those with some college, 63 percent for high school graduates, and less than 40 percent for high school dropouts.

45. As Keynes noted, there is no need to justify all government employment in terms of what is 'profitable' employment (Keynes, 1980, p. 270). See Wray (1997) for further discussion of possible ELR jobs.

7 The Logic of the Taxes-Drive-Money View

This chapter will create a simple, hypothetical 'model' to demonstrate the logical basis of claims previously made in this book. To call this a 'model' may be overly pretentious, and might scare some readers, so some assurance may be required. No higher maths will be used! Rather, by 'model' we mean to imply that we use a highly stylistic approach whereby we focus only on features of the economy with which we are immediately concerned. We will begin with the simplest sort of economy, in which there is a self-sufficient population that has no government, no money and no markets. We then introduce government, money and taxes in the most straightforward manner. We gradually build the argument until we obtain the main features of our modern economy: a central bank, required reserves, fiscal and monetary operations of the government, and a private banking system through which most transactions are conducted. We conclude with our main policy proposal, which generates full employment and enhances price stability through creation of a labour buffer stock. While this present chapter is not meant to present a 'history' of the evolution from primitive times to the present, the development here actually does seem to accord in a general way with historical evidence.

THE SIMPLE ECONOMY

Assume a very simple economy in which households are self-sufficient, using neither markets nor money. A government is formed which would like to undertake several needed projects for the benefit of the population.[1] This requires that the government obtain labour services and raw materials from the population, so it imposes a per capita tax of $1 per week. It realizes, of course, that the population has no dollars with which to pay the tax, so it must at the same time define what is to be done to obtain dollars, and also ensure that the dollars become available. The government prints a fiat (dollar) money, used to buy goods and services from the population, thereby providing the dollars required to pay taxes. It is clear to the government that the tax liability induces the population to provide goods and services in exchange for the dollars; the population needs the money provided by the government in order to pay taxes, while the government does not need the tax revenue in order to spend. Thus the government's purchases are not constrained by its tax revenue. The government uses taxes only to draw forth a supply of goods and services.

Let us assume that, over the initial year, the government plans to run a 'balanced budget', imposing a tax of $1 per week on each of the 100 citizens, and planning to spend $100 during each week, for a total planned (and balanced) budget of $5 200 dollars for the year. Soon, however, the government is likely to begin to find that weekly tax revenues fall short of its spending. On investigation, it finds that some individuals who have been recipients of government spending in excess of their own individual tax liabilities have hoarded some extra dollars; the government also finds that some of the dollars are simply unaccounted for, and presumably have been lost in the wash, eaten by pets or met with other unfortunate ends. Thus the government finds that it is running a deficit, while some of the population cannot meet the tax liability. As the government realizes it does not 'need' the tax revenue, the solution is either to increase spending or to reduce taxes – that is, to accept a government deficit as 'normal'.

At the aggregate level, the maximum the government can hope to collect in the form of taxes is exactly equal to its purchases of goods and services. In other words, the 'best' the government can plan to do is to run a balanced budget; there is no hope of running a surplus because the government cannot possibly collect more than the income it has created as it paid out dollars. Indeed, it is much more likely that tax revenues will fall short of spending. The government's deficit will rise above zero to cover all 'leakages' of dollars (to hoards and unintended loss) so that a persistent deficit is the expected norm. Understanding all of this, the government deficit is not viewed as a terrible thing. So long as the government was obtaining the goods and services it needed to provide the projects it desired, there would be no need to worry about the deficit. Indeed, the deficit could merely be seen as a measure of the population's desire to 'net nominal save' in the form of money (as defined in Chapter 4).

Indeed, the government would not care at all about collecting taxes except that it recognizes that the population is supplying goods and services to the government only to obtain dollars in order to meet tax liabilities. If the government allowed widespread tax evasion, it would thereby reduce its ability to spend – not because of a financing constraint, but because those who are able to evade taxes are also unlikely to want the government's money. Thus diligent enforcement of the tax liabilities is required to ensure that the offer of dollars will be met by an offer of goods and services.[2]

FISCAL PRUDENCE

Over time, it is possible that some of those in our hypothetical economy would 'forget' that the population has no other source of dollars than the government's spending, and that the purpose of the tax is to create a supply of goods and services flowing to the government. Instead they come erroneously to believe that the purpose of the tax is to recoup the costs of spending – that is, they come to believe that taxes 'finance' government spending. These people react to a deficit with horror! Surely deficits are a sign of fiscal imprudence and a path to certain ruin. The frugal household ensures that its receipts are in excess of its expenditures so that it accumulates dollar hoards as net savings.[3] Certainly, no household can run continuous deficits, therefore, it is asserted, no government can do so either. They label those in government 'free spenders', and, let us suppose, run on a campaign of 'fiscal responsibility' and are able to take over the government.

Our new, fiscally responsible, but fundamentally misguided, officials demand spending cuts and tax hikes, scaling back the planned projects. Indeed, they believe that they had better run surpluses for a period to match the deficits that have been incurred in order to retire all the outstanding government debt (the fiat money hoarded or lost by the public). To drive our point home, let us imagine they take one further step. Noting that the population is ageing, they suggest that it might be best to run surpluses even beyond that required to retire the outstanding national debt, perhaps for the next 20 or 30 years in order to accumulate hoards of dollars that might be used when the 'baby boom' retires (to provide nursing homes for the aged, for example). Just as the prudent household accumulates net nominal saving, it is argued, prudent fiscal policy requires accumulation of a social security surplus. Spending is cut and tax liabilities are raised to achieve the surpluses believed to be required.

To their surprise, spending cuts do not improve the budget as tax collections consistently fall below expectations because ever-increasing numbers find dollar receipts too low to meet tax liabilities, forcing them to evade taxes. The government has to confiscate private assets and tries to sell them for tax arrears; however, it finds no buyers. Thus it incarcerates an ever larger portion of the population for tax evasion. The public reacts to fiscal austerity by trying to hoard more dollars on the (rational) belief that dollars will become increasingly difficult to obtain, thus today's hoards reduce the probability of imprisonment tomorrow. The government finds long queues of those offering goods and services to the government, desperately trying to obtain dollars; however, the government cannot 'afford' to purchase the goods and services offered because fiscal prudence requires spending cuts to match the tax shortfall.

Further, the government is unable to accumulate any dollar hoards to provide for the future retirees, leading to much hand-wringing about what is to be done when the baby boom retires. People try to accumulate hoards for individual retirement accounts (in our example, to pay taxes after retirement), but cannot sell goods and services to the government to obtain the dollars to be hoarded. Taxes cannot be paid, the government continues to cut spending, and still the deficit cannot be eliminated until, finally, government spending and tax receipts inexorably reach zero. Our little economy faces a bleak future, indeed. If this does not sound familiar, it should, because the 'fiscal responsibility' party (or its equivalent) is in control of all modern nations.

As our 'free spending' government officials correctly understood, deficits should be the expected norm. It is true that if the government runs a deficit in 'year one', then households can use the accumulated dollars to pay more in taxes in 'year two' than received from government purchases in 'year two'.[4] However, it is obvious that over a run of several years, the balanced budget is the 'best' the government can do, while a persistent deficit is a more likely outcome. Unless no dollars are ever lost or hoarded, the government must, on average, run deficits.

Let us suppose that our 'free spending' officials are returned to power, accepting deficits as the norm. Each year, the government spends a bit more (returning to our example, say, $5500) than it taxes (say, $5200) to allow for some dollars to be hoarded and for others to be lost. While the tax liability is not set to 'finance' the government's spending, there still remains a relation between the two that should not be violated. Recall that the purpose of the tax is to draw forth a supply of goods and services that the government can purchase with dollars. Given a tax liability, if the government tries to increase spending 'too much' (say, to $6000), then it might find that beyond some point the public refuses to supply goods and services in exchange for dollars. That is, after paying taxes, losing some dollars, and accumulating as many dollars as desired in hoards, the public would refuse to accept any more dollars.

In our simple model, it would be easy for the government to gauge the 'saturation' point, for it would offer dollars in exchange for goods and services, but would find no takers. Thus it could simply impose a tax liability and then spend up to the point where the population was satisfied with the number of dollars supplied. Before that point was reached, the government would find queues of individuals showing up to offer goods and services to obtain dollars; beyond that point, the government would find no queue. Thus at the correct level of deficit spending, the population would have just the right amount of hoarded dollars left as net nominal saving after paying taxes (and, perhaps, losing some dollars in the wash).

PRICES AND THE VALUE OF THE CURRENCY

In the example above, we assumed that the public accepts government fiat money (dollars) in exchange for the goods and services it produces. What determines the price (in dollars) at which they relinquish goods and services to the government? Once the government realizes that its spending decision determines the quantity of fiat money available to meet the tax obligations it imposes, it can exogenously set the prices of those goods and services it buys from the private sector. This determines the value of the currency. The government may choose to devalue the currency, or cause inflation, by paying more for a given quantity of goods and services or to revalue the currency by offering lower prices.

A very simple example might help. Assume as in the discussion above that the government imposes a tax on the population and then provides fiat money – which can be used to retire tax obligations – to purchase labour services from the population. If the government pays out $100 and predicts that approximately $20 of this will 'leak out' (in the form of hoards, as discussed above), then it can set the tax at $80 and ensure that there will be a demand for the $100. If 100 hours of labour is desired by government, then it can set the price of an hour of labour at $1. If the government lowered the tax (say, to $40), while trying to hold its spending constant, it would almost certainly find it could not spend $100 because the average household would supply far less labour to the government because each would find it so much easier to meet the tax liability (which was now half what it had been). However, the government's inability to spend would not be due to its inability to 'finance' its spending through tax revenue, rather, the lower tax burden would reduce the total 'effort' devoted to earning the means of tax payment.

Note also that it would do no good for the government to offer to pay more per unit of labour purchased (for example, to offer to pay $2 per hour of labour services); this would only further reduce 'work effort'. Thus with a reduced tax liability, the government would find that it buys less whether at a constant price or at an increased price. Surprisingly, the solution would be to lower prices in order to increase the quantity of labour offered to the government: once the government lowers the tax liability (for example, to $40), it would almost certainly also have to lower the number of dollars supplied (or increase the 'work effort' required to obtain dollars) by lowering its offer prices. By analogy, holding taxes constant (at $80), if the government tries to double its spending (to $200) it may find that after some point, the population refuses the government's offer to purchase labour.[5] For example, if the government offers to pay $2 an hour for labour, the population may stop working after something like 50 hours of labour have been purchased.

In general, holding taxes constant, and holding desired net nominal saving constant, the government will increase the value of the currency if it reduces the price it offers to pay. On the other hand, raising the price it is willing to pay will devalue the currency. For the same amount of nominal spending, it will obtain fewer real labour services (or goods).

Our wiser, 'free spending' government, then, would impose a tax liability and announce how much effort would be required to obtain each dollar (for example, an hour of work in exchange for a dollar, or a dollar for a product that required on average an hour of work). It would then stand ready to purchase all the goods and services offered at these prices, without worrying about the size of its deficit. It would expect that it would normally run a deficit, but this would be strictly determined by the amount of 'net saving' (or hoards of dollars) desired by the public. If this did not call forth the quantity of goods and services required by the government (that is, if the public met its tax liabilities and accumulated the quantity of net saving desired before the government had purchased the quantity of goods and services it desires), the government would lower the prices it was willing to pay. It would be quite silly to react to the insufficient supply by raising prices, that is, to devalue the dollar, for this would be likely to reduce the quantity of goods and services offered. The government could restrain its total spending by limiting the quantity purchased (rather than by lowering purchase prices), but this would make little sense unless it felt that the population was devoting too much effort to supplying goods and services to the government (for example, if the population did not have adequate time left over for other pursuits, such as sleeping, providing for family consumption and recreation).

GOVERNMENT BONDS

So far, in our model, households that hoard dollars earn no interest on their hoards. There are at least three ways in which we can introduce interest to our exposition. First, the government might offer to lend dollars at interest to households that are temporarily short of them in order that they might meet tax liabilities; indebtedness would be an alternative to imprisonment for tax arrears.[6] Second, households with excess dollars might lend them to deficient households to pay taxes, and charge interest. Third, the government may wish to encourage saving through payment of interest on savings. Of course, we can easily introduce all three possibilities into our exposition. Market 'arbitrage' should ensure that interest rates for each of these three types of financial transaction will be similar, adjusted for variations in credit risk.

Let us assume, then, that the government begins to sell 'bonds' that pay some interest rate to households with net nominal savings (dollar hoards). In this case, some of the dollar money 'refluxes' back to the government so that a portion of the government's deficit is accumulated in the form of household bond holdings rather than in the form of dollars. Clearly, such bond sales are not necessary to finance the government's deficit, for the government spends first, and then provides interest-earning bonds. Further, the government will be able to sell bonds up to an amount equal to its deficit, less any loss or leakage of fiat money to desired non-interest-earning hoards. Households could hold either dollars or bonds to the extent that their incomes exceed tax liabilities; rational households will choose to accumulate most excess income in the form of interest-earning bonds. If the deficit doubled, the government could approximately double its bond sales.

The higher the interest rate offered by the government, the more bonds it might be able to sell (all else equal) by inducing households to part with dollars.[7] On the other hand, a low interest rate might convince households to hold more dollars and fewer bonds. Note that the government does not have to pay higher interest rates to finance its deficit, rather, it chooses exogenously what interest rate to offer – households will prefer any positive interest rate over the zero interest rate on dollars, but higher rates might encourage households to convert more dollars to bonds. In any case, bond sales are not required to finance a deficit, but rather are the means through which the government provides an interest-earning asset to the public, and thus more dollar income to the public. The market cannot dictate to the government what interest rate it should pay; the market will be happy to obtain any positive interest rate – but even if the market doesn't want interest, this is no problem as the government does not need to sell bonds.[8]

Obviously, the government will have no trouble making interest payments – it can issue dollars to pay interest on outstanding debt. These promised interest payments would add to the government's future deficits if no adjustment were made to its spending and taxing activities. Because household interest receipts are in addition to any household income resulting from sales of goods and services to the government, the government may have to raise tax liabilities (or lower its non-interest spending) in the future to avoid any depreciation of the value of the currency (because interest income is an alternative to provision of goods and services to the government as a source of dollars to pay taxes).

However, the increased tax liability (or budget cuts) has nothing to do with the 'necessity' of raising funds to pay interest; increasing taxes may be required to prevent the devaluation of the currency that would result from rising incomes (which would otherwise allow households to reduce work effort involved in earning income to pay taxes).

PRIVATE MARKETS

Up to this point, we have examined only a very simple economy that bears little apparent relation to our real economy precisely because it does not allow for private production for private markets. Let us continue by supposing that some households begin to produce for the market; those with excess dollars (that is, more than what is required to pay taxes) might purchase goods and services from neighbours. The problem with most simple expositions is that they have great difficulty in explaining why some households would suddenly decide to produce for the market in order to obtain money. These stories have typically relied on some sort of spontaneous social consensus to use a physical commodity as a medium of exchange to reduce the inefficiencies associated with barter.[9] However, our previous argument makes it clear why one would exchange produced goods and services for something that has no intrinsic value. Dollars are demanded in this economy because they are the means of paying taxes. Even if one did not have a tax liability (perhaps one was a favourite of the king, and, thus, exempt from tax payment), so long as others in society do have tax liabilities, the dollar will have a 'real', albeit 'extrinsic' value because others will offer goods and services to obtain the dollar.

Once households have a demand for government fiat money to pay taxes, it is easy to see why fiat money might also serve households as a medium of exchange, a means of payment, and a unit of account. One household's income might be insufficient to pay taxes in a given year, while another's income could be in excess of tax liabilities – even if the overall tax take is exactly at the correct level to allow the government to obtain the quantity of goods and services it requires, there is no guarantee that each individual's fiat money income will be sufficient to pay the tax liability. This then provides an incentive for deficient households to engage in private market activity to try to earn the needed fiat money to pay taxes. Surplus households can provide the demand for the output produced by the deficient households. In this way, the fiat money is redistributed among households so that tax liabilities can be met. Note, however, that use of the fiat money as a medium of exchange derives from its use to satisfy tax liabilities – households use the fiat money in private markets because it is the means of settlement of tax liabilities.

DEVELOPMENT OF BANKING

As alluded to above and in Chapter 3, the first loans seem to have been public loans to provide deficient households with the means to pay taxes. It is also possible that the tax liabilities can generate private lending. The deficient household could issue a liability denominated in the fiat-money-of-account to be held by the household with excessive income in return for a loan of dollars used to meet the tax liability of the deficient household.[10] The interest rate on this loan will be some mark-up over the government's bond rate to compensate the private lender for the chance of default by the borrower and also to compensate the lender for the 'insecurity' of parting with dollars (because net saving is the protection against unfavourable outcomes that might make it difficult to meet tax liabilities in the future). In the subsequent year, the fiat-money-of-account-denominated liability (principal and interest) can be retired by using fiat money as a means of payment. The surplus households hold either fiat money or claims on fiat money because they, too, have tax liabilities to the government – and thus can be in debt to the government in the future.

The household with a large hoard of dollars might specialize in lending, attracting both deficient and surplus households. It would accept deposits of dollars and make loans of dollars, matching maturities while maintaining a positive interest rate spread (loan rate less deposit rate) to generate income. At first the deposits might be at risk (with depositors losing their deposits when borrowers default), but eventually our 'banker' could offer to bear the default risk at a somewhat higher interest rate spread. The next step would be for the banker to offer demand deposits so that depositors could withdraw dollars at any time; the banker would pay less interest on these, to maintain a higher interest rate spread to compensate for mismatched maturity. At this point, the banker would have to maintain reserves of dollars to meet anticipated withdrawals – with mismatched maturity he could not lend out all of his deposits. A fractional reserve system is created.

Just as in any fractional reserve system, there is a danger that depositors will demand more dollars than the banker has on hand. The banker might try to prearrange credit lines with other surplus households and bankers, such that should the need arise, she would be able temporarily to borrow dollars by pledging her 'assets' (the IOUs she holds against the loans she has made). Larger 'money centre' banks could specialize in offering to hold reserves of smaller banks, and, more important, agree to lend reserves against assets when the need arose.

At first banks might actually lend the government's dollars, but they would soon realize that they could issue dollar-denominated banknotes to be paid out when they made loans. The public had already become accustomed to use of government dollars in exchange, and would eventually come to see the notes issued by banks, and backed by dollar reserves and dollar-denominated assets held by the bank, as substitutes so long as bank failures were rare. This would allow banks to 'loan' their own notes while accepting either deposits of dollars or of their own notes.[11] Banknotes would then circulate alongside government dollars in private markets; the notes would be acceptable not only because they could be converted to dollars but also because banks would accept them as deposits and as payment against principal and interest on loans.[12]

At the same time, banking business could be spread in another direction. Transactors in private markets could complete transactions solely on the 'books' of their bank. For example, in a small community with only one bank, a transaction could take place by debiting the deposit of a 'buyer' and crediting the deposit of a 'seller' with no dollars or even banknotes actually changing hands. A bank could arrange to perform such 'giro' transactions for depositors for a small monthly fee (or in return for accepting a lower deposit interest rate). The next step would be to allow a depositor to make a payment to a depositor of another bank; this could be done by writing a cheque on one's bank account to be deposited in another's bank. This would require that banks arrange for cheque clearing, perhaps through a money centre bank with which each had a reserve account. In this case, the clearing would be accomplished by debiting the reserve of the bank against which the cheque was issued, and crediting the reserve of the bank receiving the deposit. Clearing among money centre banks could then be done at some central clearing bank. Money centre banks, as discussed above, could lend reserves at interest to reserve deficient banks while the central clearing bank could lend reserves at interest to deficient money centre banks.

Banks could develop an interbank market for fiat money reserves; these would allow reserves to 'reflux' back to individual banks suffering a clearing drain to other banks in the system. Banks with excess reserves could lend them short-term to banks with insufficient reserves, leading to development of a short-term, or overnight, lending rate. This rate, in turn, would be determined relative to the rate at which the government loaned fiat money,[13] and to the rate paid by government on the bonds it issued. Banks could also try to induce households to part with hoards of fiat money by offering interest-earning deposits (but as mentioned above, the desire to hoard in the form of fiat money may not be very interest-sensitive).

Eventually, most of the reserves of the banks would be nothing more than credits on the books of money centre banks, with actual dollars held only by the central clearing bank (except for small reserves of dollars held at individual banks for daily withdrawals). Thus reserves would be 'pyramided' on the central clearing bank. This bank would be able to stop runs on individual banks by lending reserves as necessary; however, its ability to stop a systemic run might be constrained by its dollar reserves. After a number of disruptive bank crises, the government might realize that one solution would be to take over the functions of the central clearing bank, establishing a government central bank that would run the national clearing system, operate as a lender of last resort to provide dollars as necessary to halt systemic runs, and perhaps to regulate financial practices – for example, it might require some minimum required reserve ratio. In addition, the central bank might offer to run a 'discount window', lending reserves against bank assets (such as loans or government bonds). Note that loans by the government-run central bank would never be constrained by the quantity of dollars the bank held in its vaults; as the supplier of dollars, the government could always create as many dollars as required. This is why a government-run central bank could always stop bank runs, while the private central clearing bank could not.

RESERVES AND CENTRAL BANKING

Settling of accounts among households moves reserves among banks, but does not affect the aggregate quantity of bank reserves. However, each conversion of banknotes or deposits to fiat money dollars to pay taxes will result in a clearing drain from the banking system. The private banking system cannot, by itself, affect the aggregate availability of reserves – which is determined by the quantity of fiat money provided by the government, less leakages due to tax payments, dollars hoarded by the households and loss or destruction of fiat money.

Reserves can be provided directly through government purchases of bonds from the banking system or by lending reserves to banks, and indirectly through government purchases of goods and services from households, or through government purchases of bonds from households (since in either case, dollars in excess of immediate needs to meet tax liabilities and desired dollar hoards will flow into banking system interest-earning deposit accounts). Dollars (either paper dollars or bank reserves) are drained through tax payments or bond sales.

Although government is the only source of reserves, it will have no discretionary control over the quantity of reserves held by the banking system. This is easiest to see in the case where the government enforces a required reserve ratio. When the government sets reserve requirements equal to a fraction of bank deposits, then banks must obtain reserves as legally required. If the sum of required reserves across all banks is greater than the available reserves, then it is impossible for all banks to meet legal requirements – at least one bank will be short. The government will provide more reserves (for example, through a direct loan as an overdraft, or by purchasing bonds in the open market) to ensure that no bank is forced to break the law. For this reason, legally required reserve ratios as a matter of logic force the government to supply reserves on demand. As we saw in Chapter 5, our results stand even without required reserves. If government accepts bank money in payment of taxes, then reserves must be supplied on demand. On the other hand, our analysis thus far does not explain why the central bank might not force an aggregate excess reserve position on banks – we now turn to an analysis of monetary policy.

FISCAL AND MONETARY POLICY

The government might decide to separate its operations so that it could keep two interdependent books. One book could deal with fiscal operations: government purchases of goods and services, taxes and primary bond sales. The other book would deal with secondary bond sales and purchases, loans of reserves in the overnight market and operation of a clearing mechanism for banks. The first book would be kept as the Treasury's balance sheet, while the second would be kept as the central bank's balance sheet. When the government bought goods and services from the public, this would be recorded on the Treasury's book as a government purchase; the purchase would be 'financed' by increasing the reserve liability on the central bank's balance sheet. These entries would be offset by a Treasury liability held as an asset by the central bank. The quantity of fiat money (say, dollar notes or Treasury cheques) received by households would rise, most of which would flow to (or remain in) banks as reserves. Tax payments would then absorb reserves. Most of the remaining reserves would be excess reserves, placing downward pressure on the overnight rate (with bids dropping to zero in the absence of borrowers).

To maintain the overnight rate, the Treasury could then sell bonds to banks or the public, causing a reserve drain.[14] As needed (for interest rate fine-tuning, but not to 'finance' the government deficit), the central bank could add or subtract reserves through open market purchases or sales of bonds in the secondary market.

If government spending and taxing were perfectly coordinated, most of the fiat money created for purposes of spending would be immediately drained in tax payments; it would appear that spending and taxing were simultaneous, or even that taxes 'financed' spending. Only the government's deficit would appear to have been financed by creating money that showed up as excess reserves that then needed to be drained through bond sales. However, if taxes were typically paid quarterly or at the end of the year, then the fiat money injected as the government spent rather continuously throughout the year would flow to banks to earn interest, generating excess reserves and forcing the Treasury and/or central bank to drain the reserves through bond sales. Then, when taxes were paid, reserves will have to be injected to restore the positions of banks. Thus the technical details become quite complicated and obfuscate what in reality is quite easy to understand: the government cannot tax or sell bonds until it spends; the spending 'finances' tax payments and bond sales, rather than the other way round.

In this example, 'Treasury operations' have primarily to do with determining the quantity and value of fiat money, while 'central bank operations' have primarily to do with determining short-term interest rates. Although primary bond sales are normally treated as fiscal policy, they are really a part of monetary policy. Indeed, rather than thinking of bond sales as equivalent to 'deficit finance', it may perhaps be more instructive to think of bonds as nothing more than interest-earning currency when held by the public, or interest-earning reserves (held in special government accounts) when held by banks. Clearly, none of this changes anything of significance – the 'government' can be treated as the consolidated Treasury and central bank balance sheets without losing any of the argument.

Most government spending and tax payments flow through, and thus affect the banking system. When the government decides to allow households to pay taxes by writing cheques on deposit accounts, this effectively allows 'bank money' (deposits or banknotes) to be perfectly substitutable, so far as households are concerned, for government fiat money. Indeed, because taxes could be paid using bank money, the public would no longer need to obtain fiat money (except, perhaps, for illegal transactions and vending machines). This would reduce the reserve drain from banks to hoards. The 'Treasury operations' and 'central bank operations' would remain as described above. Now, government could also operate through the banking system – buying goods and services with a cheque on the Fed that would be immediately deposited in banks, increasing their reserves; conversely, tax payment by a cheque drawn on a private bank would lead to an immediate reserve drain. Nothing of significance regarding the government's ability to 'run deficits' is changed when deposit money substitutes for fiat money.

THE VALUE OF BANK MONEY AS A STATE MONEY

Once bank money is accepted as state money in payment of taxes, government policy also determines the value of bank money. There is then no possibility that bank money can fall below 'par' with fiat money because the government chooses to accept it at par in payment of taxes. Bank money and government fiat money become interchangeable, except that any payment to government ultimately reduces government fiat money, while any payment by government increases government fiat money – and this is true even if households do not use any fiat money at all, for all the fiat money will end up as bank reserves, and some of this will then be exchanged for interest-earning bonds.

As private markets expand, it is possible that government purchases become relatively small as a percentage of total GDP, but this changes none of our conclusions above – even if money initially comes solely from government, with the demand for it determined solely by its use in taxes, we can expand our exposition to the point where the vast majority of transactions involving money occur in private markets that have nothing to do with government without dropping our 'taxes-drive-money' view. In this case, government fiat money will fall as a percentage of the total 'money supply', with bank money comprising the larger part. Because bank money is convertible on demand to fiat money, banks will have to have access to reserves as required. Individual banks can suffer a clearing drain to hoards, to cheque clearing, and to tax payments; the system as a whole will lose reserves to hoards, taxes and purchases of government bonds.

If the government has agreed to accept bank money as state money (acceptable in payment cf taxes), it really has no choice but to maintain par clearing and to provide reserves on demand. When the household writes a cheque on a bank to pay taxes, the government deducts an equivalent amount of dollars – fiat money – from the bank's assets. If the bank did not have sufficient reserves to deduct, this would not be possible, so the government would have automatically to lend the reserves needed (that is, provide an overdraft) or the cheque could not clear. This can be done simply enough: the government merely books a loan of reserves as the bank's liability (replacing the bank's liability to the household writing the cheque). Similarly when cheques written on one bank are deposited in another, par clearing demands that an equivalent amount of reserves is transferred from the account of the first bank to the account of the second. If the first bank does not have the reserves, the government will have to loan them. Once bank money becomes a state money, par clearing and provision of reserves on demand become an automatic consequence.

INTERNATIONAL INDEBTEDNESS

Above we noted that government bonds are sold to provide interest-earning assets, rather than to 'finance' a government deficit. If, for some reason, the government did not understand that sales of government bonds were unnecessary to 'finance' the deficit, it might sell bonds in international markets. So long as these bonds are denominated in the domestic fiat money of account, this will not prove to be a problem: the government will always be able to service the debt and pay interest by providing more fiat money (initially in the form of reserves, as discussed above). The danger is that such a government might come to believe that its policies are hostage to the whims of international markets; in this case the government might mistakenly adopt an austere domestic policy, unnecessarily punishing its citizens while believing that international 'creditors' are forcing it to do so. Thus it might adopt tight monetary policy (high interest rates) and attempt to balance the budget to slow its economy in a perverse 'belt-tightening' attempt to 'reduce reliance on foreign savers'.

Worse, the government might decide that it must issue debt in some foreign currency in order to please international markets. Once this is done, the government has subjected itself to international constraints, for its ability to service the debt will depend on its ability to obtain foreign currency.[15] However, no government that is able to purchase the goods and services it requires in its own currency need ever surrender itself to international constraints. If the things it desires are sold for domestic currency, they will be for sale in terms of the domestic fiat money of account. If the things the government desires are not available in exchange for the domestic currency, then the country will be subject to real (rather than self-imposed) international constraints.

WHICH TAX DRIVES MONEY?

There is another issue to be addressed: what kind of tax drives money? A head tax clearly generates a universal demand for money and is the simplest way to generate a flow of goods and services to government. Note that it is not necessary for the head tax to be placed on all individuals. Suppose only half the population is subject to the tax. The half that does not have to pay taxes will still be willing to do things for money, because they can get the taxed half to do things for them in order to obtain money to pay taxes. Indeed, the logic leads inexorably to the conclusion that, in the extreme, a head tax on one individual is sufficient to create a demand for money and a supply of goods and services to government (suppose the government put a $1.2 trillion tax on Bill Gates!).

What about other kinds of taxes? Even a head tax on foreigners (while difficult to enforce) would generate a demand for dollars, inducing them to supply goods and services to the domestic population to obtain dollars, while the domestic population would supply things to government to get the dollars demanded by foreigners (since foreigners would supply imports to obtain the dollars). A tariff on imports, on the other hand, would not necessarily drive money: the tax could be completely avoided simply by avoiding imports; no one would have to supply things to government to obtain dollars to pay this tax.[16] A property tax, on the other hand, would work like a head tax – one would lose one's property unless the tax were paid, generating a demand for dollars to pay the tax. An income tax, like the tariff, cannot, alone, drive money. One could avoid the tax by avoiding income; a self-sufficient individual (or village) would not provide things to government to obtain money to pay a tax on income. On the other hand, once a market economy is developed such that most people have no choice but to obtain income from the market in order to consume, then an income tax or a tariff on imports can still work to generate things for sale to government. However, this brings up an important point: taxes on transactions (such as income taxes, sales taxes or financial 'turnover' transactions taxes) can be avoided by avoiding the transactions; as such, they tend to reduce private market activity and can be less effective in generating a supply of goods and services to government. If one understands that the purpose of a tax is to generate a demand for dollars so that the government can purchase goods and services it requires, rather than to 'finance' government spending, then one's view of the optimal type of tax might change. Of course, there still remains a role for so-called 'sin taxes', which by design are supposed to eliminate the undesired behaviour (rather than to raise revenue) – cattle prods would serve a similar purpose.

THE VALUE OF MONEY REVISITED

As discussed above, the government can determine the value of money by setting the price it is willing to pay. In our example above, with the government as the sole supplier of the fiat money it accepts in payment of the taxes it levies, and with it as the sole outlet for production of its citizens, the government's pricing policy determines the value of money quite directly.

The government could, in theory, exogenously set the price of each item it wished to buy – but this would be quite difficult to administer and could create a great many problems for the relative price system. For example, if the government set the price of an aircraft carrier at $1000 and the price of a hammer at $500, it is not difficult to foresee that people will queue up to supply hammers while no offers of aircraft carriers will be forthcoming. However, once the government has purchased the number of hammers it desires, people would find that they could not obtain fiat money by producing hammers and so would have to turn to production of something the government desired in order to obtain the money acceptable in payment of taxes.

Things admittedly are much more complicated in our expanded model where taxes can be paid using bank money and where the government is only one among many buyers (even if it is a relatively large buyer). When government allows tax payment in the form of bank money, this leads to a reserve drain and an automatic intervention by the central bank to inject reserves if banks are deficient. In other words, rather than supplying aircraft carriers to obtain money to pay taxes, given the way that the central bank operates it is possible to offer collateral against loans of reserves that provide the needed fiat money. The central bank could impose austere conditions on banks before agreeing to make such loans, but the private sector might have to suffer severe disruption and deflation before it would supply an aircraft carrier to the government in return for $1000.

When there are private markets, individuals can always choose to produce for markets rather than for the government, so it might appear that the government would have to set its price above the minimum (market) supply price (say, cost plus mark-up), but that is not correct because the public needs the government's money to pay taxes. As an extreme example, let us suppose the government decides to buy one aircraft carrier next year at our assumed price of $1000. Further, assume the government is the only buyer of aircraft carriers, and this is the only purchase it will make. Finally, let us first assume that only fiat money can be used to pay taxes (bank money is not state money). Then the only way the private sector can obtain dollars to pay taxes is to produce an aircraft carrier, sell it for $1000, and use the dollars to pay taxes. There is no doubt that this could be extremely disruptive, causing relative prices to adjust, and causing nominal prices to fall drastically (the price of labour may well fall to thousandths of a penny per day). And it is possible that the required price movements and organization of production would be beyond the capacity of the economy so that the aircraft carrier did not get built and the population did not pay its taxes. But the point is that if the production were possible and prices were sufficiently adjustable, the government would be able to set the price anywhere it desired. This is the logic of a 'taxes-drive-money' view.

Other items will be sold in private markets and also to the government. It might appear that the government will have to pay market price for these items; however, the price the government pays can still determine the 'market price' because its fiat money must be obtained to pay taxes (and to accumulate 'net' money hoards). Again, let us first deal with the situation in which only fiat money can be used to pay taxes. If the government sets the price below market price, then deflation results (as increasing numbers of people are jailed, as business are closed, and as assets are sold to pay taxes) until government purchases provide the fiat money the population needs to pay taxes. If, on the other hand, the government sets the price above market price, then inflation can result as private buyers might bid up prices to compete with the government's price.

As we discussed above, pricing is much 'looser' when bank money is accepted in payment of taxes, because par clearing forces the central bank to provide the fiat money. Still, beyond some point, a government price set below market price will become deflationary because banks will run out of collateral that can be offered to the central bank to obtain loans. The central bank could then 'haircut' bank capital (clear the cheques only by reducing bank net worth by the reserve deficiency) and eventually close the banks. A general deflation would result so that, eventually, the government's price would draw out some suppliers.

On the other hand, a government can always offer prices above market prices, causing inflation or currency devaluation. Government spending can thus be 'inflationary' but not necessarily due to any simple 'supply' or 'demand' effect as conventional wisdom suggests – rather, by determining the value of the currency through its fiscal policy. A government might not realize that it has the power to set prices exogenously; in this case, it might pay the market-determined price. If prices are rising, the government might believe that it must also increase the price it pays. However, as our analysis makes clear, government always has the alternative of refusing to increase the price it pays, although it is a bit more difficult for government to impose deflationary prices on the system if it accepts bank money in payment of taxes than if it were to accept only fiat money.

In conclusion, if we have a very simple economy in which there are no private markets, then, given desired net nominal saving, an increase of the price paid by government will devalue the currency because it takes less 'effort' to meet the tax liability. It is also possible that the government will find that it cannot spend as much as desired because the population will earn enough money to pay taxes and accumulate hoards before the government has met the level of spending planned. The government can revalue by reducing prices paid.

If we add a private market economy, with bank money accepted in payment of taxes, then the government's pricing decisions influence the overall value of money (as indicated by a consumer price index, for example) more indirectly. There is also an asymmetry involved: it is easier to cause inflation than it is to cause deflation. If the government continuously raises the price it is willing to pay for each item it purchases, this is quite likely also to cause prices of items sold in private markets to rise-due both to demand effects (household income and thus demand is higher) and supply effects (private buyers will have to compete to some degree with government for at least some of the things sold). On the other hand, if the government lowers its buy prices, sellers might at first prefer to sell to private buyers (where possible). As government spending shrinks, the flow supply of fiat money is reduced, leading to insufficient reserves (as taxes are paid). Given that the central bank automatically supplies reserves as necessary, this leads to discount window loans (and open market purchases) and eventually to central bank pressure on banks to reduce lending (for example, as the central bank 'haircuts' capital). As household income is reduced (because government spending has fallen), private spending also falls. Eventually, market prices also decline as a general deflation spreads throughout the private economy. After some point, the government's announced buy prices become 'competitive'. Thus, although the mechanism is more complex than in our simplest model, government pricing decisions still affect the value of the currency.

In our simplest economy with only a government-supplied fiat money and with the government as the only purchaser of output, it is quite obvious that taxes drive money since the public demands money only because it can be used in payment of taxes. Adding markets such that fiat money can be used to purchase goods for private consumption complicates the analysis, while allowing for bank-supplied money adds still another layer of complexity. At the macro level, the economy still needs fiat money to pay taxes so it must provide the goods, services and assets desired by government in order to obtain the money accepted by government in payment of taxes. Thus, the government can set the terms on which it will provide that money. At the micro level, however, some individuals may be driven to produce things for sale to government and private markets in order to obtain the fiat money required to pay taxes, but most individuals will seek money in order to buy things in private markets. Further, most individuals will happily accept bank money instead of fiat money since it is the responsibility of banks and the central bank to finally clear accounts in the fiat money. Thus, when one looks to the micro level, it is not obvious that taxes drive money – especially bank money – and it is not obvious that government fiscal policy would be an important determinant of the value of money. However, when one turns to the macro analysis, the importance of taxes and fiat money comes forward.

BUFFER STOCKS TO STABILIZE PRICES

This leads to an interesting policy proposition. The government could choose to peg one important price in order to impart greater price stability across the spectrum of prices of goods and services. It could then operate a 'buffer stock' policy for that one item, as an alternative to attempting to administer exogenously a wide range of prices. For example, the government can set a price at which it is willing to hire labour services. Assume (as above) that it sets the residual price of labour at $1 per hour, then agrees to hire all labour at that price. Each worker will decide individually how many hours to work; the government will impose a head tax to ensure that all citizens have an incentive to work for fiat money. Involuntary unemployment would be eliminated because anyone willing to work could work for the government. The value of money would be set in terms of the price of unskilled labour at $1 per hour. All private employers would have to pay at least $1 per hour for labour to attract workers (there might be some possibility of a wage below this for attractive private sector employment). Skilled labour would earn a wage above $1 per hour (whether working for private employers or for the government in jobs requiring skilled workers); the government's residual demand price would become the going wage for a unit of unskilled, homogeneous labour. Only in depressed market conditions would skilled labour be forced to work for $1 per hour.

Establishment of an infinitely elastic demand for labour at a residual wage might lead to a one-time devaluation or revaluation of the currency; however, to the extent that the government leaves the residual wage at $1 per hour, its full employment policy would not generate inflation (continuous devaluation of the currency). At any point, the government might decide to raise the residual wage and thereby cause a one-time devaluation of the currency. There is, however, no 'trade-off' of employment for inflation under this scheme – full employment is obtainable without inducing inflation.

CONCLUSIONS

These results are admittedly for a very simple, hypothetical economy. It is our claim, however, that all of the essential points hold true for a modern capitalist economy.

NOTES

1. Of course, the projects need not be beneficial to the population; the government might want to raise an army to conduct a foreign war.
2. We will return below to a discussion of the determination of the 'value' of the dollar.
3. In our simple exposition, household receipts come only from sales to government, while household expenditures consist solely of tax payments. In an expanded model, with use of the fiat money in private markets, purchase of consumption goods by households merely redistributes the fiat money within the household sector.
4. As Chapter 3 showed, this was the case in the nineteenth century.
5. We are assuming that desired net nominal saving does not expand, for example, to $120.
6. Indeed, according to existing historical records, tax indebtedness appears to be the earliest source of lending at interest.
7. This depends on the interest-elasticity of the demand for fiat money hoards, or the degree of liquidity preference; it is probably quite small.
8. We have not actually introduced a private market, but our results hold even after we introduce private asset markets and market interest rates. As the monopoly supplier of that which is required to purchase government bonds (fiat money), and as the monopoly supplier of government bonds, the government can set the interest rate anywhere it likes.
9. As we saw in Chapter 3 above, this does not appear to be plausible as the origin of the use of money. History seems to indicate that use of money did indeed derive from imposition of a tax.
10. As Innes argued, banks originate as intermediaries between the state and its subjects. See Chapter 3.
11. This would be a 'horizontal' leveraging activity, as discussed in Chapter 5 above. The 'vertically-supplied' government fiat money would allow for long and short leveraged positions.
12. While each bank would at first see notes of other banks as competitive rivals (thus each might at first refuse to accept deposits of others' notes), eventually it would be realized that deposited notes of rivals could always be presented for payment, which would take them out of circulation; thus by accepting the notes of competitors the bank would actually reduce the circulation of rival notes (further, acceptance of rival notes would be in the interests of expanding bank business generally).
13. For example, the government might loan money to households needing them to pay taxes; but more importantly, it would make loans to the banking system when it was short of reserves – see below.
14. The Treasury's liability to the central bank would be reduced while its liability to the public or to banks would rise; the central bank's assets and liabilities would be reduced by the amount of the bond sale.
15. This is exactly what Mexico and Russia did on the belief that international creditors were forcing them to issue dollar-denominated debt. It is also what the member states of the new European Monetary Union plan to do. They will abandon their domestic currencies and issue government debt in a foreign currency (the *euro*). This will subject the individual nations

to the same sort of constraints faced by Russia and Mexico.
16. Still, if one wants to import, one must obtain that which is accepted in payment of tariffs.

8 Conclusions

In this book we have argued that it is possible to move immediately to full employment (or zero unemployment), in the sense that anyone ready, willing and able to work at the government's announced wage would be able to obtain a job. This is far beyond what most economists call full employment, as only voluntary unemployment would remain – that is, those who prefer to remain unemployed while looking for another job.

Certainly, this is also far beyond NAIRU or that rate of unemployment below which inflation will accelerate. Economists currently debate over whether or not there really is a NAIRU and, if so, what is the NAIRU. Others prefer to argue that an economy subject to market forces will naturally reach equilibrium at full employment, such that all unemployment is voluntary because it refuses to work at the market wage – but it is not clear how low wages would have to fall and how much labour market deregulation would have to take place before the elusive natural rate could be reached.

If, however, the government were to act as employer of last resort, offering to hire anyone who shows up ready, willing and able to work, at say the minimum wage, truly full employment would be achieved with a job available to anyone ready, willing and able to work. As we have discussed, ELR cannot resolve all employment problems (including loss of high-paying jobs or working below skill level); however, it can put into place a comprehensive employment safety net while economists and other policymakers debate about the best methods of resolving other employment problems.

With ELR in place, the government will no longer rely on unemployment to stabilize prices. Rather, the primary price stabilization tool will be the price anchor provided by the ELR wage. This does not mean that the government must abandon other macroeconomic tools. For example, countercyclical fiscal policy and monetary policy still can be used if desired in an attempt to manipulate private sector demand (and the size of the ELR pool) to achieve greater price stability. It would also be possible to include incomes policy, ranging from rigid wage and price controls to centralized wage bargaining. While we do not necessarily endorse such schemes, there is nothing in our proposal that would preclude such policies.

If the ELR wage anchor does not achieve the degree of price stability desired, the government can adjust spending, taxes or interest rates – but, rather than causing unemployment to fluctuate, it will cause the size of the ELR pool to change in a countercyclical manner. Indeed, we believe that the ELR programme will enhance the effectiveness of traditional aggregate demand policies precisely because it relies on an employed buffer stock rather than on an unemployed reserve army.[1] Thus our preference for ELR over unemployment is not merely that it is more humane to offer employment, but also that it is more effective as a means to stabilize prices.

This is because ELR workers can maintain and increase their human capital stock, while human capital of the unemployed deteriorates rapidly. In addition, if the ELR programme is well-run, ELR workers can make a positive contribution to the nation's potential output – increasing public and private sector productivity and lowering private sector costs. At least some of the costs of unemployment would be reduced (for example, crime rates would fall). It appears obvious that, at the very least, it is preferable to pay people for showing up to work than to pay them to stay home. The only case that can be made in favour of using unemployment rather than ELR employment to stabilize prices seems to be based on the belief that the reserve army of the unemployed is a better labour disciplining tool. This is unlikely. Not only will ELR workers maintain and enhance their human capital, they will also demonstrate daily their availability for work. Furthermore, they can provide to potential employers their records of ELR employment, including any training or education received. While it is true that private sector workers can be emboldened by the availability of ELR employment should they be fired, employers can also use the legitimate threat of replacing obstinate workers with ELR workers. It is difficult to believe that enforced idleness produces better potential employees than could be produced by even a poorly run ELR programme.

In this book, we have argued that ELR is affordable. However, our argument has not been based on a careful estimate of programme costs and calculation of federal government revenues and expenditures, but rather on development of an alternative view of the nature of modern money, which built upon the Chartalist approach to money and Abba Lerner's functional finance approach to government spending. We have argued the government can 'afford' anything that is for sale in terms of the government's own money. This means that neither taxes nor bond sales are required to finance government spending. Tax levies generate private sector supply of goods, services and assets to government in order to obtain that which is necessary to pay taxes – fiat money. Bond sales are really part of monetary policy, which drain excess reserves as they provide an interest-earning alternative to non-interest-earning fiat money.

We have also argued that unemployment is evidence that the government's deficit is too small, or, that private sector desired net saving is higher than actual net saving (as these terms were defined in Chapter 4). Whenever there is unemployment, the deficit can be increased. The danger in the past was that such 'Keynesian' stimulation would cause inflation by creating tight labour markets. This is because Keynesian policies induce private sector firms to 'hire off the top', that is, to compete for the most desirable workers. Only extremely high aggregate demand could induce the private sector to 'hire off the bottom' – which is why inflation might set in before the chronically unemployed would find jobs. In contrast, the ELR programme is designed to 'hire off the bottom', taking the workers not needed by the private sector. In periods of high aggregate demand, the ELR pool shrinks as the private sector takes the most desirable workers; this automatically reduces the government's deficit so that it remains in line with private sector desired net saving. In periods of declining aggregate demand, the ELR pool grows, increasing the government's deficit as private sector desired net saving rises. This dampens the fall of aggregate demand. Furthermore, as the ELR pool grows, its average productivity rises (because workers of higher productivity have moved from the private sector to ELR employment). Firms can shop the ELR pool for the most desirable workers, who can be obtained at a mark-up over the ELR wage. As discussed, if the automatic fluctuations of the ELR pool are not deemed sufficient, they can be supplemented with traditional demand management policies (although we would not necessarily favour this). If the pool shrinks too much, government can tighten fiscal and/or monetary policy to slow demand; if the pool becomes too large, government can stimulate demand.

It is possible, of course, that our analysis is flawed, so it is worthwhile to examine the possible consequences. What if ELR does turn out to be more inflationary than the current arrangement? That is, what if the reserve army of the unemployed really is more effective as a buffer stock than the ELR proves to be? As we have argued, implementation of ELR does not preclude use of traditional means of price control, including countercyclical demand management as well as incomes policy. If the ELR pool is not as effective in stabilizing wages as unemployment has been, then the number of workers in the pool will have to be greater than the number of unemployed in order to have the same wage dampening effect. This, in turn, will require greater amplitude of swings of the government's budget (or, presumably, larger swings of interest rates). If 6 million unemployed are required for price stability, then perhaps 8 million ELR workers will be required. Two questions then come to mind: is it better to have, say, 6 million unemployed or 8 million employed in ELR?, and what is the budgetary impact of the larger pool? We believe the answer to the first question is obvious, unless problems of administration or supervision were insurmountable (see below). And if our functional finance approach is correct, the second question is unimportant.

What if we have erred in our understanding of money, and in our analysis of government budgets? In this case, we must take ELR programme costs seriously. Our rough estimate put the net cost at $50 billion for the US, which is in line with other estimates including those of Gordon (1997) and Harvey (1989). While Harvey's analysis was much more careful than ours, it is possible that administration, supervision and capital and equipment costs will prove to be much higher than anyone has imagined. Let us presume that actual net costs will be three to four times higher, so that ELR adds $150 billion to $200 billion to the US government's budget. No serious economist would question whether this is affordable, even on conventional analysis. The US budget is projected to run a surplus over the next few years, so ELR would merely restore a small deficit relative to the government's budget, to GDP, or to the deficits that were common under the Reagan and Bush administrations.

Admittedly, however, the analysis might be different for countries that already have high unemployment in conjunction with high deficits, such as some European countries. On the other hand, these countries typically have more generous benefits for the unemployed so that the net cost of replacing unemployment with ELR employment may not be so high as to move deficit-to-GDP ratios significantly. To at least some degree, high deficits result from low growth and high unemployment. If ELR put people to work and stimulated private demand sufficiently, it is possible, perhaps even likely, that deficits would fall. However, we do admit that ELR becomes a difficult programme to sell, except in special cases, unless one understands the principles of functional finance and Chartal money.

What if we have seriously miscalculated the number of people who will accept ELR employment? If the economists who accept the natural rate approach are correct, few of the officially and unofficially unemployed will show up for ELR work since they are actually voluntarily unemployed. If so, we have overestimated programme costs as well as the ability of the buffer stock pool to stabilize wages. If desired, the pool could be increased by slowing aggregate demand. In any case, it would be difficult to oppose the programme (since its impacts must be quite small if virtually no one shows up for work) except on some matter of principle. On the other hand, it is possible that far more than 8 million people will demand jobs. This would mean that official and even unofficial estimates of unemployment are too low, indicating both that the waste of human resources is far greater than previously believed and that the unemployment cost of holding inflation at bay is far higher than supposed. ELR, combined with fiscal and monetary stimulus, would be the recommended policy to reduce this waste. Again, if 12 million workers accepted ELR jobs, there is no danger that this would bankrupt the government, even on conventional analysis.

Frequent objections to implementation of an ELR programme include the difficulty of administering the programme, of supervising workers and of finding sufficient work for ELR workers to do. These objections remind one of the climate of opinion that gripped the UK in the late 1920s or the US in the early 1930s. Keynes (with Hubert Henderson) wrote a pamphlet to support Lloyd George in the 1929 general election on a platform which proposed to reduce unemployment through government spending. He lambasted the opposition:

> The Conservative belief that there is some law of nature which prevents men from being employed, that it is 'rash' to employ men, and that it is financially 'sound' to maintain a tenth of the population in idleness for an indefinite period, is crazily improbable – the sort of thing which no man could believe who had not had his head fuddled with nonsense for years and years.
>
> The objections which are raised are mostly not the objections of experience or of practical men. They are based on highly abstract theories – venerable, academic inventions, half misunderstood by those who are applying them today, and based on assumptions which are contrary to the facts . . .
>
> Our main task, therefore, will be to confirm the reader's instinct that what seems sensible is sensible, and what seems nonsense is nonsense. We shall try to show him that the conclusion, that if new forms of employment are offered more men will be employed, is as obvious as it sounds and contains no hidden snags; that to set unemployed men to work on useful tasks does what it appears to do, namely, increases the national wealth; and that the notion, that we shall, for intricate reasons, ruin ourselves financially if we use this means to increase our well-being, is what it looks like – a bogy. (Keynes, 1972, pp. 90–92)

To those who doubted that sufficient work could be found to employ all the unemployed, Keynes responded:

> There are innumerable schemes pigeonholed in government offices, the children of the most active and progressive brains in the country, which only have to be fished out to provide a great quantity of employment widely distributed in kind and locality.
>
> As soon as we have a new atmosphere of doing things, instead of one of smothering negation, everybody's brains will get busy, and there will be masses of claimants for attention, the precise character of which it would be impossible to specify beforehand. (Ibid., p. 99)

It is very difficult to take seriously the proposition that it is impossible to find sufficient work for 8 million new workers. As Keynes said, if we can clear away the atmosphere of smothering negation, we will think of things for them to do that will improve the quality of life. And there is no reason to limit our thinking to the innumerable schemes pigeonholed in government offices, rather, we can include the 'thousand points of light' provided by our not-for-profit, volunteer organizations. Decentralization is also an important way to keep the costs and problems of organization and supervision manageable.[2] Just as an atmosphere of doing will help us to list things to do, it will also help us to find ways of doing these things.

Still, we are left with the political feasibility of the programme. On one hand, advocating government employment and deficit spending goes against the highly abstract theories and venerable institutions that have been guiding policy in the western world for many years. On the other hand, a programme that favours employment over unemployment, production over waste and wages over hand-outs should have appeal in the current climate of opinion.

Furthermore, there is nothing in our proposal which runs counter to a free market ideology; indeed, in some important respects it reduces, or could reduce, government intervention. First, there will be no need for a minimum wage law. Second, if we rely on the ELR wage and buffer stock to help stabilize prices, then there is no need for frequent changes of interest rates as monetary policy reacts to inflation news. Perhaps more importantly, if ELR does help stabilize prices, there might not be any need to use discretionary fiscal policy in a countercyclical manner. In a sense, with ELR in place, it is the private sector rather than government which determines the size of the government's deficit (by determining the number of workers the private sector does not want). Third, with ELR in place there might be less pressure on firms to retain unwanted workers in the face of technological advance or foreign competition. Finally, if our analysis is correct, prices will be more stable with ELR than they have been in the past – which should appeal to most groups in society.

At the same time, the programme should appeal to those who are concerned with unemployment. While we admit that ELR alone cannot resolve all unemployment problems – especially the problem of 'downsizing' of highly skilled, high income professionals (who probably could not even avoid bankruptcy if they tried to live on an ELR wage) – we believe it addresses the most important unemployment problem, which is the lack of job opportunities for the worker with relatively low skills and low educational achievement, who may have long spells of unemployment and/or long and frequent spells out of the labour force. We believe this is a serious problem, even in the US, that is not necessarily captured in official unemployment statistics (see below).

The programme will also appeal to those who believe there is much that can be done to increase living standards, national wealth, and the general quality of life. Many desirable projects might be undertaken which are not profitable or which cannot be afforded at the local level. These could include provision of public services, environmental clean-up and restoration of public infrastructure.

There remains the question of 'why now?', or, better yet, 'where should ELR be tried first?' Many would question the political feasibility of an ELR programme in the US, which has apparently achieved high employment and stable prices while purportedly relying on market forces. It might be more realistic to propose such a programme in a country with high unemployment, or with high inflation (or better still both). Perhaps a desperate country, such as Indonesia or South Korea, would be more willing to experiment with what appears on the surface to be a radical change. Or a country like France or Spain, with high, long-term unemployment. The problem with trying to implement the programme in the European countries that will become part of the EMU has already been addressed – these will soon lose the power to individually create fiat money (and so will be constrained by their ability to borrow). On the other hand, as Kregel (1998b) argues, the EU could implement a system-wide ELR programme funded by the ECB. The two main impediments to implementation of ELR in high unemployment countries are, first, the high net costs of the programme will scare all those who do not understand the principles of functional finance and, second, questions about the organizational and supervisorial problems associated with developing a new programme that might employ 10 or 20 or even 30 per cent of the population would be raised by opponents. For this reason, it might actually be more politically feasible to first propose the programme in a country with relatively low unemployment.

And this is not as difficult to justify as it might appear. If it is the case that the US is now enjoying a 'new economy', with the lowest inflation and lowest unemployment in decades, and if it is the case that this is the best performance that can be expected from the 'free market economy', then it means that more than 6 million people are officially unemployed (and many more are unofficially unemployed) in the best of all possible worlds. No matter how one looks at it, this is a tremendous waste of resource that should not be tolerated without a very strong justification. The primary justifications offered in defence of maintenance of unemployment are that the involuntarily unemployed help to fight inflation and more generally help to maintain labour discipline (voluntarily unemployed would do little in either regard). However, as we have argued, the ELR pool helps to stabilize prices and discipline labour by offering to employers the opportunity of hiring from the pool rather than from the ranks of the unemployed – and we believe it is much more effective in both respects.

Furthermore, we believe that the official unemployment figures mask the extent of the unemployment problem – especially at the low end of the skills continuum. For example, in the US approximately 17 per cent of the noninstitutional population over age 25 did not finish high school and another 34 per cent finished high school but did not go to college; in contrast, 25 per cent attended college without earning a degree, and 25 per cent have a college degree. (Ritter, 1998, p. 1) The employment–population ratio during the first four months of 1998 for each of these groups was 39.6, 62.9, 72.3 and 78.7 per cent from lowest to highest level of educational achievement. From these data, it is quite clear that educational attainment (which is a proxy for skill level) is an important determinant of the likelihood that one will be employed.

Furthermore, while the employment–population ratio for college graduates is double that of high school dropouts, '[u]nemployment rates produce a less dramatic picture ranging from 7.1 per cent for those who did not finish high school down to only 1.9 per cent for those with a college degree' (ibid.). In other words, the vast majority of high school dropouts who do not have jobs are simply out of the labour force, rather than unemployed.

As we discussed in Chapter 6, it is impossible to guess how many people would be drawn into the labour force if ELR were implemented with universal job opportunity, but it is likely that employment–population ratios can be raised when the supply of jobs increases. If the employment–population ratio of high school dropouts and graduates were increased to anything close to the ratio achieved by college graduates, nearly 25 million additional workers would be contributing to the production of national wealth – and this is on top of the 6 million officially unemployed (Pigeon and Wray, 1998).

Can the US really 'afford' not only the millions officially unemployed, but also the more than 30 million non–elderly adults who are currently out of the labour force? Unlike the government's deficit, this waste of resources is a real burden. Can we envision a true 'new economy' in which all those who are ready, willing and able to work have a real opportunity to contribute to society?

NOTES

1. In addition, it will enhance the automatic stabilizer since ELR workers will receive greater income than currently received by the unemployed – when private demand is low, the ELR pool grows, increasing the government deficit more than would be the case in the absence of ELR. We would prefer to rely on the automatic fluctuations of the ELR pool to stabilize demand and prices; however, we emphasize that the traditional macroeconomic stabilization tools will still be available if they are desired.

2. As just one example, decentralization can make it easier to discipline ELR workers since the management of each independent organization would be free to dismiss any worker for just cause. Indeed, management would be able to discipline ELR workers using any and all legal methods at the disposal of any other private or public sector employer. For some reason, a common objection raised to the ELR proposal is that workers cannot be disciplined because they cannot be fired. On the contrary, we view the ELR programme as a job opportunity programme rather than as a guarantee of a job to every individual no matter how badly behaved! While cases of dismissal for spurious reasons could be remedied in the courts – just as they are now – we see no valid reason for preventing dismissal of workers who do not perform up to reasonable standards. Even within the ELR programme, there could be 'last resort' jobs requiring minimal education and skills – but these would still have performance standards (for example, requiring that one show up on time, dressed and sober). As discussed in Chapter 6 above, after a certain number of dismissals, an individual would become ineligible for ELR employment and would have to rely on another income source.

Bibliography

Adams, John (1998), AFEEMAIL, 27 January.

Angell, Norman (1929), *The Story of Money*, New York: Frederick A. Stokes.

Arestis, Philip and Malcolm Sawyer (1998), 'Prospects for the Single European Currency and some Proposals for a New Maastricht', paper presented at The Fifth Post Keynesian Workshop, Knoxville, Tennessee, 25 June–1 July.

Aschauer, David Alan (1998), 'Public Capital and Economic Growth: Issues of Quantity, Finance, and Efficiency', Working Paper No. 233, Jerome Levy Economics Institute, Annandale-on-Hudson, NY, April.

Aston, T.H. and C.H.E. Philpin (1987), *The Brenner Debate, Agrarian Class Structure and Economic Development in Pre-Industrial Europe*, Cambridge: Cambridge University Press.

Bank of Canada (1997), 'Monetary Policy Report: Summary', Bank of Canada, http://www.bank-banque-canada.ca/english/mprsum.htm, May, pp. 1–4.

Bell, Stephanie (1998), 'How the Government Really Spends: A Balance Sheet Approach', draft manuscript.

Bernanke, Ben S. (1981), 'Bankruptcy, Liquidity, and Recession', *American Economic Association Papers and Proceedings*, vol. 71, no. 2, May, pp. 155–9.

Blinder, Alan and Joseph Stiglitz (1983), 'Money, Credit Instruments, and Economic Activity', *American Economic Association Papers and Proceedings*, vol. 73, no. 2, May, pp. 297–308.

Boulding, Kenneth (1950), *A Reconstruction of Economics*, New York: John Wiley & Sons.

Bowen, William G., Richard G. Davis, and David H. Kopf (1960), 'The Public Debt: A Burden on Future Generations?', *American Economic Review, 50*, pp. 701–6.

Bowen, William G., Richard G. Davis, and David H. Kopf (1962), 'The Distribution of the Debt Burden: A Reply', *The Review of Economics and Statistics, 44*, pp. 98-9.

Braudel, Fernand (1982), *The Wheels of Commerce: Civilization and Capitalism, 15th–18th Century*, New York: Harper & Row.

Brothwell, John F., (1994) 'Unemployment', in Geoffrey M. Hodgson, Warren J. Samuels and Marc R. Tool (eds), *The Elgar Companion to Institutional and Evolutionary Economics L–Z*, Aldershot: Edward Elgar, pp. 357–62.

Brunner, Karl (1968), 'The Role of Money and Monetary Policy', *Federal Reserve Bank of St. Louis Review, 50* (7), July, pp. 9–24.

Calomiris, Charles, R., Glenn Hubbard and James H. Stock (1986),'The Farm Debt Crisis and Public Policy', *Brookings Papers on Economic Activity*, vol. 2, pp. 441–79.

Cameron, Rondo (ed.) (1967), *Banking in the Early Stages of Industrialization: A Study in Comparative Economic History*, New York: Oxford University Press.

Cannan, Edwin (1921), 'The Application of the Theoretical Apparatus of Supply and Demand to Units of Currency', *Economic Journal, 31*, pp. 453–62, reprinted in Friedrich A. Lutz and Lloyd W. Mints (eds) (1983), The American Economic Association, *Readings in Monetary Theory*, New York & London: Garland Publishing, pp. 3–13 (originally issued by The Blakiston Company, New York, Philadelphia and Toronto, 1951).

Cavanaugh, Francis X. (1996), *The Truth about the National Debt: Five Myths and One Reality*, Boston, MA: Harvard Business School Press.

Clinton, Kevin (1997), 'Implementation of Monetary Policy in a Regime with Zero Reserve Requirements', Bank of Canada Working Paper, April, pp. 97–8.

Colander, David (1997) 'Functional Finance', in Thomas Cate, Geoff Harcourt, and David C. Colander (eds), *An Encyclopaedia of Keynesian Economics*, Cheltenham, UK and Brookfield, US: Edward Elgar, pp. 201–4.

Cook, R.M. (1958), 'Speculation on the Origins of Coinage', *Historia, 7*, pp. 257–62.

Crawford, M. (1970), 'Money and Exchange in the Roman World', *Journal of Roman Studies, 60*, pp. 40–48.

Davidson, Paul (1978), *Money and the Real World*, London: Macmillan.

Davies, Glyn (1997), *A History of Money: From Ancient Times to the Present Day*, Cardiff: University of Wales Press.

Deleplace, Ghislain and Edward J. Nell (eds) (1996), *Money in Motion: The Post Keynesian and Circulation Approaches*, New York: St Martin's Press.

Epstein, Gene (1997), 'A Free-Market Guru's Immodest Proposal: Billions in Tax Breaks to Help the Poor', *Barron's*, October, p. 65.

Forstater, Mathew (1998), 'Selective Use of Discretionary Public Employment and Economic Flexibility', paper presented at The Fifth Post Keynesian Workshop, Knoxville, Tennessee, 25 June–1 July.

Furness, William Henry (1910), *The Island of Stone Money*, Philadelphia and London: J.P. Lippincott.

Galbraith, James K. (1997), 'Dangerous Metaphor: The Fiction of the Labour Market', *Public Policy Brief*, Jerome Levy Economics Institute, Annandale-on-Hudson, NY, No. 36.

Ginsburg, Helen (1983), *Full Employment and Public Policy: The United States and Sweden*, Lexington, MA: Lexington Books.

Godley, Wynne (1997), 'Curried EMU - the meal that fails to nourish', *Observer*, 31 August, Business p. 2.

Goodhart, C.A.E. (1989), *Money, Information and Uncertainty*, Cambridge, MA: The MIT Press.

Goodhart, C.A.E. (1996), 'The Two Concepts of Money, and the Future of Europe', draft manuscript.

Goodhart, Charles (1997), 'One Government, One Money', *Prospect*, March, http://www.prospect-magazine.co.uk/highlights/one_gov_one/index.html, pp. 1–3.

Gordon, Wendell (1997), 'Job Assurance – the Job Guarantee Revisited', *Journal of Economic Issues, 31*, September, pp. 826–34.

Grierson, Philip (1965), 'Money and Coinage under Charlemagne', in W. Braunfels (ed.), *Karl der Grosse*, vol. 1, Dusseldorf, pp. 501–36; reprinted as Chapter XVIII in *Dark Age Numismatics*, pp. 530–3.

Grierson, Philip (1977), *The Origins of Money*, London: The Athlone Press.

Grierson, P. (1975), *Numismatics*, London: Oxford University Press.

Grierson, Philip (1979), *Dark Age Numismatics*, London: Variorum Reprints.

Harvey, Philip (1989), *Securing the Right to Employment*, Princeton: Princeton University Press.

Heilbroner, Robert and Peter Bernstein (1989), *The Debt and the Deficit*, New York: W.W. Norton.

Heinsohn, Gunnar and Otto Steiger (1983), *Private Property, Debts and Interest or: The Origin of Money and the Rise and Fall of Monetary Economies*, Naples, Italy: University of Bremen.

Hoppe, Goran and John Langton (1994), *Peasantry to Capitalism: Western Ostergotland in the Nineteenth Century*, NY: Cambridge University Press.

Hudson, Michael (1998), 'Bronze Age Finance, 2500–1200', manuscript.

Iliffe, John (1987), *The African Poor: A History*, Cambridge: Cambridge University Press.

Innes, A. Mitchell (1913), 'What is Money', *Banking Law Journal*, May, pp. 377–408.

Kaldor, N. (1985), *The Scourge of Monetarism*, London: Oxford University Press.

Keynes, John Maynard ([1930] 1976), *A Treatise on Money*, Volumes I and II, New York: Harcourt, Brace & Company.

Keynes, John Maynard (1964), *The General Theory*, New York: Harcourt-Brace-Jovanovich.

Keynes, J.M. (1972) *The Collected Writings of John Maynard Keynes, Volume IX: Essays in Persuasion*, edited by Donald Moggridge, London and Basingstoke: Macmillan/St. Martin's Press.

Keynes, John Maynard (1973), *The Collected Writings of John Maynard Keynes, Volume XIV: The General Theory and After: Part II Defence and Development*, edited by Donald Moggridge, London and Basingstoke: Macmillan/Cambridge University Press.

Keynes, J.M. (1980), *The Collected Writings of John Maynard Keynes, Volume XXVII: Activities 1940–46, Shaping the Post-war World:*

Employment and Commodities, edited by Donald Moggridge, London and Basingstoke: Macmillan/Cambridge University Press.

Keynes, John Maynard (1982), *The Collected Writings of John Maynard Keynes, Volume XXVIII*, edited by Donald Moggridge, London and Basingstoke: Macmillan/Cambridge University Press.

Keynes, John Maynard (1983), *The Collected Writings of John Maynard Keynes, Volume XI: Economic Articles and Correspondence, Academic*, edited by Donald Moggridge, London and Basingstoke: Macmillan/Cambridge University Press.

Knapp, George Friedrich ([1924]1973), *The State Theory of Money*, Clifton, NY: Augustus M. Kelley.

Kraay, C.M. (1964), 'Hoards, Small Change and the Origin of Coinage', *Journal of Hellenic Studies, 84*, pp. 76–91.

Kregel, Jan A (1998a), 'East Asia is not Mexico: The Difference between Balance of Payments Crises and Debt Deflations', Working Paper No. 235, Jerome Levy Economics Institute, Annandale-on-Hudson, NY, May.

Kregel, Jan A (1998b), 'Price Stability and Full Employment as Complements in a New Europe', paper presented at The Fifth Post Keynesian Workshop, Knoxville, Tennessee, 25 June–1 July.

Lerner, Abba (1943), 'Functional Finance and the Federal Debt', *Social Research*, vol. 10, pp. 38–51.

Lerner, Abba P. (1947), 'Money as a Creature of the State', *American Economic Review, 37(2)*, May, pp. 312–17.

Lerner, Abba P. (1961), 'The Burden of the Debt', *Review of Economics and Statistics, 43*, pp. 139–41.

Lerner, Eugene M. (1954), 'The Monetary and Fiscal Programs of the Confederate Government, 1861–1865', *Journal of Political Economy, 62*, pp. 506–22.

Leys, Colin (1975), *Underdevelopment in Kenya*, California: University of California Press.

MacDonald, George (1916), *The Evolution of Coinage*, Cambridge and New York: University Press, G.P. Putnam's Sons.

Magubane, Bernard (1979), *The Political Economy of Race and Class in South Africa*, New York: Monthly Review Press.

Mankiw, Gregory (1997), 'Alan Greenspan's Tradoff', *Fortune*, December 8, p. 36.

Marx, Karl (1909), *Capital, Volume III*, Chicago: Charles H. Kerr and Company.

Mayer, Martin (1998), 'The Asian Disease: Plausible Diagnoses, Possible Remedies', Working Paper No. 232, Jerome Levy Economics Institute, Annandale-on-Hudson, NY, April.

McIntosh, Marjorie K. (1988), 'Money Lending on the Periphery of London, 1300–1600', *Albion*, *20(4)*, Winter, pp. 557–71.

Meulendyke, Anne-Marie (1989), 'US Monetary Policy and Financial Markets', New York: Federal Reserve Bank of New York.

Minsky, Hyman P. (1986), *Stabilizing an Unstable Economy*, New Haven, CT: Yale University Press.

Minsky, Hyman P. (1987), 'Securitization', mimeo, Washington University, September.

Mitchell, William F. (1997), 'Unemployment and Inflation: A Demand Side Focus', paper presented on the PKT Seminar, January, http:\\csf.colorado.edu/authors/Mitchell.bill/title.html.

Mitchell, William F. and Martin J. Watts (1997), 'The Path to Full Employment', manuscript, University of Newcastle, November.

Montador, Bruce (1995), 'The Implementation of Monetary Policy in Canada', *Canadian Public Policy-Analyse de Politiques*, *21(1)*, March , pp. 107–20.

Moore, Basil J. (1988), *Horizontalists and Verticalists: The Macroeconomics of Credit Money*, Cambridge: Cambridge University Press.

Mosler, Warren (1995), *Soft Currency Economics*, 3rd edn., West Palm Beach, FL (self published). Http:\\www.warrenmosler.com.

Mosler, Warren (1997–8), 'Full Employment and Price Stability' *Journal of Post Keynesian Economics*, *20(2)*, Winter, pp. 167–82.

Mosler, Warren and Mathew Forstater (1988), 'A General Analytical Framework for the Analysis of Currencies and Other Commodities', draft manuscript, Summer.

Munroe, John H. (1979), 'Bullionism and the Bill of Exchange in England, 1272–1663: A Study in Monetary Management and Popular Prejudice', in *The Dawn of Modern Banking*, Center for Medieval and Renaissance Studies, University of California, Los Angeles. New Haven and London: Yale University Press, pp. 169–239.

Neale, Walter C. (1976), *Monies in Societies*, The University of Tennessee, San Francisco, CA: Chandler & Sharp.

Papadimitriou, Dimitri, Ronnie Phillips and L. Randall Wray, (1993), 'A Path to Community Development: The Community Reinvestment Act, Lending Discrimination, and the Role of Community Development Banks', *Public Policy Brief*, Jerome Levy Economics Institute, Annandale-on Hundson, NY, No. 6.

Papadimitriou, Dimitri and L. Randall Wray (1996), 'Targeting Inflation: The Effects of Monetary Policy on the CPI and its Housing Component', *Public Policy Brief*, Jerome Levy Economics Institute, Annandale-on-Hudson, NY, No. 27.

Phelps, Edmund S. (1997), *Rewarding Work*, Cambridge, MA: Harvard University Press.

Pigeon, Marc-Andre and Randall L. Wray (1998), 'Did the Clinton Rising Tide Raise all Boats?', *Public Policy Brief*, Jerome Levy Economics Institute, Annandale-on-Hudson, NY, forthcoming.

Redish, Angela (1987), 'Coinage, Development of', in John Eatwell, Murray Millgate and Peter Newman (eds), *The New Palgrave*, New York: W.W. Norton, pp. 376-7.

Ritter, Joseph A. (1998), 'School and Work', *National Economic Trends*, The Federal Reserve Bank of St. Louis, June, p. 1.

Rodney, Walter (1974), *How Europe Underdeveloped Africa*, Washington, DC: Howard University Press.

Rousseas, Stephen (1986), *Post Keynesian Monetary Economics*, Armonk, NY: M.E. Sharpe.

Samuelson, Paul A. (1973), *Economics*, Ninth Edition, New York: McGraw-Hill.

Schumpeter, J.A. (1934), *The Theory of Economic Development: An Inquiry into Profits, Capital, Credit, Interest and the Business Cycle*, Cambridge, MA: Harvard University Press.

Smith, Adam (1937), *The Wealth of Nations*, The Cannan Edition, New York: The Modern Library.

Stabile, Donald R. and Jeffrey A. Cantor (1991), *The Public Debt of the United States: An Historical Perspective 1775–1990*, New York: Praeger.

Stichter, Sharon (1985), *Migrant Laborers*, New York: Cambridge University Press.

Stiglitz, J.E. and A. Weiss (1981), 'Credit Rationing in Markets with Imperfect Information', *American Economic Review*, *71*, (3), June, pp. 393–410.

Studenksi, Paul and Herman E. Kroos (1963), *Financial History of the United States: Fiscal, Monetary, Banking, and Tariff, Including Financial Administration and State and Local Finance*, New York: McGraw-Hill.

Thomas, Clive Y. (1984) *The Rise of the Authoritarian State in Peripheral Societies*, London, Monthly Review Press.

Tobin, James (1987), *Essays in Economics, Volume 1: Macroeconomics*, Cambridge, MA: The MIT Press.

Tobin, J. (1998), *Money, Credit, and Capital*, Boston, MA: Irwin McGraw–Hill.

Vickrey, William (1997), 'A Trans–Keynesian Manifesto (Thoughts about an Asset-based Macroeconomics)', *Journal of Post Keynesian Economics, 19(4)*, Summer, pp. 495–510.

Wray, L. Randall (1990), *Money and Credit in Capitalist Economies: The Endogenous Money Approach*, Aldershot, UK and Brookfield, US: Edward Elgar.

Wray, L. Randall (1993), 'The Origins of Money and the Development of the Modern Financial System', Working Paper No. 86, Jerome Levy Economics Institute, Annadale-on-Hudson, NY, March.

Wray, L. Randall (1997), 'Government as Employer of Last Resort: Full Employment without Inflation', Working Paper No. 213, Jerome Levy Economics Institute, Annandale-on-Hudson, NY, December.

Index